From
TAPAS
to MEZE

From
TAPAS
to MEZE

Small Plates from the Mediterranean

Joanne Weir

Photographs by Caren Alpert

TEN SPEED PRESS
Berkeley | Toronto

A Kirsty Melville Book

Ten Speed Press
Box 7123
Berkeley, California 94707
www.tenspeed.com

Distributed in Australia by Simon and Schuster Australia, in Canada by Ten Speed
Press Canada, in New Zealand by Southern Publishers Group, in South Africa by Real
Books, and in the United Kingdom and Europe by Publishers Group UK.

Cover and text design by Betsy Stromberg
Food photography by Caren Alpert
Food styling by Pouké
Prop styling by Peggi Jeung
Photography assistance by Chugrad McAndrews
Food styling assistance by Jeffrey Larsen and Bruce Fielding

Special thanks to Sur La Table (www.surlatable.com) for donating the props used on
pages 21 (cutting board), 46 (platter), 86 (ramekin), 102 (bottle), and 112 (bowl).

Special thanks to Gumps (135 Post Street, San Francisco, CA, www.gumps.com) for
donating the props used on pages 21 (pitcher), 31 (bowl), 36 (plates), 86 (placemat),
99 (soup bowl and plates), 117 (plate), 153 (glass), 197 (bowl), and 249 (bowl).

Library of Congress Cataloging-in-Publication Data

Weir, Joanne.
  From Tapas to Meze : small plates from the Mediterranean / Joanne Weir.
     p. cm.
  Includes index.
  ISBN-10: 1-58008-586-5
  ISBN-13: 978-1-58008-586-1
  1. Cookery, Mediterranean. 2. Entrées (Cookery) I. Title.
  TX725.M35W4523 2004
  641.59'1822—dc22
                             2004009717

Printed in China

3 4 5 6 7 8 9 10 — 09 08 07

ACKNOWLEDGMENTS

I celebrate this day! It is exactly ten years ago that the original *From Tapas to Meze* was released. This was my first book and, for me, an amazing triumph. A book is a sum of many parts, and its inspiration comes from many places. This book is no exception. Initially, I was inspired to write the book from my years as a cook at Chez Panisse. It is here that I fell in love with Mediterranean food and embraced the lifestyle. I would like to thank my dear friend and mentor, Alice Waters, who inspires us all every single day with her manifesto, her perseverance, and her drive. I would like to thank all of the cooks at Chez Panisse who inspired me to write this book, supported me, and continue to inspire me.

There are so many other extraordinary people who helped me along the way. To Kirsty Melville, who approached me at a reception over a glass of wine and a small plate and asked me if I would like to do a rewrite of my favorite book. And to everyone else at Ten Speed: my editor, the kind and gentle Julie Bennett; designer Betsy Stromberg; art director Nancy Austin; and Sharron Wood, the copyeditor. Thank you to Caren Alpert for her lovely photography, Peggi Jeung for her props, and Pouké for her food styling.

Sometimes I feel so lucky to have Doe Coover on my side. She isn't only my agent, she's a great friend. From my heart, thanks Doe! And thanks to Frances Kennedy for being so kind and so helpful.

Special thanks to Barbara Ignatius for her keen eye, listening ear, quick wit, and attention to every detail, and to Tracey McKeown for watering my plants and traveling with me to Italy. Both of you have taken some of the everyday details and made my life so much better. It is wonderful working with friends! Bruce Fielding deserves a medal for his help with testing, cooking, styling, and of course, his friendship and loyalty. And thanks to Alisa Barry of Bella Cucina Artful Food for her delicious preserved lemons!

Julia Child recognized this book as one of her twelve favorite books the year it was published, and we all honor you. Thanks to Erica Marcus, my original editor from Crown Publishing. Wherever you are, Erica, this book is for you!

To my family and friends, who tasted many a small plate over the years. Whether it was at a *baccaro* in Venice, a *tasca* in Madrid, a *taverna* in Athens, or in my own kitchen, your support and love have meant more than you will ever know. And finally, to all of the wonderful cooks and chefs all over the Mediterranean who so graciously shared their love of food with me, and sometimes even a great family recipe. Cin Cin! Salud! Cheers!

CONTENTS

INTRODUCTION

One autumn evening I sat around a table with a group of chef friends after our shift at Chez Panisse, Alice Water's famous Berkeley, California, restaurant where I worked for several years. We were enjoying a couple of first courses: an escarole, endive, and fresh grilled anchovy salad and a pizza with wild mushrooms and pancetta. I had been thinking for some time about writing a book about the food of the Mediterranean, but I had not yet decided on my focus. Inspiration came to me that night: first courses of the Mediterranean!

When I began working on the book, I knew I wanted to include all of my favorite foods—pizzas, salads, pastas, risottos, flat breads, polenta, and soups. But where should I stop? Should I include Turkey? The Middle East? Morocco? As I looked at maps of the Mediterranean and studied the foods common to the countries that border it, I realized my book wouldn't be complete without the foods of Turkey and the Middle East, areas that had fascinated me since I was eighteen years old. Nor could I ignore the exotic countries of North Africa that I'd longed to visit ever since reading Paula Wolfert's books years earlier.

Life at the Mediterranean Table

I traveled to the Mediterranean many times to learn about the food, but on my first trip there I discovered that there was much more to first courses than met the mouth. I was in Spain, standing against the tapas bar at Las Truchas in Madrid eating *boquerones*—tiny deep-fried fish—and wiping my fingertips on flimsy waxed napkins a bit larger than a playing card. Why was the bar packed five feet deep with people? The fish was delicious, but there was more going on here than mere eating.

In Greece, friends and I sat for hours at a rustic outdoor taverna and ordered plate after plate of sumptuous *meze*: mussels with feta cheese, *taramasalata* (a heavenly purée of cod fish roe), *saganaki* (fried cheese that comes to the table aflame), and pickled squid. In Sicily and again in Apulia, as the

sun met the horizon, we shared bowls of pasta, grilled artichokes and sardines, or a pizza. All of these evenings had more to do with feeding our hearts and souls than our stomachs. Indeed, life at the table appeared very different around the Mediterranean than in central Europe or in America. I soon realized that my simple subject matter was really much more than a collection of recipes.

First Courses of the Mediterranean

Mealtime around the Mediterranean is a major part of daily life. Drinking is not excessive here, and one wouldn't think of drinking without eating. In every country that touches the Mediterranean, small plates of flavor-packed foods provide a perfect accompaniment to the local drink, be it sherry, pastis, wine, prosecco, ouzo, or raki. In Spain we find tapas; in France, hors d'oeuvres and entrées; in Italy, antipasti, *primi piatti*, and *cichetti*; in Greece, Turkey, and the Middle East, *meze*; and in North Africa, *mukabalatt*.

First courses are meant to stimulate the appetite, not satiate it. The host often prepares them ahead of time to avoid being trapped in the kitchen and missing all the fun. First courses are often served at room temperature, so that the flavors aren't dulled by extremes of hot and cold and so that they can be consumed at leisure. The first course of a meal is to be savored, and the memories of these small plates linger long after the table has been cleared.

The Ingredients of Mediterranean Cuisine

The countries that surround the Mediterranean Sea share the azure waters and are linked by a sun-baked landscape with a temperate climate. Generally, Mediterranean summers are hot and dry, and the winters are mild and wet, punctuated by the dusty African sirocco and the chilling winds of the French mistral. Blessed by the strong southern sun and the gentle waters that lap the shores, the arid land can be made—with considerable effort—to yield unsurpassed results. This bounty is seen in the tiniest home garden plots; in the sprawling outdoor markets; and in the exquisite produce, cheeses, meats, and seafood that grace the table.

Spain, France, Italy, Greece, Turkey, the Middle East, and North Africa produce dishes that are loyal to the seasons. In summer, eggplants, peppers, tomatoes, onions, garlic, and squash abound. In the fall, artichokes, squash, and fennel are grown, and wild mushrooms are hunted by the intrepid. In the winter, perfumed groves of lemons and oranges produce a wealth of citrus, and in the spring, radishes, lettuces, and asparagus flourish. The makeshift stalls at the outdoor markets of Seville, Nice, Palermo, Istanbul, Cairo, and Fez are flooded with seasonal produce that implicitly instructs cooks what they should serve that day. To round out the menu and extend the seasons, legumes are dried, wines and spirits are distilled, fish is salted and cured, fruits and vegetables are preserved, fresh milk is made into cheese, bundled herbs are hung in the kitchen to dry, and olives are both cured for the table and pressed for their oil.

The Importance of Olive Oil

The symbols of Mediterranean agriculture and the most fundamental ingredients in the larder are the olive and the green-gold, luscious oil that it produces. A small amount of other fats—lard and butter—is used in various regions, but olive oil is used almost exclusively in cooking. Olive oil brings out the flavor of other ingredients; imparts its own fruity qualities; and is a natural complement to robust regional ingredients such as tomatoes, onions, peppers, eggplant, and garlic.

The precise origin of the olive tree has been lost over time. There is speculation that the original home of the olive tree is Syria, but some hypothesize that it is indigenous to the entire Mediterranean basin. Still others say it was brought to Egypt by the Hyksos, a nomadic Asian tribe. The Greeks say that the goddess Athena produced the olive tree as her most sacred gift to humanity. In the book of Genesis, Noah sent a dove from the ark, and it returned with an olive branch, now considered an international symbol of peace. Whatever its origins, the olive tree holds a unique symbolic position in each Mediterranean country's culture.

The Syrians were the first to cultivate the trees and produce olive oil, but the Greeks and Romans were unrivaled in spreading the cultivation of the olive around the Mediterranean and producing vast quantities of olive oil. Early on, olive oil was used in religious rites, as medicine, ointment, and fuel for oil lamps. Olive tree leaves were winter fodder for the goats and sheep, its branches and roots a source of heat. It wasn't until later that olive oil became a significant part of the Mediterranean diet.

The extraction of oil from the olive must follow certain steps to yield a high-quality product. Around the Mediterranean, olives are harvested from the fall to winter, depending upon the country and whether they are picked green, brown, deep-violet, or black. Optimally, the olives are sorted and washed within hours of picking. Next they are crushed to produce a paste that is traditionally spread between hemp mats. The mats are layered one on top of another and pressed, resulting in a water and olive oil mixture. The oil, being lighter than the water, rises to the surface and is decanted. Today, due to higher demand and mechanization, the paste is either pressed hydraulically or put through a centrifuge to extract the oil. New automated oil mills are bright with stainless steel and operated by computers—a bit less romantic, but they result in a more consistent finished product.

Extra virgin olive oil is made from the first pressing of the olives. This pressing produces a darker, purer, fruitier olive oil, one that is cleaner on the palate. More expensive than lesser grades, extra virgin oil is usually saved for special dishes, mainly uncooked ones, where the flavor of the oil is on display. The oil that is extracted from the second, third, and fourth pressings of the olive paste deteriorates progressively. These oils must be treated chemically to neutralize high acid levels, and extra virgin olive oil is added to them to boost the flavor. Oils are graded according to acid levels, oleic acid being of importance. A strict system for classifying olive oils was established in 1959 by the United Nations Conference on Trade and Development and is administered by the International Olive Oil Council.

Olive oil has an honored place in the Mediterranean diet, but so do table or eating olives. To remove their bitterness and render them palatable, raw olives must be either brined (soaked in an alkaline solution) or salt cured (layered in a basket with salt). Olives are then marinated, stuffed, cooked, or simply served on a small plate with drinks. The most common eating olives grown around the Mediterranean are niçoise, picholine, and Lucques (France); Frantoio (Italy); Manzanilla and Arbequina (Spain); and kalamata (Greece).

The Mediterranean Trinity

The trinity that forms the backbone of Mediterranean cuisine is composed of olive oil, garlic, and tomatoes, and there is hardly a dish that doesn't include at least one of these ingredients. Garlic has been used here for aeons and appears with olive oil as an inseparable and incomparable partner: in *allioli* and *romesco* from Spain; *anchoïade, aioli, aillade,* and *tapenade* from the south of France; *agliata* and *aglio e oglio* from Italy; *skorthalia* from Greece; *tatator* from Turkey; *tahini* from the Levant; and *harissa* and *chermoula* from North Africa. Tomatoes are relative newcomers to the Mediterranean, arriving from the Americas in the early sixteenth century. They took the area by storm, not only for their versatility and flavor, but also because they are a natural complement to olive oil.

Other vegetables that give form and flavor to Mediterranean cuisine are onions, leeks, greens, beans, peppers, artichokes, eggplant, squash, mushrooms, and fennel. Herbs figure prominently in Mediterranean cuisine—parsley, basil, oregano, dill, bay leaves, mint, marjoram, rosemary, thyme, and sage on the northern shores, and in the southern Mediterranean, the aforementioned plus coriander or, as we call it in the United States, cilantro. Saffron, black pepper, crushed red pepper, and, especially around the southern and eastern Mediterranean, paprika, ginger, cumin, cinnamon, allspice, and turmeric are also used liberally. Other essential Mediterranean ingredients include capers; almonds; pine nuts; aromatic honeys; orange and rose waters; figs; citrus; lamb; anchovies; fresh and salted fish; shellfish; grapes; and a tremendous assortment of rice, legumes, and grains.

Mediterranean ingredients are not particularly unusual ones; most are readily available in the United States. But what makes Mediterranean food interesting is the way that each country puts the ingredients together to form its own unique cuisine with its own nuances and flavors. Ingredients are treated with integrity; each dish strives to maintain the full and pure flavor of the separate components.

Cheeses from the Mediterranean Shores

The Mediterranean shores have produced a relatively narrow variety of cheese, but nowhere is the quality higher. These cheeses—made from the milk of cows, goats, and sheep—are gutsy and straightforward and tend to be, as much as any cheese can, on the lean side. Italy boasts ricotta; mascarpone; Gorgonzola; fontina; Bel Paese; provolone; Asiago; the famed buffalo milk mozzarella; and the incomparable eating and grating cheeses, Parmigiano-Reggiano, grana padano, and pecorino. Southern France produces a wide variety of goat cheeses and Roquefort, and Corsicans make a ricotta-like cheese, broccio. Greece is famed for its briny feta, kasseri, and kephalotyri, and Spain for its manchego, a hard sheep's milk cheese. Turkey is noted for kajmak, a soft, fresh, incredibly rich cheese, and tulim, a sheep's milk cheese. Egypt makes domiati, a cow's milk cheese. The eastern shores of the Mediterranean produce some delicious thick yogurt that, when drained, produces a creamy spreadable yogurt cheese called *labneh*.

A Healthy Cuisine

With an abundance of fish, vegetables, pulses, rice, and legumes; liberal use of olive oil; and limited use of red meat and dairy products, Mediterranean cuisine is healthy. Olive oil, high in monounsaturates and containing no cholesterol, is the most nutritionally beneficial oil in the pantry. Onions and garlic cleanse the bloodstream and are known to have curative and protective qualities. The moderate consumption of wine aids digestion, stimulates the appetite, and reduces stress. The gentle pace of daily life around the Mediterranean leaves time for social and sensual pleasures. With this healthy cuisine and a relaxed attitude, it is no wonder that the countries of the Mediterranean have the lowest incidence of heart disease and cancer in Europe.

The Mediterranean Spirit

The Mediterranean embraces fifteen countries and touches three continents, Europe, Africa, and Asia. It is a vast sea stretching from the Strait of Gibraltar to the Bosphorus, from Marseilles to Tunis. Of the Christians, Jews, and Muslims who live there, some look to the vast desert, some to the mountains, and some to the sea. Some see fishing villages clinging to the rocks, some see ancient ruins, and some see the perimeters of their own island. But everywhere one looks, one appreciates the robust Mediterranean spirit, its unparalleled history, and the hospitality with which it offers its remarkable cuisines.

As you sample these dishes, imagine that you are sitting under an arbor sipping wine or passing time in a small taverna, caught up in conversation, or standing with friends and enjoying morsels of food at a tapas bar. Food is integral to life around the Mediterranean, and so it can be in your own home. All you need are a simple table set with many small plates and perhaps a bottle of wine, at which friends may gather at the end of the day.

SPAIN

*W*alk down any side street in Seville, Málaga, or even Murcia and you will find it nearly impossible to pass the local *tasca*, or tavern, because a noisy, happy throng will have spilled out onto the streets. Inside, people will be jammed against one another in a sea of glasses and small plates of food, loudly discussing the events of the day or arguing about their favorite team or the latest film they've seen. I have seen *tascas* so packed that getting to the bar required the skill of an acrobat.

Indulging in tapas is one of Spain's favorite sports. Think bullfighting or soccer and you'll get an idea of the crowds and passion they inspire. The tradition of offering many small dishes or first courses began in the mid-1800s, when tavern owners would put a slice of ham or a simple plate of salted almonds over the top of a glass of sherry to keep the flies out (*tapa* means "to cover"). These early tapas were free of charge, meant to promote thirst and increase drink sales. Over the next hundred years, tapas evolved to become part of everyday life, not only as the covering for a glass of sherry or wine, but as the main event of a visit to a *tasca*.

Each *tasca* has its own specialties determined by the local cooking style and what's in season. A few glass cases will display various tapas, and a blackboard will announce the daily specials, ranging from the simple—plates of perfectly salted and roasted almonds, bright red radishes, or glistening meaty green olives—to the complex—plates of golden deep-fried anchovies; a salad of salt cod, olives, and oranges; or a potato "omelette." Choices are made, and within seconds the tapas appear. The bartender runs back and forth, taking care of everyone at the same time and somehow remembering what each patron has had so that he can present each with a grand total as they leave for home or the next *tasca*.

"*Tasca*-hopping," going from *tasca* to *tasca*, is a favorite way to spend an evening with friends. "I found a wonderful little tapas bar where they serve the very best *pastel*," someone will say. "Great! Let's go there, and after that, let's go to that tiny little place on the corner where they serve *patates bravas* just like my mother used to make." Dinner gets put on the back burner (maybe that's why Spaniards eat so late in the evening!) or postponed entirely.

Tapas: More than Just Appetizers

Today, tapas are available almost any time of the day, but they're still most popular before the noon or evening meal. With lunch and dinner served so late in Spain, tapas are meant to stave off hunger, whet the appetite, and bring immediate gratification. These aren't really dishes to be lingered over, but instead consumed quickly so that you can move on to the next tapa, washing each down with a cool sip of sherry, beer, or wine.

Still, tapas are more than just appetizers: they draw people together in one of the most pleasant and convivial customs surrounding food. It's hard to imagine eating tapas by yourself. You want to be part of that boisterous crowd, arguing happily about sports, politics, or the arts and savoring the incredible variety of tapas.

The Influence of the Romans and Arab Moors

Life in Spain hasn't always been so carefree and easy. In its long history, Spain has seen many invasions, the Romans and the Arab Moors of North Africa leaving the most profound effect. In the first half of the first millennium, the occupying Romans instituted the first large-scale propagation of olive trees and grape vines and taught the Spanish the fine art of curing Serrano hams, similar to Italian prosciutto.

The Arab Moors ruled Spain for nearly 800 years, from 711 to 1492, and left the most pervasive cultural imprint on Spain. They introduced eggplant; almonds; hazelnuts; citrus; sugarcane; and spices such as cumin, cinnamon, black pepper, saffron, and nutmeg. They perfected the Roman irrigation system, making the land around Valencia perfect for growing rice.

In 1492, the Moors were expelled from Spain. It was, of course, the same year that Columbus set sail for the New World. Columbus returned to Spain, and in subsequent years the cuisine of Spain and the rest of the Mediterranean was changed by the introduction of foods from the New World: tomatoes, peppers, potatoes, corn, varieties of squash, various dried beans, avocado, chocolate, and turkey.

Catalonia

The Spanish states that border the Mediterranean—Catalonia, Valencia, Murcia, Andalusia, and the Balearic Islands—vary immensely. Catalonia, which inhabits the northeast corner of Spain, is a cultural kingdom whose loyalties cross political borders to include parts of Roussillon in the southwest corner of France, a portion of Valencia, Andorra, and even a single city on the Italian island of Sardinia. More closely related to Languedoc and Provence than Spain, the Catalans have their own distinct style of food, which is highly aromatic and flavorful, employing unexpected combinations. Some believe that Catalan cuisine is the most sophisticated and original food of Spain. Eating is taken seriously in Catalonia, and, due to the influence of bordering France, a "proper" meal in the past was never consumed while standing. Thus first courses were mostly taken at the table, and tapas, which weren't so much a part of daily life, are now becoming increasingly popular. Barcelona is bursting with tapas bars.

Valencia

Along the east coast of Spain, Valencia is a fertile semitropical plane of sugarcane, date palms, citrus groves, and, most importantly, rice fields. Rice has been grown here since Moorish times, and many recipes are based around it. Paella, the national dish of Spain, is made with short-grain rice and saffron grown in nearby Murcia. This quasi-risotto of Spain is occasionally eaten as a tapa when it is formed into balls, breaded, and deep-fried, but mostly it is eaten as a dramatic main course. As we head south to Murcia, rice paddies give way to vegetable fields, fruit orchards, and groves of date palms. Murcia relies heavily on the *huerta*, or garden. The strong Arabic influence is seen in the generous use of sweet spices and chickpeas, and the tremendous array of seafood helps to mold a unique and varied cuisine.

Andalusia

In Andalusia, horses, dancing, flamenco guitar, and merrymaking are at the forefront. The Andalusian has a real zest for life. Food is not generally the cerebral art that it is in other parts of Spain such as Catalonia, but tapas are taken seriously here, especially in Seville. One of the most popular tapas in all of Spain is a simple plate of paper-thin slices of Serrano ham from Andalusia (Jabugo is the finest). The pigs are fattened for a year on acorns before being slaughtered. The haunches and shoulders of the pig are cured by salting, washing, and drying and then are matured for one to three years in underground cellars, where they acquire a distinctive aroma and flavor. But Andalusian tapas don't end with ham. Andalusia is renowned for its perfectly deep-fried fish, and egg dishes abound, especially the tortilla. Gazpacho, the cold liquid salad introduced by the Moors, was born here, and the Moorish influence can also be tasted in highly spiced Andalusian kebabs.

The Balearic Islands

The Balearic Islands—Majorca, Minorca, Ibiza, and Formentera—are a haven for romantics, with serrated coasts, coves, and cliffs descending to the sea. It's no surprise that the main culinary focus is the Mediterranean. Fish and shellfish, especially a spiny type of lobster called *llogosta*, and capers that grow wild on the island make their way into much of the cuisine. The islands have strong ties to Catalonia, and many of their dishes are similar to the down-to-earth and flavorful foods of that region. It is thought that mayonnaise or *salsa mahonesa*— a sauce served with many tapas—originated in Port Mahon on Minorca. The French, however, claim mayonnaise as well.

A Colorful and Uncomplicated Cuisine

The rich legacy of many classical Mediterranean countries is seen in both Spain's culture and its food. It is not a peppery or hot cuisine. Instead, it is subtly colored with saffron and paprika and perfumed with olive oil. It features the mild sweetness of pimiento, almonds, tomatoes, and caramelized onions; the earthiness of wild asparagus, mushrooms, and herbs; and the zest of lots of sherry vinegar and garlic. Pork products such as Serrano ham and chorizo, game, fish, shellfish, and salt cod are mainstays, while citrus and other fruits make their way into both sweet and savory dishes. Spain's is an uncomplicated cuisine, composed of the best ingredients and the simplest techniques, virtues that are heroically evident in tapas.

COLD ICED TOMATO SOUP FROM ANDALUSIA

Gazpacho Andaluz

In Spain there are more than thirty varieties of gazpacho, but there is one common denominator. One would think that it is tomatoes, but in fact it is stale crusty bread, soaked in water. Gazpacho was originally made with garlic, bread, olive oil, water, and salt—and no tomatoes at all. When Columbus returned to Spain from the New World, he brought with him the tomato and pepper. With these new ingredients, the future of gazpacho changed and became much rosier.

2¹/₂ pounds fresh ripe tomatoes, peeled, seeded, and chopped (page 259), about 3 cups, or one 28-ounce can Italian plum tomatoes, chopped, juice reserved

1 green bell pepper, seeded and coarsely chopped

1 medium red onion, coarsely chopped

1 hothouse cucumber, peeled, halved, seeded, and coarsely chopped

5 to 6 tablespoons red wine vinegar

3 large cloves garlic, minced

1¹/₄ cups tomato juice

¹/₄ cup extra virgin olive oil

1 slice rustic country-style bread, crusts removed, soaked in water and squeezed dry

Salt and freshly ground black pepper

Garnishes

1 tablespoon extra virgin olive oil

1 tablespoon unsalted butter

3 cloves garlic, peeled and crushed

6 slices rustic country-style bread, crusts removed, cut or torn into small cubes

Salt

¹/₂ cup peeled, seeded, and diced cucumber

¹/₂ cup diced green bell pepper

¹/₂ cup halved cherry tomatoes

¹/₂ cup diced red onion

In a large bowl, stir together the tomatoes, green pepper, onion, cucumber, 5 tablespoons of the vinegar, garlic, tomato juice, olive oil, and bread. Put the mixture in batches in a blender and blend on high speed until very smooth, 3 to 4 minutes. Season with additional salt, pepper, and vinegar as needed. Chill.

Preheat the oven to 400°F. Heat the olive oil and butter in a frying pan. Add the crushed garlic and cook until the garlic is golden brown, 4 to 5 minutes. Remove the garlic and discard. Toss the oil with the bread cubes. Place on a baking sheet, season with salt, and bake, stirring occasionally, until the bread cubes are golden and crispy, 12 to 15 minutes. Cool.

Serve the soup garnished with the cucumber, green pepper, tomatoes, red onion, and the toasted bread cubes.

Serves 6

CHILLED WHITE GAZPACHO WITH ALMONDS AND GRAPES

Gazpacho Ajo Blanco con Uvas

In my estimation, ajo blanco, the Spanish white garlic soup, has never received its due. Traditionally a noon meal for peasants, it was prepared in the fields in a wooden bowl and eaten directly from the bowl with wooden spoons. This seductive blend of garlic, almonds, sherry vinegar, and iced water goes back 1,000 years to the Moorish occupation. A must is the splash of sherry vinegar, which comes from Jerez, a very quick jaunt west of the Strait of Gibraltar. This recipe comes from Málaga, where it's garnished with sweet muscat grapes. Use whatever sweet green grapes you can find.

3/4 cup almonds, blanched

3 cloves garlic, peeled

Salt

4 slices stale rustic country-style bread, crusts removed, about 4 ounces

4 cups ice water

5 tablespoons extra virgin olive oil

2 to 3 tablespoons white wine vinegar

2 tablespoons sherry vinegar

1 tablespoon unsalted butter

6 thick slices rustic country-style bread, crusts removed, cut in cubes, about 6 ounces

1 1/2 cups seedless green grapes

In a food processor, pulverize the almonds, 2 of the garlic cloves, and 1/2 teaspoon salt. Soak the stale bread in 1 cup of the ice water and squeeze to extract the moisture. Discard the water. Add the bread to the food processor. With the motor running, add 4 tablespoons of the olive oil and 1 cup of the ice water slowly in a steady stream. Add the white wine and sherry vinegars and mix on high speed until very smooth, 2 minutes. Add another 1 cup of the ice water and mix 2 minutes more. Place the soup in a bowl, add the remaining 1 cup ice water, and mix well. Season with additional salt and vinegar, if needed. Chill.

The soup can be prepared to this point and chilled up to 6 hours before serving.

Preheat the oven to 400°F. Melt the butter and heat the remaining 1 tablespoon olive oil in a frying pan over medium heat. Crush the remaining 1 clove garlic and add to the pan, stirring until golden. Remove and discard the garlic. Add the bread, tossing to coat with the butter and oil, and place on a baking sheet. Bake, stirring occasionally, until the bread cubes are golden and crispy, 12 to 15 minutes.

Serve the soup ice cold garnished with the toasted bread cubes and grapes.

Serves 6

SMOKED HAM SOUP WITH WHITE BEANS AND MINT

Judías Blancas y Menta

It was really chilly that January evening in southern Spain. When we arrived for dinner at Beatriz and Jose Luis's in Ecija, the table was already set. Jose Luis greeted us at the door, while Beatriz was in the kitchen finishing up the soup. When Beatriz brought the soup, we all took our seats at the table. Curiously, Jose Luis and Beatriz covered their laps with the overhanging edges of the tablecloth, so I followed suit. Much to my delight, the tablecloth was heated, like an electric blanket. I laughed and wondered why we didn't have heated tablecloths in the United States to keep the winter chill away. By the way, the soup was perfect that evening, and I am not sure if it was the hot soup or the tablecloth, but I never felt a single bit cold!

3/4 cup dried white beans, about 5 ounces

6 sprigs fresh flat-leaf parsley

Pinch of dried thyme

2 bay leaves

1 tablespoon extra virgin olive oil

1/4 pound thickly sliced smoked bacon, cut into 1/4-inch dice

1 medium yellow onion, chopped

3 cloves garlic, minced

2 smoked ham hocks, about 1 pound total

1 1/2 cups peeled, seeded, and chopped tomatoes (page 259), fresh or canned

6 cups chicken stock (page 255)

3 sprigs fresh mint, bruised with the back of a knife

Salt and freshly ground black pepper

5 tablespoons chopped fresh mint

Pick over the beans and discard any stones. Cover with water and soak 8 hours or overnight. The next day, drain the beans, place them in a saucepan with the parsley sprigs, thyme, bay leaves, and enough water to cover by 2 inches. Simmer until the skins just begin to crack and the beans are tender, 35 to 45 minutes.

Heat a soup pot over medium heat and add the olive oil, bacon, and onion. Cook until the onion is soft and the bacon has rendered its fat, about 10 minutes. Add the garlic and continue to cook for 3 minutes, just until the bacon begins to turn golden. Add the ham hocks, tomatoes, chicken stock, and mint sprigs. Decrease the heat to low and simmer 1 hour.

Add the beans and continue to simmer 1 hour. Remove and discard the parsley sprigs, mint sprigs, and bay leaves. Remove the ham hocks. Discard the skin and bones, cut the ham into bite-size pieces, and add the ham to the soup. Season to taste with salt and pepper. Ladle the soup into bowls and garnish with chopped mint.

Serves 6

VEAL AND GREEN PEPPER TURNOVERS OF MURCIA

Pastel de Carne y Pimientos Murcianos

In Spain, a pastel is a flaky meat pie filled with veal, spicy chorizo, onions, hard-cooked eggs, and spices. The pastel dates way back to the 1400s, when the Moors occupied Spain. Today, the influence of the Moors can be seen in Spain not only in all kinds of recipes, but also in architecture, art, music, and even the faces of the people, especially in the southern provinces of Andalusia and Murcia. The pastel resembles the Moroccan bastilla, hence the similarity in spelling. See the note below about making them ahead.

2 tablespoons extra virgin olive oil

1 medium yellow onion, minced

2 cloves garlic, minced

2 green bell peppers, seeded and finely chopped

4 ounces chorizo, casing removed

4 ounces finely diced Serrano ham, prosciutto, or Black Forest ham

1/2 pound ground veal

Pinch of saffron threads

3/4 cup peeled, seeded, and chopped tomatoes (page 259), fresh or canned

1/4 cup finely chopped pitted green olives with pimiento

1/2 teaspoon ground cumin

2 hard-cooked eggs, finely chopped

Salt and freshly ground black pepper

1 recipe Quick Puff Pastry (recipe follows), or one 10-ounce package frozen puff pastry sheets, thawed

2 eggs, lightly beaten

1 tablespoon water

Heat the oil in a frying pan over medium-low heat. Add the onion, garlic, and bell peppers and cook, stirring occasionally, until soft, 7 minutes. Increase the heat to medium and add the chorizo, ham, and veal. Cook, stirring occasionally, for 5 minutes. Place the saffron in a small, dry frying pan over medium heat, shaking the pan frequently, for 30 to 60 seconds. Add the saffron, tomatoes, olives, and cumin to the meat mixture and simmer, covered, for 10 minutes. Uncover and continue to cook until the moisture is gone, 3 to 4 minutes. Add the hard-cooked eggs and mix well. Season with salt and pepper.

Preheat the oven to 350°F. On a floured surface with a floured rolling pin, roll the puff pastry to 1/8 inch thick. Using a 3 1/2-inch round cookie cutter or a clean empty can, cut circles of dough. Place a tablespoon of the filling to the side of the center of each circle. Whisk the eggs with the water. Brush the edges of half of each circle with the egg wash. Fold the circles over, enclosing the filling, and seal the edges. Place the turnovers on an ungreased baking sheet and bake until golden brown, 12 to 15 minutes.

Makes 24 turnovers

NOTE: The turnovers can be assembled several hours ahead of time, refrigerated, and baked at the last minute. Alternatively, they can be assembled up to a week ahead of time and stored in freezer bags in the freezer. Remove from the freezer, place on baking sheets in a single layer, and bake frozen, adding 5 to 7 minutes to the baking time. If they get cold while being served, reheat on the top rack of a 400°F oven.

QUICK PUFF PASTRY

I use this recipe anytime I need a quick and easy flaky pastry, whether for a sweet or savory dish. This recipe should dispel any concerns you might have about puff pastry being difficult to make. One note of caution: You must work quickly so that the butter doesn't get warm and soft. If the dough gets sticky, dust it well with flour and place it in the refrigerator for 10 to 15 minutes.

1 cup all-purpose flour

$1/2$ cup cake flour

$1/4$ teaspoon salt

14 tablespoons unsalted butter,
    cut into $1/2$-inch pieces

2 teaspoons lemon juice

$1/4$ to $1/3$ cup ice water

Mix the flours and salt together in a bowl and place in the freezer for 1 hour. Place the butter in the freezer for 1 hour.

Place the cold flour in a mixing bowl with the cold butter and cut the butter into the flour with 2 forks, or place in a food processor bowl and pulse, until the butter is in $1/4$-inch pieces. Combine the lemon juice and ice water and add it, a little at a time, to the flour mixture, mixing only until the dough is moistened and just begins to hold together to form a rough ball.

Place the dough on a floured work surface and press together as best you can to form a rough rectangle. There will be large chunks of butter showing. Do not knead. Roll out the dough into a $1/2$-inch thick rectangle approximately 8 inches by 10 inches. Fold the two narrow ends in to meet in the center. Fold in half again so that there are 4 layers. Turn the dough one quarter turn. This is your first turn. Repeat exactly the same way twice more. Finally, roll the dough once again into a $1/2$-inch thick rectangle. This time, fold the dough into thirds as you would a business letter. Wrap the dough in plastic wrap and refrigerate for 1 hour.

Makes approximately 1 pound

> NOTE: The dough can be stored in the refrigerator for up to 3 days or frozen for up to 1 month.

SUMMER VEGETABLE FLAT BREAD

Coca de la Huerta

This Catalan coca, or flat bread, is traditional fare on the Balearic Islands. It's shaped into a long, narrow oval and baked in a wood-fired oven. Cheese and herbs aren't used here as they are in Italy; instead, the coca is topped with either the summer's bounty or the cook's leftovers.

Dough

1 tablespoon active dry yeast

2 tablespoons plus 1 cup warm water

3 cups all-purpose flour

1 teaspoon salt

1/4 cup extra virgin olive oil

Topping

2 cups tightly packed Swiss chard, washed, dried, and stems removed

3 tablespoons extra virgin olive oil

5 cloves garlic, minced

1 small zucchini, unpeeled, sliced paper-thin

1 large green bell pepper, seeded and thinly sliced

1 large yellow onion, thinly sliced

Salt and freshly ground black pepper

2 ripe tomatoes, thinly sliced

2 teaspoons white wine vinegar

1/4 cup pine nuts, toasted (page 258)

NOTE: To use a pizza stone, preheat the stone to 400°F. Place one oval of dough on a heavily floured pizza peel or paddle and add the vegetables as directed. Transfer the dough from the paddle directly onto the stone. Repeat with the other piece of dough. Bake 15 to 20 minutes, until golden.

To make the dough, in a large bowl, dissolve the yeast in 2 tablespoons of the warm water. Let stand 10 minutes until frothy. Add the flour, salt, the remaining 1 cup warm water, and the olive oil. Knead on a floured surface until smooth, elastic, and slightly tacky to the touch, 7 to 10 minutes. Place the dough in an oiled bowl, turning it once to coat with oil. Cover with plastic wrap and place in a warm place (75°F). Allow the dough to rise until doubled in volume, about 1 hour.

To make the topping, preheat the oven to 400°F. Pile the Swiss chard leaves on top of one another, roll them up, and slice into 1/2-inch strips. In a large frying pan, heat 1 tablespoon of the oil. Add the Swiss chard and garlic and toss together. Cover and cook 2 minutes. Remove the cover and continue to cook until the Swiss chard is tender, 2 to 3 minutes. Remove from the pan and place in a bowl. Add 1 tablespoon of the oil to the frying pan, add the zucchini, and cook over medium heat until just done, 4 minutes. Remove from the pan and reserve with the Swiss chard. Add the pepper and onion to the pan and cook until tender, 7 to 8 minutes. Add to the other vegetables and season with salt and pepper. Reserve.

After 1 hour, punch down the dough and cut it into 2 pieces. Flour a surface and roll each portion into an oval shape, 8 inches by 10 inches by 3/8 inch. Crimp the edges slightly. Place the pieces of dough side by side on a large oiled baking sheet. (See Note if you are using a pizza stone or oven tiles.) Divide the cooked vegetables between the two pieces of dough and distribute evenly, leaving a 1/2-inch border around the edges. Distribute the tomatoes over the vegetables. Drizzle with the vinegar. Sprinkle the pine nuts on top and drizzle with 1/2 tablespoon olive oil each. Season with salt and pepper. Bake until golden, 20 to 25 minutes.

Remove from the pan and cut into wedges. Serve immediately or at room temperature.

Makes 2 *coca* to serve 8

GRILLED BREAD WITH RIPE TOMATOES AND OLIVE OIL

Pan con Tomate

The cousin to Rome's bruschetta *or Florence's* fettunta, *Catalonia's* pan con tomate *is kind of the American equivalent to potato chips or pretzels. Served before the meal to whet the appetite,* pan con tomate *is ideally toasted over a wood fire, smeared with the best fruity olive oil, and topped with perfectly ripe crushed tomatoes. Using rustic country-style bread is essential, and don't forget a liberal sprinkling of salt. Garlic is optional.* Pan con tomate *can be a perfect accompaniment to a salad or bowl of soup for lunch, especially when it is topped with paper-thin slices of* manchego *cheese or Serrano ham.*

2 cloves garlic, peeled

Salt and freshly ground black pepper

$^1/_4$ cup extra virgin olive oil

12 slices rustic country-style bread, $^3/_4$-inch thick

6 very ripe tomatoes

Garnishes

$^1/_2$ cup pitted green Spanish olives

12 anchovy fillets, soaked in cold water 10 minutes and patted dry

6 paper-thin slices Serrano ham, prosciutto, or Black Forest ham

12 paper-thin slices manchego or Parmigiano-Reggiano cheese (see Note)

Mash the garlic and a pinch of salt in a mortar and pestle or with the back of a knife on your cutting board to make a fine paste. Mix with the olive oil. Set aside.

Grill the bread until golden brown over a wood-burning fire or a gas grill, or toast the bread under a broiler until golden on each side, 45 to 60 seconds.

Cut the tomatoes in half and, cupping a half in your palm, rub both sides of the toast with the tomato, squeezing slightly as you go along to leave pulp, seeds, and juice. Drizzle the toast with the garlic–olive oil mixture and sprinkle with salt and pepper. Serve immediately garnished with the olives, anchovy fillets, ham, and cheese.

Serves 6

NOTE: Manchego cheese is a sheep's milk cheese available in specialty cheese shops.

CHORIZO AND CHEESE PUFFS

Buñuelos con Chorizo y Queso

Spaniards love pork sausages of all kinds, red, black, or white. Botifarra is a simple white pork sausage, while botifarra negra is a coarser, fattier sausage made with bread soaked in pig's blood. Morcilla is another blood sausage made with manteca, a red lard heavily seasoned with paprika. Sobrassada, a Majorcan specialty, is a soft, almost pastelike sausage flavored with garlic and paprika that is often spread on bread. But the most popular Spanish sausage is undoubtedly chorizo, a pork sausage heavily spiced with red pepper, cumin, and garlic and made red with paprika. Chorizo and manchego cheese pair up in this recipe to make a tasty tapa.

1 cup all-purpose flour

1/4 teaspoon crushed red pepper flakes

3 eggs, separated

2 tablespoons extra virgin olive oil

3/4 cup warm beer

1/2 teaspoon salt

Freshly ground black pepper

4 cups peanut or corn oil

10 ounces chorizo, casing removed and finely chopped

3 tablespoons chopped fresh flat-leaf parsley, plus extra leaves

1 cup grated manchego or Parmigiano-Reggiano cheese

Sift the flour into a bowl. Add the red pepper flakes and mix well. Lightly beat the egg yolks. Make a well in the center of the flour mixture and add the egg yolks, olive oil, beer, the salt, and pepper. With a spoon, mix well, but do not allow the batter to get stringy. Let rest for 1 hour at room temperature.

In a deep saucepan, heat the oil to 375°F. A drop of batter should sizzle when dropped into the oil.

Heat a frying pan over medium heat and cook the chorizo, stirring occasionally, until it begins to turn golden, 3 minutes.

In a clean bowl, beat the egg whites until they form stiff peaks. Fold the egg whites, chorizo, parsley, and cheese into the batter. Drop the batter by heaping table-spoonfuls into the hot oil. Cook, turning occasionally, until golden, 2 to 3 minutes. Drain on paper towels.

Place on a platter and garnish with parsley leaves. Serve immediately.

Makes 25 to 30 puffs to serve 6 to 8

CARAMELIZED ONION OMELETTE FROM ANDALUSIA

Tortilla de Cebollas a la Andaluza

Eggs are one of the most basic Spanish ingredients. The tortilla, a 1-inch-thick egg pie—like an unfolded French omelette or an Italian frittata—can be flavored with a variety of ingredients. Traditionally, the tortilla was taken to the fields and eaten at lunch by farm workers. Today, the tortilla can be found in white-tablecloth restaurants and country roadhouses. This one, common in Andalusia, is made sweet by cooking several pounds of onions until they are caramelized and almost melting. Get ready for a good cry. This is a lot of onions to chop.

3 pounds yellow onions

6 tablespoons extra virgin olive oil

6 eggs

Salt and freshly ground black pepper

Finely chop the onions. Alternatively, they can be chopped in the food processor by pulsing several times. In a frying pan, heat 4 tablespoons of the olive oil over medium heat, add the onions, and stir to combine. Cover and cook 15 minutes. Do not stir. Remove the cover, stir, and reduce the heat to low. Cover and continue to cook, stirring occasionally, until the onions are very soft and golden, 1 to 1 1/4 hours total. Remove from the heat and cool 10 minutes.

In a bowl, whisk the eggs and season with salt and pepper. Add the onions. Let stand 15 minutes. In a 10-inch nonstick frying pan, heat the remaining 2 tablespoons oil until it just begins to smoke, 2 minutes. Pour the eggs into the pan and cook over medium heat, using a spatula to loosen the edges, for 10 to 15 minutes. When the tortilla is almost firm, put a plate a little larger than the circumference of the frying pan over the top of the pan. Holding the plate and frying pan together, carefully invert the plate and frying pan so that the tortilla is now inverted onto the plate. Slide the tortilla back into the frying pan, browned side up. Cook until done, 3 to 4 minutes. It should be slightly wet inside.

Slide the tortilla onto a platter, cut into wedges, and serve hot or at room temperature.

Serves 6

NOTE: This dish can be prepared 1 day in advance and stored covered in the refrigerator. Bring to room temperature before serving.

SPANISH OMELETTE, GYPSY-STYLE

Just the word flamenca conjures up images of colorful dancers, gypsies, robust guitar music, and an energy like no other. Huevos a la flamenca originated in Seville, home of the flamenco dance, where this vivacious dish is a whirl of red, green, orange, white, and yellow. Not only a delight to look at, this dish also tastes just wonderful.

3 tablespoons extra virgin olive oil

1 medium yellow onion, minced

2 cloves garlic, minced

1¼ cups peeled, seeded, and chopped tomatoes (page 259), about 3 medium tomatoes, fresh or canned

1 teaspoon sweet paprika

Salt and freshly ground black pepper

¹/3 cup chicken stock (page 255)

4 ounces Serrano ham, cut into ¹/4-inch dice

4 ounces chorizo, cut into ¹/4-inch slices

¹/2 cup fresh or frozen peas

8 asparagus spears, cut into 1¹/2-inch lengths

8 eggs

Pinch of cayenne

1 small red bell pepper, roasted (page 259) and cut into strips

2 tablespoons chopped fresh flat-leaf parsley

Preheat the oven to 400°F. Heat 2 tablespoons of the oil in a frying pan over medium heat and cook the onion, stirring occasionally, until soft, 7 minutes. Add the garlic and cook 1 minute longer. Add the tomatoes, paprika, salt, and pepper and cook, stirring occasionally, for 2 to 3 minutes. Add the chicken stock, cover, and simmer slowly for 5 minutes.

In another frying pan, heat the remaining 1 tablespoon oil and cook the ham and chorizo until golden, 5 minutes. Bring a pot of salted water to a boil. Add the peas and simmer 30 seconds. Remove with a slotted spoon. Add the asparagus to the boiling water and simmer until almost tender, 2 to 3 minutes. Drain and reserve.

Pour the sauce into a 2-quart baking dish. Break one egg at a time into a small bowl and slip them one at a time into the sauce, distributing the eggs evenly in the tomato sauce. Season with cayenne. Arrange the ham, chorizo, peas, asparagus, and roasted pepper strips decoratively around and between the eggs. Season with salt and pepper. Sprinkle with parsley.

Bake until the egg whites are lightly set and the yolks are still runny, 10 minutes. Garnish with parsley and serve immediately.

Serves 4

TINY SPICED MEATBALLS WITH TOMATOES

Albóndigas

I was invited for a simple dinner at the country house of my friend Beatriz Tamarit, who lives outside Seville. I know Beatriz enough to know that anything she does is far from simple. On the long table she spread at least fifteen different tapas, including these tiny succulent meatballs. I closed my eyes as I tasted one and was immediately transported to other parts of the Mediterranean. Spiced with coriander, nutmeg, cumin, and cayenne, these tiny meatballs are also made in North Africa, the Middle East, Turkey, and Greece, where they are known as kefta.

1/2 pound ground pork

1/2 pound ground beef

1/2 pound ground veal

1 cup dry bread crumbs

6 cloves garlic, minced

2 tablespoons chopped fresh flat-leaf parsley

1 1/2 teaspoons ground coriander seeds

1/2 teaspoon freshly grated nutmeg

1/2 teaspoon ground cumin

Pinch of cayenne

1/2 teaspoon salt

Freshly ground black pepper

3 tablespoons extra virgin olive oil

1 medium yellow onion, minced

1 cup dry white wine

3 cups Italian plum tomatoes, peeled, seeded, and chopped (page 259), fresh or canned

Preheat the oven to 350°F. In a bowl, combine the pork, beef, veal, bread crumbs, half of the garlic, the parsley, ground coriander, nutmeg, cumin, cayenne, 3/4 teaspoon salt, and 1/4 teaspoon pepper. Form the mixture into 32 one-inch meatballs and place on an oiled baking sheet. Bake for 10 to 12 minutes. Remove from the oven and reserve.

Heat the olive oil in a frying pan over medium heat. Add the onion and the remaining garlic and cook, stirring occasionally, until soft, 7 minutes. Add the wine and the tomatoes and simmer slowly for 15 minutes. Add the meatballs, the salt, and pepper to taste and continue to simmer slowly for 10 minutes.

Serve immediately or at room temperature.

Serves 6

> NOTE: This recipe can be made up to 2 days in advance and stored covered in the refrigerator. Reheat before serving.

SPICY PORK KEBABS WITH MOORISH FLAVORS

Pinchitos are heavily seasoned miniature meat kebabs cooked over a charcoal grill. The spice mixture is reminiscent of North Africa and the Middle East, but the use of pork is not. Pork consumption is forbidden by Islam, and thus it is absent in North African cuisine. In Spain, pork is much favored. Be sure to soak the skewers in water before placing them on the hot grill, otherwise they might go up in flames.

2 cloves garlic, sliced

Salt

1 teaspoon whole coriander seeds

3/4 teaspoon sweet paprika

3/4 teaspoon cumin seeds

1/2 teaspoon dried thyme

1/4 teaspoon crushed red pepper flakes

1 teaspoon curry powder

3 tablespoons extra virgin olive oil

1 tablespoon lemon juice

1 tablespoon chopped fresh flat-leaf parsley

Freshly ground black pepper

1 pound pork tenderloin, cut into 3/4- to 1-inch cubes

Soak twelve 7-inch bamboo skewers in water for 30 minutes.

Mash the garlic and a pinch of salt in a mortar and pestle or with the back of a knife on your cutting board to make a fine paste.

In a dry frying pan, heat the coriander seeds, paprika, cumin seeds, thyme, red pepper flakes, and curry powder until hot and aromatic, 30 seconds. Remove from the pan; put the mixture into an electric spice grinder, a coffee grinder, or a mortar and pestle; and grind to make a fine powder. In a bowl, combine the garlic, spices, olive oil, lemon juice, parsley, 3/4 teaspoon salt, pepper, and the pork cubes. Toss well to coat the pork completely and marinate covered in the refrigerator, tossing occasionally, for 2 to 3 hours.

Thread the pork onto the skewers. Broil or grill the pork skewers over hot coals, turning every 2 to 3 minutes and basting occasionally with the marinade, until well browned but still juicy, 10 to 15 minutes. Serve immediately.

Makes 12 skewers to serve 6

PORK TENDERLOIN STUFFED WITH ONION MARMALADE

Solomillo de Cerdo Relleno de Mermelada de Cebolla

Combine paprika, cumin, cayenne, cloves, raisins, citrus, and caramelized onions, and the outcome is a lusty blending of sweet, savory, and sour flavors. I tasted this in the hill town of Arcos de la Frontera in Andalusia, in the very south of Spain, and loved the way that it reflected a North African influence. This dish is substantial enough to be served as a main course.

1 large pork tenderloin, about 1 pound, trimmed

3 tablespoons extra virgin olive oil

1 clove garlic, minced

$1/4$ teaspoon sweet paprika

$1/4$ teaspoon ground cumin

Large pinch of cayenne

$1/4$ teaspoon ground cloves

Pinch of freshly ground black pepper

1 orange

3 tablespoons sultana or golden raisins

2 tablespoons sherry vinegar

1 medium yellow onion, thinly sliced

1 teaspoon sugar

$1/4$ cup water

5 cloves garlic, peeled

3 sprigs fresh flat-leaf parsley

1 bay leaf

4 whole cloves

$1/4$ cup dry white wine, such as sauvignon blanc

$1^1/2$ cups chicken stock (page 255)

Salt

Butterfly the pork by slitting the pork lengthwise almost from end to end so it opens up to make a flat piece. Flatten slightly with a meat pounder. In a bowl, combine 1 tablespoon of the olive oil, the garlic, paprika, cumin, cayenne, cloves, and pepper. Rub the pork with the mixture, place in a baking dish, cover, and refrigerate for 2 hours or up to overnight.

Using a vegetable peeler, zest one-quarter of the orange. Juice the orange. In a small saucepan, combine the orange zest and juice, raisins, and sherry vinegar. Simmer very slowly, uncovered, for 10 minutes. Heat the remaining 2 tablespoons olive oil in a frying pan over medium heat, add the onion, and cook, stirring occasionally, until very soft, 20 minutes. Add the raisin mixture, sprinkle with the sugar, and continue to cook very slowly, covered, until the onion is very soft, 30 minutes. Add the water and continue to cook, uncovered, until almost dry, 20 minutes. Season with salt and pepper.

Place the pork on a work surface, cut side up. Season with salt and pepper. Spread the onion mixture on the pork, spreading evenly. Roll the pork back up into its original shape, enclosing the filling. Tie at 1-inch intervals with kitchen string. The recipe can be prepared to this point up to 1 day in advance.

Place the pork in a sauté pan with the peeled garlic, parsley, bay leaf, whole cloves, wine, and chicken stock. Cover and bring to a boil. Turn down the heat to very low and simmer until the pork is done, 30 minutes. Remove the pork and keep warm. Reduce the liquid until it coats the back of a spoon and is reduced by half, 10 to 15 minutes. Strain. Season with salt and pepper.

Remove the strings and slice the meat into $1/2$-inch slices. Place on a platter and drizzle the sauce over the top.

Serves 6

STEWED CHICKPEAS WITH CHORIZO

Habas con Chorizo

The Phoenicians were the traveling salesmen of the Mediterranean. In the south of Spain, they traded their glass, metal, and cloth for copper extracted from Spanish mines and salt from the coastal marshes. They also introduced chickpeas to the Spanish, who called them garbanzo beans. Chickpeas and other pulses remain a staple of Spanish cuisine, especially in Catalonia.

2 cups dried chickpeas, about 12 ounces

1 small yellow onion, quartered

1/8 teaspoon ground cloves

1 cinnamon stick

1 bay leaf

Pinch of dried thyme

6 sprigs fresh flat-leaf parsley

3 tablespoons extra virgin olive oil

1 medium yellow onion, minced

3 cloves garlic, minced

3 chorizo, pricked with a fork, about 12 ounces

Salt and freshly ground black pepper

Pick over the chickpeas and discard any stones. Cover with water and soak 8 hours or overnight. Drain and place in a saucepan with the onion, cloves, cinnamon stick, bay leaf, thyme, parsley, and enough water to cover by 2 inches. Simmer, uncovered, until the skins just begin to crack and the beans are tender, 40 to 45 minutes. Discard the onion, cinnamon stick, bay leaf, and parsley and reserve the chickpeas with their cooking liquid.

In a large frying pan, warm the oil over medium heat. Add the onion, garlic, and chorizo and cook, stirring occasionally, until the onion is soft, 7 minutes. Add the chickpeas and their cooking liquid and simmer slowly until the liquid is almost gone, 40 minutes. Season with salt and pepper.

Remove the chorizo from the pan and slice on the diagonal into thin slices. Return to the chickpeas and heat thoroughly, 3 to 4 minutes.

Serves 6

NOTE: This recipe can be prepared in advance and reheated to serve.

ROASTED POTATOES WITH SPICY TOMATO SAUCE

Patatas Bravas

Although this delicious tapa served all over Spain is one of the simplest dishes in this book, it is also a personal favorite. How could it not be? Crispy golden potatoes, topped with a fiery tomato sauce and smothered with a pungent garlic mayonnaise! The garlic mayonnaise is optional for some, but for me it's a must.

3 pounds red potatoes, unpeeled
   and cut into 3/4-inch cubes

4 tablespoons extra virgin olive oil

Salt and freshly ground black pepper

1/4 cup minced yellow onion

2 cloves garlic, minced

2 cups peeled, seeded, and chopped
   tomatoes (page 259), about
   1 pound, fresh or canned

1 tablespoon tomato paste

1/2 cup dry white wine

1 cup water

1/4 teaspoon crushed red pepper
   flakes

1/2 teaspoon Tabasco sauce

1 bay leaf

2 tablespoons chopped fresh
   flat-leaf parsley

1/4 teaspoon fresh chopped thyme,
   or 1/8 teaspoon dried thyme

Pinch of sugar

2 to 3 teaspoons red wine vinegar

Spanish Garlic Mayonnaise
   (page 257)

Preheat the oven to 375°F. Toss the potatoes, 2 tablespoons of the olive oil, and salt and pepper together in a baking dish. Arrange in a single layer and bake on the top rack of the oven until golden and cooked through, about 45 minutes.

Meanwhile, heat the remaining 2 tablespoons olive oil over medium heat in a frying pan and cook the onion and garlic until soft, 7 minutes. Add the tomatoes, tomato paste, wine, water, red pepper flakes, Tabasco, bay leaf, parsley, thyme, sugar, salt, and pepper. Reduce the heat to low and simmer 20 minutes. Cool for 10 minutes. Remove the bay leaf and purée in a blender until smooth. Season with salt, pepper, and vinegar.

Place the warm potatoes on a serving dish and pour the sauce over the top. Serve with the Spanish Garlic Mayonnaise on the side.

Serves 6

STUFFED EGGPLANT WITH OREGANO AND MINT

Berenjenas Rellenas

Like the rest of the Mediterranean, Spain loves stuffed vegetables. This recipe is from the one-star restaurant called L'Ampurdan, a few miles north of the town of Figueras in Catalonia. Josep Mercader, the restaurant's owner and chef, is considered the father of modern Catalan cuisine. He delved into the history of Catalonia and put together some wonderfully innovative, modern dishes that transcend time. He died in 1979, but his son-in-law, Jaume Subiros, now follows in his footsteps. If you go to his restaurant, ask him to make you his deep-fried anchovy spines.

2 large eggplants

Salt and freshly ground black pepper

5 tablespoons extra virgin olive oil

6 cloves garlic, peeled and crushed with the side of a knife

1 small yellow onion, minced

1 cup peeled, seeded, and chopped tomatoes (page 259), about 3 tomatoes, fresh or canned

1/2 teaspoon sugar

1 teaspoon chopped fresh thyme

3/4 teaspoon chopped fresh oregano

Large pinch of chopped fresh mint

8 anchovy fillets, soaked in cold water for 10 minutes and patted dry

1/2 cup fresh bread crumbs

3 tablespoons chopped fresh flat-leaf parsley

3 cloves garlic, minced

Halve the eggplants lengthwise and score the pulp of the eggplants with a knife, leaving the skin and a 1/2-inch border of the pulp intact. Salt the eggplants and let them sit in a colander, cut side down, for 30 minutes. Wash the salt off the eggplants and squeeze them dry.

Heat 2 tablespoons of the olive oil in a frying pan over medium heat and fry the eggplants on all sides until golden, 35 minutes total. Remove and let sit until the eggplants are cool enough to handle. In the same frying pan, add 1 tablespoon of the olive oil and cook the garlic cloves until light golden brown, 4 to 5 minutes. Remove and discard the garlic. With a spoon, scoop out the pulp of the eggplants, leaving the skin and 1/2 inch of the pulp intact. Do not pierce the skin. Chop the eggplant pulp very finely, return it to the frying pan with the onion, and cook, stirring occasionally, until soft, 15 minutes. Add the tomatoes, sugar, thyme, oregano, mint, anchovies, salt, and pepper and simmer slowly, 30 minutes. Season with salt and pepper.

Preheat the oven to 375°F. Fill the eggplant shells with the tomato-eggplant stuffing. Place in a greased 13 by 9-inch baking dish, stuffing side up. Combine the bread crumbs, parsley, and garlic and sprinkle over the top. Drizzle with the remaining 2 tablespoons olive oil.

Note: This recipe can be made to this point in advance. Cover with plastic wrap and place in the refrigerator. Bring to room temperature before baking.

Bake until the eggplants are soft and the tops are golden brown, 30 to 40 minutes. Serve immediately.

Serves 6

WILTED GREENS WITH RAISINS, PINE NUTS, AND FRIED BREAD

Acelgas con Pasas, Piñónes, y Migas

Wilted greens, pine nuts, raisins, and garlic are frequently combined in Catalonia, Provence, Genoa, and Sicily. This combination can be seen on a pizza in northern Italy, in a tart in Provence, and in a side dish or contorno in Genoa and Sicily. Here in Catalonia, it is most commonly served as a tapa, but is also served as a topping on coca dough, the equivalent of Catalan flat bread.

1 cup boiling water

1/4 cup sultana or golden raisins

1/4 cup dark raisins

1/4 pound stale rustic country-style bread, crusts removed

5 tablespoons extra virgin olive oil

6 cloves garlic, minced

Salt and freshly ground black pepper

3 large bunches of spinach or Swiss chard

4 anchovy fillets, soaked in cold water for 10 minutes and patted dry

1/2 cup pine nuts, toasted (page 258)

Pour the boiling water over all the raisins and let stand 15 minutes. Drain.

Preheat the oven to 400°F. Tear the bread into crouton-size pieces or cut into 1-inch cubes and place on a baking sheet. Heat 4 tablespoons of the olive oil in a frying pan, add 4 minced garlic cloves, and turn off the heat immediately. Pour over the bread cubes and toss gently. Bake, tossing occasionally, until golden and crisp, 10 to 15 minutes. Season with salt and pepper.

Remove all stems from the greens, wash, and dry well. Warm the remaining 1 tablespoon olive oil in a frying pan over medium-high heat. Add the remaining garlic and the anchovies and stir until the anchovies melt into the oil, 30 seconds. Add the greens, salt, and pepper and cook, tossing occasionally with tongs, until wilted, about 2 minutes for spinach, about 7 minutes for Swiss chard. Add the pine nuts and raisins. Toss together well and place on a platter. Garnish with the toasted bread and serve warm.

Serves 6

GRILLED LEEKS AND GREEN ONIONS WITH ROMESCO

Calcots con Romesco

Romesco, the reddish sauce that hails from Tarragona, the old Roman capital of northern Spain, has three meanings: a seafood dish, the accompanying sauce, and the red pepper that grows here and is used to give the sauce its characteristic heat. Like rouille of Provence, tarator of Turkey, and harissa of Morocco, romesco provides a good punch to the palate. Romesco differs from town to town and from cook to cook, but it is predominantly an emulsified sauce of olive oil, red pepper, bread, tomato, almonds, garlic, and vinegar. I use it for just about everything: meat, fish, and vegetables.

Sauce

3 fresh or one 16-ounce can tomatoes

5 cloves garlic, unpeeled

2 dried sweet red peppers, such as ancho peppers, or 2 teaspoons sweet paprika

1/4 teaspoon crushed red pepper flakes

3/4 cup water

6 to 7 tablespoons red wine vinegar

6 to 7 tablespoons extra virgin olive oil

1 slice rustic country-style bread

15 whole almonds, skins removed (see Note)

15 whole hazelnuts, skins removed (see Note)

1 teaspoon sweet paprika

Salt and freshly ground black pepper

Vegetables

18 small leeks

18 large green onions

1 tablespoon unsalted butter, melted

2 tablespoons extra virgin olive oil

Preheat the oven to 350°F. To make the sauce, place the tomatoes and garlic in an ungreased roasting pan and roast in the oven for 30 minutes. Remove from the oven and peel, core, and seed the tomatoes and peel the garlic.

Place the dried red peppers and red pepper flakes in a saucepan with the water and 4 tablespoons of the vinegar. Bring to a boil, cover, and simmer slowly for 10 minutes. Turn the heat off and let steep for 30 minutes. Drain the peppers, discard the seeds, and chop finely. (If using paprika, omit this step.)

Heat 2 tablespoons of the olive oil in a small frying pan and fry the bread until golden. Transfer to a food processor. In the same oil, fry the almonds and hazelnuts until golden and add to the food processor with the peppers (or, if using paprika, add the 2 teaspoons paprika and the red pepper flakes), peeled garlic, and tomatoes. With the motor running, gradually pour in the remaining 4 to 5 tablespoons olive oil and 2 to 3 tablespoons vinegar, 1 teaspoon paprika, salt, and pepper. Let sit 2 hours.

Heat an outdoor charcoal grill until very hot. While it is heating, trim the leeks and green onions and wash them well. Combine the butter and oil and brush the leeks and green onions with the mixture. When the grill is ready, place the leeks on the grill and cook, turning occasionally, for about 15 minutes. When the leeks are almost blackened, add the green onions and grill until golden, 4 to 5 minutes. Remove from the grill and wrap in newspaper or a paper bag. Allow them to steam 10 minutes.

Remove the black skin from the leeks. Place the leeks and green onions on a serving plate with the romesco sauce.

Serves 6

NOTE: If you prefer, you can bake the leeks and green onions on the top rack of a 450°F oven, turning occasionally. The green onions will cook in 10 to 15 minutes and the leeks in 35 to 40 minutes.

To remove the almond skins, blanch the almonds in boiling water for 1 minute. Puncture the skin with the tip of your fingernail and squeeze the almond from the skin. Discard the skins.

To remove the hazelnut skins, place the hazelnuts on a baking sheet and spray with a light mist of water. Bake in a 325°F oven until the skins crack, 10 to 15 minutes. Cool slightly, wrap in a kitchen towel, and rub them together inside the towel to remove the skins.

WARM CHARCOAL-GRILLED VEGETABLE SALAD

Escalivada

Escalivar is a Catalan word meaning "to cook in hot embers" or "to roast." As in the celebrated ratatouille of Provence, the vegetables in this dish are grilled and then oiled. When making escalivada, however, the vegetables are removed from the grill and composed into a warm or room-temperature salad, whereas in ratatouille the vegetables are stewed together after they are taken from the grill. In both cases, grilling imparts a smoky flavor. Both dishes are best when made in the late summer or early autumn, when the vegetables are at their peak.

1 1/2 pounds eggplant, preferably Japanese

5 small tomatoes

1 large red bell pepper

1 large green bell pepper

2 small yellow or red onions, peeled

4 tablespoons extra virgin olive oil

Salt and freshly ground black pepper

3 tablespoons chopped fresh flat-leaf parsley

2 cloves garlic, minced

18 pitted cured black olives

Start a charcoal grill (see Note). Preheat the oven to 350°F.

Wash and dry the eggplant, tomatoes, peppers, and onions and leave whole. Grill all the vegetables over a very hot fire, turning occasionally, until they are black on all sides, 7 to 12 minutes, depending upon the size. Cut the tomatoes in half. Coat the vegetables with 1 tablespoon of the olive oil. Place the vegetables in a roasting pan, with the tomatoes cut side up, and roast until the vegetables are done. (Tomatoes will cook in 20 minutes, peppers and eggplant in 45 minutes, and onions in 1 hour.) As soon as they are done, remove them from the oven.

Place the vegetables in a plastic bag and let stand 15 minutes. Core, seed, and peel the peppers. Slice into thin strips. Peel the eggplant and tear into thin strips. Slice the onions. Slip the tomatoes out of their skins and cut them into quarters.

Arrange the vegetables on a serving dish, alternating stripes of color. Season with salt and pepper and drizzle with the remaining 3 tablespoons olive oil. Combine the parsley and garlic and chop together until fine. Sprinkle over the vegetables. Garnish with the olives and serve.

Serves 6

NOTE: The vegetables can also be charred under the broiler, directly over the gas burners of the stove, or in a cast-iron pan (see Red-Hot Smoked Tomato Relish, page 206).

FAVA BEAN SALAD WITH FRESH MINT

Ensalada de Habas a la Menta

Dried legumes and ham are a classic combination in Spain, the Languedoc, and all over Italy. This version, from L'Ampurdan in Catalonia, adds a twist—mint—to this time-honored favorite. Another trademark of Josep Mercader, this salad is pretty addictive. If you can't find fresh fava beans at the market, forget about making this salad until fresh favas are available.

3¹/₂ pounds fava beans in their pods

3 sprigs of fresh mint

5 cups salted water

4 ounces thinly sliced Serrano ham, prosciutto, or Black Forest ham

1 small head of romaine lettuce, cut into thin strips

1 teaspoon Dijon mustard

5 tablespoons extra virgin olive oil

2 tablespoons red wine vinegar

Salt and freshly ground black pepper

Peel the fava beans and discard the pods. Bring a pot of water to a boil. Add the fava beans and simmer 30 seconds. Remove the fava beans and cool. To peel them, puncture the bright green skin with your fingernail and pop the bean out of the shell. Discard the shells.

Remove the leaves from the mint sprigs, but reserve the stems. Pile the leaves one on top of another and roll like a cigar. Cut into very thin strips and reserve. With the back of a knife, tap the mint stems several times to bring out their flavor. Bring the salted water and the mint stems to a boil. Add the fava beans and simmer until tender, 3 minutes. Drain, discard the mint stems, and cool.

Cut the ham into thin strips. Combine the ham, lettuce, strips of mint, and fava beans.

Whisk together the mustard, olive oil, and vinegar. Season with salt and pepper. Toss the vinaigrette with the fava bean mixture and serve immediately.

Serves 6

SHREDDED COD SALAD WITH TOMATOES, PEPPERS, AND ONIONS

Esqueixada

Spain began to import salt cod from the south of France in the fifteenth century. Today, salt cod appears all over the Mediterranean; only in Catalonia, however, is it eaten soaked but uncooked. It is imperative that the fish soak in many changes of cold water for 2 to 3 days before use. Esqueixada (pronounced es-kwe-sada) is a popular summer salad in Catalonia. The cod should be torn or shredded (esqueixar); a knife must never be used.

3/4 pound dry salt cod (see Note)

1 small red onion, thinly sliced

3 medium tomatoes, peeled, seeded, and chopped (page 259)

1 red bell pepper, seeded and diced

2 cloves garlic, minced

6 tablespoons extra virgin olive oil

3 tablespoons red wine vinegar

24 pitted cured black olives

Salt and freshly ground black pepper

12 slices rustic country-style bread, toasted

Soak the salt cod in cold water for 2 or 3 days, changing and replenishing the water a few times each day. Drain the cod and press it with your hands to rid it of any excess water. Remove the skin and bones and discard. Tear the cod into thin strips and place in a bowl.

Soak the onion in salted water for 30 minutes. Drain and pat dry. Place the onion in the bowl with the cod. Add the tomatoes, pepper, garlic, oil, vinegar, and olives. Season with salt and pepper. Let marinate 2 to 3 hours in the refrigerator.

Remove from the refrigerator and bring to room temperature. Serve with the toasted bread.

Serves 6

NOTE: Dry salt cod is available in fish markets and Italian or Spanish specialty shops.

SALT COD SALAD WITH ORANGES AND OLIVES

Bacalao de Granada

A Spanish friend told me that if I were ever in Granada in the south of Spain, I really must try the salt cod salad that the city is famous for. When I got to Granada, I scoured every restaurant menu until I found exactly the salad I was looking for. The rustic little restaurant where I ate this, tucked into a side street of the bustling city, actually served two varieties of Granada's trademark salad, one with olives, red onions, oranges, and sherry vinaigrette, and this one with revived salt cod.

1 pound dry salt cod (see Note, page 39)

3 cups milk

6 sprigs fresh flat-leaf parsley

Pinch of thyme

1 bay leaf

1 clove garlic, minced

1 tablespoon sherry vinegar

3 tablespoons white wine vinegar

3 tablespoons orange juice

1/2 cup extra virgin olive oil

Salt and freshly ground black pepper

1/2 small red onion, thinly sliced

24 pitted cured black olives

3 oranges, peeled and sectioned (page 260)

1 hard-cooked egg, peeled and chopped

Soak the salt cod in cold water for 2 or 3 days, changing and replenishing the water a few times per day. Drain and place in a saucepan with the milk, parsley, thyme, bay leaf, and enough cold water to cover. Over high heat, bring to just below the boiling point, cover, and turn off the heat. Let stand 10 minutes. Drain and chill immediately until completely cool. Remove and discard the skin and bones. Flake the fish and place in a bowl.

To make a vinaigrette, whisk together the garlic, sherry vinegar, white wine vinegar, orange juice, olive oil, salt, and pepper. Marinate the cod in the vinaigrette for 1 hour.

Add the onion, olives, and oranges to the cod and vinaigrette. Adjust the seasonings with salt, pepper, and vinegar. Place on a serving plate and garnish with the hard-cooked egg.

Serves 6

STUFFED MUSSELS WITH ROASTED GARLIC MAYONNAISE

Mejillones Rellenos

As the waves rolled along the shore in the little village of Sitges in Catalonia, I watched the waiters at Cal Pinxo restaurant set the tables outside with starched white tablecloths and candles, getting ready for a busy evening. The rumor was that the chef here made delicious stuffed mussels broiled with garlic mayonnaise. When I finally got my table under the stars and tasted the mussels, I realized why they were so talked about. He used the freshest mussels, roasted the garlic for the mayonnaise, and added the perfect amount of Serrano ham, an excellent cured ham from the Spanish mountains.

Mayonnaise

1 large head garlic

10 tablespoons pure olive oil

1/4 cup water

1/2 teaspoon dried thyme

1 bay leaf

Salt and freshly ground black pepper

1 egg yolk

1 to 2 teaspoons white wine vinegar

Mussels

3/4 cup dry white wine, such as sauvignon blanc

1 small yellow onion, minced

6 sprigs fresh flat-leaf parsley

Pinch of thyme

1 bay leaf

36 large mussels (3 pounds), scrubbed and beards removed

1 tablespoon extra virgin olive oil

2 cups fresh spinach, washed and dried

3 tablespoons minced Serrano ham, prosciutto, or Black Forest ham

2 tablespoons unsalted butter

2 tablespoons all-purpose flour

3/4 cup milk

Salt and freshly ground black pepper

Preheat the oven to 375°F. Break up the head of garlic into separate cloves. Place the garlic cloves in a small baking dish and drizzle with 1 tablespoon of the olive oil, the water, thyme, bay leaf, salt, and pepper. Cover and bake until soft, 20 to 30 minutes. Cool. Remove the garlic from the skins by scraping the garlic with a knife or pressing the garlic through a food mill to extract the pulp. Reserve the pulp and discard the skins. Place the egg yolk and 1 tablespoon of the olive oil in a bowl. Whisk well to form an emulsion. Drop by drop, add the remaining 8 tablespoons olive oil to the egg yolk emulsion, whisking constantly until all the oil has been added. Add the roasted garlic purée, salt, pepper, and vinegar and mix well. Reserve.

Bring the white wine, half of the onion, parsley, thyme, bay leaf, and mussels to a boil in a large covered saucepan over high heat. Steam, shaking the pan frequently, until the mussels open. Remove the mussels as they open, discarding any unopened mussels. Cool the mussels. Reduce the cooking liquid until 2 tablespoons remain. Strain and reserve the liquid. Remove the mussels from their shells and save two-thirds of the shells. Separate each shell into 2 halves. Chop the mussels coarsely.

Heat the olive oil in a frying pan. Cook the remaining onion until soft, 7 minutes. Finely chop the spinach. Add the ham and spinach to the onion, cover, and cook until wilted, 1 minute. Remove from the pan and place in a bowl with the chopped mussels.

Preheat the broiler. Heat the butter in a saucepan. Add the flour and cook slowly 2 minutes, stirring. Add the milk and the reserved cooking liquid and cook until smooth and very thick. Add to the mussels and mix well. Season with salt and pepper.

Stuff the shells with the mixture. Spread the mayonnaise on top of the mussels and place on a baking sheet. Broil until hot and golden, 10 to 20 seconds; watch closely, as they brown very quickly. Serve immediately.

Serves 6

CLAMS STEWED WITH TOMATOES AND GARLIC

Almejas Marineras L'Avi Pau

The tomato was introduced to Spain in the sixteenth century, and from that time forward it became the inspiration for a huge variety of dishes. Later the tomato migrated from Spain to Italy. Marineras is very similar to marinara sauce, made in Campania in southern Italy: both sauces are based on tomatoes, olive oil, and garlic and were originally made by fishermen who had only a few ingredients available to them.

4 tablespoons extra virgin olive oil

1 medium yellow onion, chopped

2 large tomatoes, peeled, seeded, and chopped (page 259), about ³/4 cup, fresh or canned

1 tablespoon tomato paste

¹/2 cup dry white wine, such as sauvignon blanc

1 cup fish stock (page 255) or bottled clam juice

Salt and freshly ground black pepper

1 large clove garlic, minced

2 tablespoons chopped fresh flat-leaf parsley

2 pounds fresh clams, scrubbed

Rustic country-style bread

Heat 2 tablespoons of the olive oil in a frying pan over medium heat. Add the onion and cook, stirring occasionally, until it just begins to turn golden, 12 to 15 minutes. Add the tomatoes and tomato paste and continue to cook 5 to 6 minutes. Add the wine and simmer until the mixture is reduced by half, 5 minutes. Increase the heat to medium-high and add the fish stock. Simmer for 5 minutes. Cool for 5 minutes. Transfer the sauce to a blender or food processor and purée until smooth. Season with salt and pepper.

Heat the remaining 2 tablespoons olive oil in a frying pan large enough to hold the clams in one layer. Add the garlic, parsley, and clams. Cover and cook over high heat until the clams open, 5 to 10 minutes, depending upon their size. Discard any unopened clams.

With a slotted spoon, remove the clams and keep them warm. Add the tomato sauce to the frying pan and reduce the sauce by one-quarter, 3 to 4 minutes. Add the clams and mix well.

Serve immediately with crusty bread.

Serves 6

SHRIMP AND GREEN ONION PANCAKES

Tortillitas con Camarones y Cebollitas

An absolute must when visiting Seville is eating at Bodega La Albariza. While the patrons stand around old sherry barrels sipping fino, waiters scurry through the crowd delivering plates of alca-parrones (golden deep-fried sardines) and these tortillas made with tiny shrimp, cooked green onions, and chickpea flour brought to Spain by the Moors.

2 tablespoons extra virgin olive oil

$3/4$ cup thinly sliced green onions, white and green parts

$3/4$ cup all-purpose flour

$3/4$ cup chickpea flour (see Note)

$1/2$ teaspoon baking powder

$1/2$ teaspoon salt

Freshly ground black pepper

3 tablespoons minced fresh flat-leaf parsley

$1^1/2$ teaspoons sweet paprika

$1/2$ teaspoon ground cumin

Large pinch of cayenne

8 ounces small fresh shrimp, shelled and finely chopped

$1^1/2$ cups cold water

Olive oil for frying

Heat the olive oil in a small frying pan over medium heat. Add the green onions and cook, covered, until soft, 3 minutes. Cool slightly.

Combine the all-purpose and chickpea flours, baking powder, the salt, and pepper. Add the green onions, parsley, paprika, cumin, cayenne, shrimp, and water. Stir well. The batter should be the consistency of very heavy cream. Let rest 1 to 2 hours at room temperature.

Heat the oil $1/4$ inch deep in a large frying pan over medium-high heat. Drop 2 tablespoons of batter into the oil, spreading it out to form a $2^1/2$-inch-diameter pancake. Repeat with the remaining batter. Fry until golden, turning once, 2 minutes on each side. Drain on paper towels. Serve immediately.

Makes 18 to 20 pancakes to serve 6

> NOTE: Chickpea flour is available at any health food store. It is also called garbanzo flour.

GRILLED TUNA WITH GREEN OLIVE RELISH

Atún Asadas con Condimento Aceitunas Verdes

Spain is the world's largest producer of olive oil. It is the first country to have established a strict grading system, the Spanish Denominación de Origen. Almost all of the table olives in Spain, mostly the Manzanilla variety, come from Andalusia. Other olives grown here are the Gordal, Hojiblanca, Arbequina, and Blanguetas. To vary the recipe slightly, reduce the amount of olive oil in the relish and spread it on grilled bread. It will then resemble tapenade of Provence, France, and garum of Lazio, Italy, and it's terrific with these grilled tuna skewers. Remember to soak the skewers in water before placing them on the hot grill.

1 lemon, plus 6 lemon wedges

1 pound fresh tuna, cut into 3/4-inch chunks

6 tablespoons extra virgin olive oil

2 cloves garlic, crushed, plus 1 clove garlic, minced

Salt and freshly ground black pepper

2 anchovy fillets, soaked in cold water 10 minutes and patted dry

1/2 cup pitted (page 260) and finely chopped green olives

1/2 cup chopped fresh flat-leaf parsley, plus flat-leaf parsley leaves for garnish

1 tablespoon white wine vinegar

Soak twelve 7-inch bamboo skewers in water for 30 minutes.

Peel the lemon with a vegetable peeler into long pieces, avoiding the pith. Marinate the tuna with the lemon peel, 2 tablespoons of the olive oil, the 2 cloves crushed garlic, salt, and pepper for 2 hours or up to overnight in the refrigerator.

Mash the anchovies and place in a small bowl. Add the olives, the 1 clove minced garlic, the chopped parsley, vinegar, the juice of 1/2 lemon, and the remaining 4 tablespoons olive oil. Mix well. Season with salt, pepper, and additional lemon juice as needed.

Thread the tuna onto the skewers. Broil or grill over hot coals, turning every 2 minutes, until cooked through but still juicy, 5 to 6 minutes total.

Serve warm or at room temperature garnished with the relish, lemon wedges, and parsley leaves.

Serves 6

SOUTHERN FRANCE

*I*n southern France, the Mediterranean laps against the three provinces of Roussillon, Languedoc, and Provence, with French-run Corsica sitting just off the horizon. The countryside is a painter's dream of rolling herb-scented hills; citrus and olive groves; vineyards; and terra-cotta-roofed farmhouses sun-dried to shades of ocher, mauve, amber, and viridian. A translucent haze hangs over the landscape, and the quality of light is compelling. It isn't hard to see why Cézanne, Matisse, and Renoir were all drawn to paint here.

The sun is relentless. It penetrates deeply into the land and the lives of the people who live and work here. During the day, the hard work in the fields is interrupted as families gather to share the midday meal. Seeking shade under an arbor, men come in from work and children from school or play. Women dash back and forth from the kitchen bringing platters of appetite-arousing hors d'oeuvres and entrées, setting them on a table covered with a flowered oilcloth. Stories are exchanged and bodies and minds revived for the afternoon.

Later, as the workday ends and the sun begins to settle into the skyline, everyone meets again under the arbor. Well-tanned faces turn from the long day of work and contemplate the bounty before them. Here are plates of well-seasoned, full-flavored hors d'oeuvres and entrées meant to tease and please the appetite and to take the edge off the sweltering day: croutons with *tapenade* or eggplant caviar; roasted vegetable salad; an onion, tomato, and anchovy pie. Glasses are filled with slightly chilled rosé, light red or white wine, or pastis, a favorite licorice-flavored liqueur. Both food and drink seem to reflect the strong sunshine and the bold character of the landscape, which contrasts with the gentleness of the Mediterranean.

Hors d'Oeuvres and Entrées: Overture to the Meal

In France, first courses go by two names: hors d'oeuvre and entrée. *Hors d'oeuvre* literally means "apart from the work." Hors d'oeuvres, simple bites of food that require little preparation, are served to amuse the palate before the meal. *Entrée* means "to enter," specifically, to enter the meal. Both terms are used to refer to a wide range of starters served before the main course. These include soups, crudités (raw vegetables), charcuterie, salads, savory pies, egg dishes, fish dishes both raw and cooked, grilled breads with various toppings, and even pasta.

Versatility, Flavor, and Simplicity

Hors d'oeuvres and entrées can be as light as a few raw vegetables served with an anchovy and olive oil sauce or as hearty as a robust vegetable and bean soup served over a crust of bread doused in olive oil. They can be as simple as a saucer of tiny jet-black niçoise olives marinated and warmed in herbaceous olive oil or as complex as a *galette*, a thin pie that might be filled with goat cheese and wild thyme from the hillsides.

In Provence, Languedoc, and Roussillon, hors d'oeuvres and entrées center around two major themes: flavor and simplicity. Bold, assertive, and forthright flavors—sour, bitter, spicy, and salty—are accomplished with aromatics such as wild herbs, tender garlic, salt-packed anchovies, lemons, and pungent gold olive oil. And simplicity is the guiding principle of cooks, who take the excellent ingredients from the land and sea and prepare them in a way to accentuate their natural flavors: freshly shucked oysters on the half shell garnished with a wedge or two of lemon and thin slices of rye bread spread with sweet butter, or a salad of sweet grilled peppers with anchovies and briny black niçoise olives.

Where It Began

Hors d'oeuvres and entrées are very much a part of everyday life in southern France today, but their roots go back many civilizations. The Greeks and the Phoenicians were probably the first to travel to southern France, sailing across the Mediterranean to the old port of Massalia (Marseilles today) in the seventh century BC to set up trade settlements. They brought olive trees and grape vines—matchless gifts, as it turned out. They also introduced the custom of spreading the table with an array of first plates. Five hundred years later, the Romans were summoned to help the Greeks defend this land from the Celts and Ligurians. The Romans came and stayed, later settling parts of Provence as well as Languedoc. Their endowment, too, was tremendous, and they profoundly influenced architecture, engineering, culture, and food traditions. The Romans refined the table and reiterated the value of first courses, incorporating legumes, anchovies, herbs, and perhaps dried orange peel into various dishes.

The Arabs and North Africans arrived in Languedoc in the eighth century AD to set up trade colonies, and their legacy can still be seen in the piles of spices in the market and even in the Arabic-derived street signs. Arabic and North African influences can be seen in Languedoc with the rich use of spices, rice, eggplant, legumes, citrus, almonds, and sweet-and-sour flavor combinations.

The Spanish were also very influential in southern France, particularly in Roussillon, the province that borders Spain and was once part of Catalonia. Roussillon did not become part of France until 1659, and Spanish and Catalan roots here are still very deep, evidenced in the use of red pimientos, cayenne pepper, green olives, ham, sausage, snails, anchovies, bitter orange peel, eggplant, tomatoes, and garlic and in the liberal use of olive oil. A favorite first course in Roussillon is a slice of grilled bread rubbed with whole garlic cloves, doused with coarse salt and olive oil, and rubbed with ripe tomato. In Roussillon it is called *pain Catalan*, in Catalonia *pan con tomate*.

An Infinity of Ingredients

Provence, Languedoc, and Roussillon are all distinctive for the abundance of produce, the bounty from the sea, and the traditions of their cooking techniques. The Mediterranean trinity of olives, tomatoes, and garlic is combined in many ways that entice the palate. The Provençal, Languedoc, and Roussillon cook uses garlic liberally, but due to the strong sun and fiery summer climate, the garlic here doesn't have the same harshness as elsewhere: it tends to be sweeter, and it doesn't linger with the senses after it has been consumed. Artichokes are ubiquitous and are served frequently. Other common vegetables are asparagus, onions, broad beans, green beans, eggplant, peppers, wild fennel, wild mushrooms, tomatoes, squash, and cardoon. Mesclun is a traditional niçoise salad mix of small leaves of rocket or arugula, dandelion greens, chervil, mâche or lamb's lettuce, wild chicory, and purslane or oak leaf lettuce. These greens, which vary in color, texture, and flavor, are both grown together and picked together. The climate in Provence is perfect for a profusion of wild herbs, and the array is endless: mint, chervil, savory, lavender, rosemary, thyme, tarragon, chives, basil, marjoram, oregano, and sage. A specific combination of herbs called herbes de Provence—thyme, rosemary, bay, basil, savory, and lavender— is sold in colorful sachets in the market and used to enhance many dishes.

Bounty from the Sea

From Nice to the Spanish border, the Mediterranean is home to more than fifty species of fish. Most cities along the sea feature outdoor fish markets with their own specialty, but Marseilles is the place where one can sample the widest variety. Wander down to the Vieux Port and try a plate of *coquillage*, an intriguing array of bivalves, as an appetizer: impeccably fresh Bouzigues oysters; shiny black mussels; violets, the leathery little sea-floor creatures; and *oursin*, or sea urchin, a golf ball–size delicacy with a tough, spiny, repellent exterior that when opened exposes a sweet, salmon-colored coral. There are all kinds of clams, for example, *oursin* and large praires. Sardines are grilled, stuffed, or served raw doused with good virgin olive oil. *Poutargue*, a specialty from the Etang de Berre, is compressed salted roe from the gray mullet and is considered a real treat, a poor man's caviar.

Aioli

Aioli, garlic-flavored mayonnaise similar to Spanish *allioli*, is Provence's most popular sauce. In addition to its use as a garnish for seafood soup, aioli is the centerpiece of a favorite dish, also know as aioli, that is served on Fridays: a large bowl of silky smooth aioli surrounded by an assortment of hard-cooked eggs, freshened salt cod, snails, Jerusalem artichokes, beetroot, chickpeas, small red potatoes, carrots, green beans, artichokes, and olives. When roasted red pepper, cayenne, and fish stock are added to aioli it becomes *rouille* (French for "rust") and is used as garnish for bouillabaisse, their seafood stew.

Techniques and Basic Equipment

Favored cooking techniques in Provence, Languedoc, and Roussillon are spit roasting, grilling, and slow simmering. Most kitchens are equipped with a fireplace or grill and can turn out first courses as delectable and simple as a plate of grilled sardines brushed with a fennel branch dipped in fruity virgin olive oil. Soups and stews hold a time-honored place in the kitchen; examples include *aigo boulido*, a garlic broth with olive oil–doused crusts of bread; ratatouille, a mélange of squash, onions, garlic, bell peppers, eggplant, tomatoes, and herbs;

and *tian*, a casserole unique to the area that consists of leftover ingredients cooked slowly in olive oil.

The mortar and pestle, brought to France by the Romans, are fundamental implements in the southern French kitchen. They are essential for making *pistou*—a Provençal mix of basil, garlic, olive oil, and cheese pounded into a paste—which can be swirled into a minestrone-style soup or served as a sauce for gnocchi and pasta, Italian dishes made in the area. *Pistou* resembles pesto, made just across the border in Genoa, except it doesn't have pine nuts. The mortar and pestle are also used to make *tapenade*, an aromatic spread of olives, capers, garlic, anchovies, and lemon, and *anchoïade*, made of anchovies, garlic, parsley, and olive oil. Both are spread on grilled bread. With the addition of warm olive oil, *anchoïade* becomes *bagna cauda*, a dipping sauce for vegetables in Italy. *Brandade de morue* is dried salt cod, boiled potatoes, olive oil, and plenty of garlic ground into a creamy spread. It is much favored by people in Provence and Languedoc.

Goat's and Sheep's Milk Cheese

The southern French are avid cheese makers. Most Provençal cheeses are made from goat's milk, but those of Languedoc, including the world-renowned Roquefort, are made of ewe's milk. These cheeses are aromatic and can be cooked into various dishes or served on their own, especially as goat cheese marinated in herbs de Provence and olive oil. They are also used in salads, tarts, and sauces for gnocchi and pasta.

Corsica

Corsica is a dramatic island that seems to jump out of the Mediterranean Sea with great force. It is extremely diverse, with lovely sand beaches on the coast and rugged mountains in the interior. Lying between France and Italy, Corsica has been owned by France since the middle of the eighteenth century, though it is closer to Italy geographically and in its traditions. The island's traditions also reflect the influences of fifty different invaders. Strong and intriguing flavors are combined to create simple country fare such as pasta, minestrone, risotto, and polenta from Italy; bouillabaisse or *ziminu*, *anchoïade*, stuffed vegetables, and garlic sauces from the south of France; pimiento and salt cod from Spain; and *galettes*, or flat pies, and aromatic spices from North Africa. Their charcuterie, the cheese Brin d'amour, and *brocciu*, a ricotta-like cheese, are prized in the Mediterranean.

An Informal Cuisine

In comparison to the cuisine of northern France, the food of the south rarely aspires to the same classical principles and formal presentation. In fact, the food of southern France has more in common with the cuisines of its Mediterranean neighbors than it does with, say, the cuisines of Normandy or Alsace-Lorraine. If you asked a Parisian his feelings about the food of the south he might turn up his nose a bit—but he probably spends his summer holiday enjoying a nice slice of *pissaladière* in Nice.

BAKED SQUASH AND TOASTED BREAD SOUP

Panade à la Gourde et Oignons au Gratin

Baked in layers and resembling a gratin, this soup provides important sustenance during the winter months. And because nothing is thrown away in the kitchens of the countries that border the Mediterranean, this is an ingenious way to use up any leftovers you might have on hand.

3 tablespoons extra virgin olive oil

3 pounds red onions, sliced

Salt and freshly ground black pepper

Large pinch of chopped fresh rosemary

Large pinch of chopped fresh sage

Large pinch of chopped fresh thyme

1 1/2 pounds butternut, acorn, or turban squash, peeled, halved, and seeded

6 cups chicken stock (page 255)

3/4 cup fruity red wine, such as Côtes du Rhône or Beaujolais

6 slices rustic country-style bread, toasted

2 cloves garlic

1/2 cup grated Parmigiano-Reggiano cheese

Chopped fresh flat-leaf parsley

Heat the olive oil in a large frying pan over medium-low heat. Add the onions, salt, pepper, rosemary, sage, and thyme. Cook covered, stirring occasionally, until the onions are very soft, 40 minutes. Remove the cover and continue to cook until light golden, 10 to 20 minutes.

Slice the squash into 1/4-inch slices. Bring the chicken stock to a boil in a large saucepan over high heat. Add the squash and simmer slowly until almost soft yet still crisp, 8 to 10 minutes. Remove the squash with a slotted spoon and reserve the broth.

When the onions have cooked for 1 hour, remove the cover, increase the heat to high, add the wine, and stir for 2 minutes. Add the reserved broth, salt, and pepper.

Preheat the oven to 350°F. Rub the toasted bread with the garlic cloves. Break the toast into rough pieces and place on the bottom of a 13 by 9-inch baking dish. With a slotted spoon, cover the bread with half of the onions and then half of the squash. Ladle 1 cup of the stock over the squash and sprinkle with half of the cheese. Repeat the layering with the remaining bread, onions, 1 cup stock, and the other half of the cheese. Reserve the remaining stock for later, when serving the soup. Bake until almost all of the stock has been absorbed and the top is golden, 1 to 1 1/4 hours.

To serve, with a large spoon, scoop a portion of the gratin into soup bowls. Heat the reserved broth and distribute evenly. Garnish with the parsley and serve immediately.

Serves 8

SUMMER TOMATO AND GARLIC SOUP

Soupe d'Été

Pastel-colored cities with a thousand-year patina dot the hillsides one after the other along the coastline. Many villages balance on the very edge of the cliff, looking as though the next blast of wind might send them plummeting down into the blue depths of the Mediterranean. This describes Antibes, a town steeped in history, art, and sumptuous food. I tasted this soup in Antibes at the height of summer, when the tomatoes were brilliant red, herbs covered the hills, and the garlic was still slightly green and sweet. It's a simple recipe, so its success depends upon using the freshest and most flavorful summer ingredients.

3 tablespoons extra virgin olive oil

1/2 pound garlic cloves, peeled and halved

1 small yellow onion, minced

2 1/2 cups tomatoes, peeled, seeded, and chopped (page 259), about 5 tomatoes, fresh or canned

3 cups chicken stock (page 255)

1 cup water

2 ounces dry semolina spaghetti or linguine, broken into 1-inch pieces

2 tablespoons mixed chopped fresh herbs, such as flat-leaf parsley, thyme, savory, chives, oregano, and marjoram

1 tablespoon red wine vinegar

1/4 cup fruity red wine, such as Côtes du Rhône

Salt and freshly ground black pepper

Heat the olive oil in a soup pot over medium-low heat. Add the garlic and onion and cook, stirring occasionally, until the onion is very soft, 15 minutes.

Increase the heat to high; add the tomatoes, chicken stock, and water; and bring the soup to a boil. Reduce the heat to low and simmer for 10 minutes. Add the pasta and herbs and continue to simmer until the pasta is tender, 10 minutes.

Add the vinegar and red wine and stir. Season with salt and pepper and simmer 2 minutes. Serve the soup immediately.

Serves 6

ANCHOVY CRUSTS

If you're an anchovy lover, you're in luck! If anchovies aren't your favorite, this dish might change your mind. The anchovies, whether they are packed in salt or olive oil, are soaked in cold water for 10 minutes, then patted dry. The addition of garlic, red wine vinegar, and parsley also tempers the fishy flavor. This Provençal classic is simple and very flavorful, so give it a try. I have changed many minds with this dish.

4 ounces flat anchovy fillets, soaked in cold water for 10 minutes and patted dry

2 shallots, minced

3 tablespoons extra virgin olive oil

1 tablespoon red wine vinegar

4 cloves garlic, minced

$1/3$ cup chopped fresh flat-leaf parsley

Freshly ground black pepper

1 baguette, cut diagonally into $1/4$-inch slices and toasted

Lemon wedges

Radishes

Niçoise olives

Finely chop the anchovies. Add the shallots and extra virgin olive oil to the anchovies on your work surface and continue to chop until the anchovies and shallots are very fine and the whole mixture is well combined. Place in a bowl. Add the vinegar, garlic, and parsley. Season with pepper and mix well.

Spread the anchovy paste on the toasted slices of bread and place them in a single layer on a baking sheet. Broil just until warm, about 1 minute. Place the bread slices on a platter and garnish with lemon slices, radishes, or olives. Serve immediately.

Serves 6

CROUTONS WITH OLIVE AND TOMATO TAPENADE

Croutons avec Tapenade d'Olive et Tomate

Tapenade comes from the word tapeno, *meaning "caper." This olive spread originally contained more capers than it does today. This recipe is a variation on the classic tapenade recipe with its inclusion of sun-dried tomatoes. It's a natural on grilled bread, as a topping for pizza, or as a stuffing for chicken breasts.*

1 cup pitted niçoise or kalamata olives (page 260)

2 cloves garlic, minced

3 anchovy fillets, soaked in cold water 10 minutes and patted dry

3 tablespoons chopped capers

1/4 teaspoon finely grated lemon zest

1/2 teaspoon herbes de Provence

Freshly ground black pepper

1 to 2 tablespoons lemon juice

1/2 cup sun-dried tomatoes in oil, finely chopped and drained, 2 tablespoons oil reserved

12 slices rustic country-style bread, cut in half on the diagonal

Lemon wedges

Fresh flat-leaf parsley leaves

Place the olives, garlic, anchovies, capers, lemon zest, and herbs de Provence in the bowl of a food processor. Pulse a few times until the mixture forms a rough paste. Remove the mixture from the work bowl and place in a mixing bowl. Add the pepper, lemon juice, tomatoes, and the reserved oil from the tomatoes.

The recipe can be prepared to this point up to 1 week in advance and stored in the refrigerator until ready to use. Bring to room temperature before using.

Toast the bread or grill over a charcoal fire. Spread with the tapenade. Place on a platter and garnish with the lemon wedges and parsley. Serve immediately.

Makes about 1 1/2 cups *tapenade* to serve 8

GRILLED BREAD WITH EGGPLANT CAVIAR

Croutons avec Caviar d'Aubergines

This is a very common small plate in Provence. Garnished with black olives, lemon wedges, and whole parsley leaves, these croutons are irresistible served on their own or as a garnish to a garden salad or a garlic-roasted leg of lamb.

1 to 1$\frac{1}{2}$ pounds eggplant

3 to 4 cloves garlic, minced

3 shallots, minced

1$\frac{1}{2}$ tablespoons chopped capers

5 anchovy fillets, soaked in cold water 10 minutes, patted dry, and minced

1 tablespoon extra virgin olive oil

2 tablespoons chopped fresh flat-leaf parsley

2 to 3 tablespoons lemon juice

Salt and freshly ground black pepper

1 baguette, cut diagonally into $\frac{1}{4}$-inch slices

Preheat the oven to 350°F. Puncture the eggplant several times with a fork, place it on a baking sheet, and bake until it can be easily skewered with a knife, 35 to 40 minutes. Remove from the oven and cool.

Peel the eggplant and discard the skin. Mash the pulp in a mixing bowl. Add the garlic, shallots, capers, anchovies, olive oil, and parsley. Season with lemon juice, salt, and pepper.

Toast or grill the bread slices. Spread the eggplant purée on the toasted bread. Serve immediately.

Serves 6 to 8

PAN-FRIED GARLIC BREAD WITH WILD MUSHROOMS

Croutons avec Cèpes et Persillade

These pan-fried garlic croutons are as habit forming as potato chips. Combine the garlic-fried bread with savory wild mushrooms and persillade, a Provençal concoction of chopped parsley and garlic added toward the end of the cooking time, and the result is a real winner. If wild mushrooms are unavailable, use cultivated mushrooms such as button or cremini.

For a little extra mushroom flavor, place a handful of dried porcini in a bowl, cover with boiling water, and let sit until the water cools. Drain the mushrooms and save the liquid for another use. Chop the mushrooms and add to the cooked mushrooms.

2 tablespoons chopped fresh flat-leaf parsley

2 cloves garlic, minced

6 slices rustic country-style bread

3 tablespoons extra virgin olive oil

2 tablespoons unsalted butter

2 cloves garlic, peeled

3/4 pound wild mushrooms (morels, chanterelles, porcini, hedgehogs), brushed clean and halved

1/2 pound button mushrooms, brushed clean and halved

1 cup chicken stock (page 255)

Salt and freshly ground black pepper

Combine the parsley and garlic and chop together until fine. Set aside.

Cut the bread slices in half on the diagonal. Heat 1 tablespoon of the oil and the butter in a large frying pan over medium heat. Place the bread in the frying pan to coat each side lightly with the oil and butter. Cook the bread until golden on each side, 4 to 5 minutes total. Remove from the pan and rub with the whole garlic cloves.

Heat the remaining 2 tablespoons oil in a large frying pan over medium-high heat. Add the mushrooms and cook, stirring occasionally, until they are soft and the mushroom liquid is evaporated, 10 to 12 minutes. Increase the heat to high, add the chicken stock, and reduce by half, 5 minutes. Season with salt and pepper and add the reserved parsley and garlic.

Place the bread on a serving plate and distribute the mushrooms and sauce evenly on top. Serve immediately.

Serves 6

CHICKPEA, OLIVE OIL, AND CUMIN PANCAKES

Socca

Theresa runs a small vending cart that travels from one market to another along the Azure Coast in southern France. You can't miss her in Antibes or Nice: her name is painted on the side of the cart in big yellow letters. She is an expert at baking these Arabic-influenced chickpea pancakes on a 20-inch-diameter pizza pan over a metal drum filled with slowly burning olive wood. Cut into half-moons and placed on waxed paper, they are doused with fruity, peppery virgin olive oil and coarsely cracked pepper.

$1^3/_4$ cups chickpea flour (see Note, page 45)

$^3/_4$ teaspoon salt

$^3/_4$ teaspoon ground cumin

$1^1/_2$ cups water

9 tablespoons extra virgin olive oil

Coarsely cracked black pepper

In a bowl, combine the chickpea flour, salt, and cumin. In another bowl, combine the water and 4 tablespoons of the olive oil. Sift the dry ingredients into the wet ingredients, whisking constantly. Let stand at room temperature for 1 hour.

Preheat the oven to 425°F. Oil a 9-inch round cake pan with 1 tablespoon of the olive oil and pour one-third of the batter into the pan, tilting the pan to coat the bottom with $^1/_4$ inch of the batter. Repeat with two more pans using 1 tablespoon olive oil and one-third of the batter in each pan. Bake them in the upper third of the oven until crisp and golden brown on top, 25 to 30 minutes.

Remove the pancakes from the pan with a spatula and cut into wedges. Drizzle with the remaining 2 tablespoons olive oil and sprinkle with black pepper. Serve immediately.

Makes three 9-inch *socca* to serve 6

RUSTIC GOAT CHEESE GALETTE

Galette de Fromage de Chèvre

Nearly two-thirds of the world's goat cheese, or chèvre, comes from France. When sold fresh, these cheeses are sweet and moist; when aged, they develop a stronger, more pungent flavor. One of my favorites is Banon, from the town of the same name. It's a creamy, nutty 4-ounce disk of goat's or ewe's milk cheese, wrapped in chestnut leaves soaked in eau-de-vie and tied with raffia. It's stored for a few months in an earthenware jar before eating. In this recipe, just about any goat's milk cheese can be used.

Pastry

1 1/2 cups all-purpose flour, placed in the freezer for 1 hour

1/4 teaspoon salt

9 tablespoons unsalted butter, cut into 1/2-inch pieces and placed in the freezer for 1 hour

1/3 to 1/2 cup ice water

Filling

5 ounces fresh goat cheese

4 ounces ricotta cheese

3 ounces mozzarella, coarsely grated

1/4 cup crème fraîche (page 257) or sour cream

3 tablespoons grated Parmigiano-Reggiano cheese

Salt and freshly ground black pepper

1/2 recipe Warm Olives with Wild Herbs (page 66)

To make the pastry, place the flour and salt on a cold work surface. With a pastry scraper, cut the butter into the flour until half of the butter is the size of peas and the other half is smaller. Make a well in the center of the flour and add half of the water. Push together with your fingertips and set aside any dough that holds together. Add the rest of the water and repeat. Form the mixture into a rough ball. Alternatively, this can be done in a food processor. On a well-floured surface, roll the dough into a 14- to 15-inch circle. Trim the edges. Place on a large sheet pan in the refrigerator.

To make the filling, mix together the goat cheese, ricotta, mozzarella, crème fraîche, and Parmigiano. Mix well and season with salt and pepper.

Preheat the oven to 350°F. Remove the pastry from the refrigerator. Spread the cheese over the pastry, leaving a 2 1/2-inch border around the edge uncovered. Fold the uncovered edge of the pastry over the cheese, pleating it to make it fit. There will be an open hole in the center.

Bake until golden brown, 35 to 40 minutes. Let cool 5 minutes, then slide the galette off the pan and onto a serving plate. Serve hot, warm, or at room temperature garnished with warm olives.

Serves 6

WARM OLIVES WITH WILD HERBS

Olives Tiedes aux Herbes Sauvages

Olive trees were introduced to Marseilles by the Greeks 2,500 years ago, and they have prolifer-ated there ever since. Ancient olive groves, with their twisted and gnarled trunks and limbs and burnished-silver leaves, cover much of the area. Today, thirty different types of olives are grown here; mellow green picholine and briny black niçoise olives are the most common. These two types of olive dominate this simple dish, which I always have on hand to serve with a glass of Syrah or Champagne.

5 ounces small black niçoise olives

5 ounces green picholine olives or other green olives with pits

3/4 cup extra virgin olive oil

Several sprigs of fresh rosemary, thyme, and savory

Small pinch of crushed red pepper flakes

1/4 teaspoon grated lemon zest

Place the olives, olive oil, herbs, red pepper flakes, and zest in a saucepan over medium heat, stirring occasion-ally until warm, 2 to 3 minutes. Let sit at room tempera-ture for 6 hours.

Before serving, discard any herbs that have turned brown and replenish with fresh herbs, if desired. Reheat the olives to serve.

Makes 1 1/4 cups

NOTE: These can be made several months in advance and stored in the refrigerator. The flavor will improve with age. Reheat the olives before serving.

CREAM TART WITH HERBS FROM THE SOUTH OF FRANCE

Tarte à la Creme aux Herbes

So many herbs grow wild in Provence that you can smell them in the wind. When you taste this tart, you will experience the best of France right there on your plate. The filling for this tart was inspired by my teacher, Madeleine Kamman, when I studied with her many years ago in France. She introduced me to the wonderful combination of equal amounts of crème fraîche or sour cream, heavy cream, and cream cheese added to eggs for the creamiest filling.

Short Crust Tart Shell

6 tablespoons unsalted butter

1 1/8 cups all-purpose flour

2 tablespoons vegetable shortening

1/8 teaspoon salt

1 to 3 tablespoons ice water

Filling

1/2 cup crème fraîche (page 257)
    or sour cream

1/2 cup heavy cream

1/2 cup cream cheese, at room
    temperature

2 eggs, lightly beaten

1/4 cup snipped fresh chives

1/4 cup assorted chopped fresh
    herbs, such as thyme, basil, flat-
    leaf parsley, marjoram, oregano,
    and savory

Salt and freshly ground black pepper

To make the tart shell, cut the butter into 1-inch pieces. Using the paddle attachment on an electric mixer, blend the butter and flour at low speed until it resembles coarse meal. Alternatively, this can be done by pulsing several times in a food processor, or it can be done with a pastry blender. Add the shortening and cut it into the flour and butter until the pieces are a little larger than coarse meal. Mix the salt and water together and add to the flour mixture a little at a time until it holds together. Blend only until the dough comes together. Cover with plastic wrap and let rest in the refrigerator for at least 30 minutes.

With a floured rolling pin, roll out the pastry into a 10-inch circle on a floured surface. Place in a 9-inch tart pan. Crimp the edges and prick the bottom of the pastry. Place in the freezer for 30 minutes.

Preheat the oven to 350°F. Completely line the bottom and sides of the pastry with parchment or aluminum foil. Fill with dried beans or metal pie weights. Bake in the middle of the oven for 25 minutes, or until the top of the crust is golden brown. Remove the beans or pie weights and remove the lining. If the bottom of the pastry is still moist and pale, return it unlined to the oven for a few minutes more until it is fully cooked and light golden.

Remove from the oven and cool completely. Raise the oven temperature to 425°F.

To make the filling, combine the crème fraîche, heavy cream, and cream cheese. Add the eggs, chives, and assorted herbs and mix thoroughly. Season with salt and pepper. Pour the mixture into the prebaked tart shell.

Place the tart in the oven and immediately turn the oven down to 375°F. Bake the tart until golden and firm to the touch, 35 to 40 minutes. Let rest 20 minutes before serving.

Serves 6

ONION, TOMATO, AND ANCHOVY PIE

A pissaladière is best when baked directly on a pizza brick set on the bottom rack of the oven. Heat the oven to the hottest temperature 30 minutes prior to baking the pizza. The results will closely resemble what you will find in Provençal bakeries that use wood-fired ovens.

1 recipe pizza dough (page 258)

5 tablespoons extra virgin olive oil

3 pounds yellow onions, thinly sliced

3 cloves garlic, minced

1 teaspoon chopped fresh thyme

$1/2$ teaspoon chopped fresh rosemary

1 cup peeled, seeded, and chopped tomatoes (page 259), fresh or canned

Salt and freshly ground black pepper

One 2-ounce can flat anchovy fillets, soaked in cold water 10 minutes, patted dry, and halved lengthwise

$1/2$ cup pitted niçoise olives (page 260)

Prepare the dough according to the recipe. After the dough has risen for 1 to $1^{1}/2$ hours, place a pizza brick on the bottom rack of the oven and preheat the oven to 500°F.

Heat 3 tablespoons of the oil in a frying pan over medium-low heat and add the onions, garlic, thyme, and rosemary and cook, stirring occasionally, until the onions are soft and golden, 50 to 60 minutes. Add the tomatoes and continue to simmer until almost dry, 20 minutes. Season with salt and pepper and cool.

On a floured surface, roll the dough out into a large rectangle $1/4$ inch thick. Place the dough on a well-floured pizza peel. Cover the dough to within $1/2$ inch of the edge with the onions and tomatoes. Arrange the anchovy fillets in a lattice fashion on top and place a pitted olive in the middle of each section. Drizzle with the remaining 2 tablespoons olive oil. Transfer the pizza onto the brick and bake until the crust is golden and the bottom is crisp, 8 to 10 minutes.

Makes 1 large rectangular pizza to serve 6

CORSICAN CANNELLONI WITH FARM CHEESE AND HERBS

Cannellonis à la Corse avec Brocciu et Herbes

My friend Josie first made these cannelloni for me at her restaurant Chez Josie in Porto Vecchio on the island of Corsica in the early fall, when the tomatoes were sweet and ripe. I asked her to tell me about the sauce. She bent over and whispered in my ear, "I can't let the village people know my secret. I put a splash of cream into the tomato sauce. It brings out the sweetness." Josie is right.

Filling

1 pound spinach, ends trimmed

1 pound ricotta, drained overnight in a cheesecloth-lined strainer

2 eggs

$1/4$ teaspoon chopped fresh mint

$1/4$ teaspoon chopped fresh oregano

$1/4$ teaspoon chopped fresh thyme

$1/4$ teaspoon chopped fresh rosemary

$1/4$ teaspoon chopped fresh savory (optional)

$3/4$ teaspoon salt

Freshly ground black pepper

$1/4$ cup grated Parmigiano-Reggiano cheese

Sauce

3 tablespoons extra virgin olive oil

1 small yellow onion, chopped

5 cloves garlic, minced

4 pounds ripe plum tomatoes, peeled, seeded, and chopped (page 259), or two 28-ounce cans Italian plum tomatoes, drained and chopped

$1/3$ cup heavy cream

Salt and freshly ground black pepper

Rich Egg Pasta

$2 1/2$ cups all-purpose flour

$3/4$ teaspoon salt

3 whole eggs (see Note)

3 egg yolks (see Note)

White rice flour for rolling out pasta

Fresh flat-leaf parsley leaves

To make the filling, heat the spinach in a dry pan over medium heat, covered, until wilted, 2 to 3 minutes. Squeeze out all the excess moisture in paper towels. Chop.

Combine the spinach with the ricotta, eggs, mint, oregano, thyme, rosemary, savory, the salt, pepper, and the Parmigiano. Set aside.

To make the sauce, heat 2 tablespoons of the olive oil in a large frying pan and cook the onion, stirring occasionally, until soft, 7 minutes. Add the garlic and cook for 2 minutes. Add the tomatoes and cook until the sauce is thick and the liquid has reduced by about half, 20 to 30 minutes. Purée the sauce in a blender or put it through a food mill fit with the smallest holes. Add the cream and season with salt and pepper.

To make the pasta, place the flour and salt on a work surface and toss to mix. Beat the eggs and egg yolks together in a bowl.

Make a well in the center of the flour and add the eggs to the well. Beat with a fork or your thumb and first finger, bringing the flour in from the sides until the mixture thickens. After the mixture has thickened, use a pastry scraper to combine all of the flour and liquid. Alternatively, this can be made in a food processor. It should be a fairly dry mixture. Knead for 2 minutes to form into a ball. Cover with plastic wrap and let rest for 30 minutes.

Using a pasta machine or a floured rolling pin, roll the pasta to a thickness of $1/16$ inch. Use rice flour to facilitate the rolling. You should just be able to see your hand through the dough when it reaches the right thickness.

Cut the pasta into 12 to 16 five-inch squares. Bring a pot of salted water to a boil. Boil the pasta for 30 seconds, immediately remove with a slotted spoon, and place in a bowl containing ice water and the remaining

1 tablespoon olive oil. Drain on slightly dampened kitchen towels. Cover with plastic wrap.

Preheat the oven to 350°F. Divide the filling into as many portions as you have squares of pasta. Roll the pasta over the filling in a tube fashion. Oil a 13 by 9-inch baking dish and place a small ladleful of sauce on the bottom of the dish. Place the cannelloni next to each other in a single layer in the dish. Pour the remaining sauce on top and bake until hot and bubbling around the edges, 20 to 30 minutes.

To serve, place 2 cannelloni on each plate and garnish with whole parsley leaves.

Serves 6 to 8

NOTE: The total volume of the eggs plus the egg yolks in the pasta recipe should be ³/₄ to ⁷/₈ cup. Water and a small amount of olive oil can be substituted for any part of this liquid, but using eggs yields the most supple and tender dough.

GNOCCHI WITH ROQUEFORT CREAM

Gnocchi avec Crème Roquefort

This recipe is one of the traditional methods for making gnocchi in France. It is basically like making a choux paste or cream puff dough. The finished gnocchi are featherlight and irresistible. If you love blue-veined cheese, you'll love this creamy and assertive sauce made with Roquefort.

1²/3 cups milk

³/4 cup (1¹/2 sticks) unsalted butter

³/4 teaspoon salt

1¹/3 cups all-purpose flour

6 eggs

2 cups heavy cream

6 ounces Roquefort cheese, crumbled

Freshly ground black pepper

¹/4 cup grated Parmigiano-Reggiano cheese

Bring a large pot of salted water to a boil. Reduce the heat to a simmer.

Bring the milk, butter, and the salt to a boil. As soon as it comes to a boil, take the pan off the heat and add the flour all at once. Mix vigorously with a wooden spoon until it forms a ball. Place the dough in the bowl of an electric mixer. While still warm, add the eggs one at a time, beating well after each addition. The mixture should be very thick and smooth.

Fit a large pastry bag with a ³/4- to 1-inch plain round tip. Fill the pastry bag with dough. Into the simmering water, squeeze out 1-inch pieces of dough, cutting them from the pastry bag with a knife. Do not overcrowd the pan. Simmer the gnocchi slowly until they begin to puff slightly and are slightly firm, 5 to 10 minutes. Remove the gnocchi from the water with a slotted spoon, drain well, and cool.

Note: The gnocchi will keep for up to 2 days in the refrigerator at this stage. They can also be frozen. Make sure that they are at room temperature before proceeding to the next step.

Preheat the oven to 425°F.

In a large saucepan, bring the cream, Roquefort, salt, and pepper to a boil. Simmer on low heat to reduce the mixture by one-quarter, or until it thickens slightly, 5 to 10 minutes. Add the cream mixture to the gnocchi and mix carefully. Divide the gnocchi and sauce among 3¹/2-inch ramekins or a 13 by 9-inch baking dish. Sprinkle with the Parmigiano and bake until the gnocchi puff and are golden brown, 10 minutes. If the gnocchi have not turned golden, brown them briefly under the broiler.

Serve immediately.

Serves 6 to 8

CARAMELIZED ONION AND GOAT CHEESE SOUFFLÉ

Soufflé d'Oignon Confit et Fromage de Chèvre

What makes this soufflé different from others is that it is baked on a large ovenproof platter on the top rack of a hot oven, resulting in a soufflé that is about 2 inches high. It happens to be one of my favorite recipes in this book. It can be made in advance up to the point of whipping the egg whites.

3 tablespoons extra virgin olive oil

3 medium yellow onions, about 1¹/₂ pounds, thinly sliced

Salt and freshly ground black pepper

1 teaspoon chopped fresh thyme

4 tablespoons plus 2 teaspoons unsalted butter

6 tablespoons all-purpose flour

1 cup milk

1 cup heavy cream

5 egg yolks

1¹/₄ cups crumbled goat cheese, about 5 ounces

6 egg whites

¹/₂ cup grated Parmigiano-Reggiano cheese

Heat the olive oil in a frying pan over medium heat and add the onions, salt, pepper, and ¹/₂ teaspoon of the thyme. Cook the onions, covered, stirring occasionally, until the onions are very soft, 30 minutes. Uncover and cook until light golden, 30 minutes. Remove the onions with a slotted spoon and place them in a strainer set over a bowl to drain. Reserve.

Butter a 10 by 18-inch oval ovenproof platter with 2 teaspoons of the butter.

Preheat the oven to 450°F. In the meantime, melt the remaining 4 tablespoons butter in a saucepan over low heat and add the flour. Stir with a whisk to combine and let the mixture bubble for 2 minutes. Add the milk and cream to the flour-butter mixture, stirring rapidly with a whisk. Cook until very thick and smooth, 2 to 3 minutes. Transfer to a bowl and add the drained onions. Mix well. Add the egg yolks, one at a time, stirring well after each addition. Add the goat cheese and mix well. Season with salt and pepper.

Beat the egg whites until stiff. Add half of them to the base and fold together. Fold in the remaining whites. Pour onto the prepared platter. Sprinkle with the Parmigiano and the remaining ¹/₂ teaspoon thyme and bake on the top rack of the oven until well browned, 10 to 14 minutes.

Serve immediately.

Serves 8

MAGALY'S STUFFED TOMATOES

Tomatoes Farcies Magaly

Magaly and Raymond Fabre are the proprietors of Domaine du Mont Redon, producing some of the finest Châteauneuf du Pape wines. The first time I met Magaly, she invited me to lunch and recommended that I arrive at 9 AM. I spent the early morning with Raymond at the winery and later cooked lunch and talked with Magaly. We grilled croutons on the hearth to be served with anchoïade, we stuffed tomatoes, and we sliced truffles for the salad. Finally, we were finished. Magaly, Raymond, and I sat at the table for the next several hours eating lunch, drinking their wine, and talking. As the sun began to set, we left the table and gathered around the fireplace. Raymond brought out a bottle of their exquisite house-made Marc de Châteauneuf du Pape, 1945. The bottle was covered with a layer of dust, and Raymond had a sly smile as he opened it. While we sipped, Magaly wrote out this excellent recipe, which we had eaten hours earlier, for me.

6 large ripe tomatoes, cored

Salt and freshly ground black pepper

2 tablespoons extra virgin olive oil

$1/2$ medium yellow onion, minced

$3/4$ pound fresh pork sausage, crumbled

$1/2$ cup milk, scalded

1 cup fresh white bread crumbs

1 egg, lightly beaten

4 tablespoons chopped fresh flat-leaf parsley

$1/4$ teaspoon chopped fresh thyme

$1/2$ teaspoon chopped fresh savory, or $1/3$ teaspoon dried savory

2 cloves garlic, minced

1 tablespoon unsalted butter

Whole sprigs of fresh thyme, flat-leaf parsley, or savory

With the core side up, cut the tomatoes in half horizontally and press just slightly to remove any excess moisture. Sprinkle the interior of the tomatoes with salt and place them, cut side down, on paper towels for at least 1 hour to drain.

Preheat the oven to 350°F. Heat 1 tablespoon of the olive oil in a frying pan over medium heat and add the tomato halves, 6 at a time, cut side down. Cook 5 minutes. Turn the tomatoes over, season with salt and pepper, and cook for an additional 3 minutes. Remove the tomatoes from the frying pan.

Oil a 13 by 9-inch baking dish with the remaining 1 tablespoon olive oil and place the tomatoes, cut side up, side by side in the dish. Add the onion to the frying pan and cook until the onion is soft, 10 minutes. Add the sausage and cook over medium heat until the sausage is cooked halfway, 5 minutes. With a slotted spoon, transfer the sausage and onion to a mixing bowl. Add the scalded milk and bread crumbs. Cool slightly. Add the egg, 2 tablespoons of the parsley, the thyme, and savory. Season with salt and pepper.

Divide the stuffing among the tomatoes. Bake the tomatoes 10 minutes. In the meantime, chop the remaining 2 tablespoons parsley and the garlic together. Remove the tomatoes from the oven. Heat the broiler. Sprinkle the parsley and the garlic on top of the tomatoes. Dot with the butter and broil until golden brown, 1 to 2 minutes.

Garnish with some whole sprigs of thyme, flat-leaf parsley, or savory and serve hot, warm, or at room temperature.

Serves 6

BASIL OMELETTE

Pistou is the cousin of Italian pesto, the only difference being that pistou doesn't include pine nuts. Pistou is made in the vicinity of Nice, where basil fills the hillsides and garlic perfumes the air. Most often, pistou is a sauce used as a garnish for thick vegetable and pasta soups, but here it is used as a delightful flavoring for an omelette.

3 cloves garlic, chopped

1 cup fresh basil leaves, washed and dried

Salt and freshly ground black pepper

4 tablespoons extra virgin olive oil

1 cup grated Parmigiano-Reggiano cheese

8 eggs

1 tablespoon water

Place the garlic, basil, salt, pepper, and 3 tablespoons of the olive oil in a blender or food processor and process until smooth. Add the cheese, a little at a time, until a very stiff paste is formed. Set aside.

Whisk the eggs with salt, pepper, and the water until foamy. Heat the remaining 1 tablespoon oil in a 10-inch omelette pan until very hot and the oil is rippling. Add the egg mixture and let it cook 5 seconds. As the eggs begin to set, with a fork lift the outer edges of the omelette and let the liquid run underneath. Continue cooking until almost set but still slightly soft inside, a total of 30 seconds. Quickly spread the eggs with the pistou.

To serve, fold the omelette onto a serving plate to form a slight roll. Serve immediately.

Makes 1 omelette to serve 4

PROVENÇAL ROASTED SUMMER VEGETABLE RAGOUT

Ratatouille

Throughout Provence there are many varieties of ratatouille. In this version, the vegetables are first sautéed separately to preserve their brilliant colors, and then they are stewed together.

One 1 1/2- to 2-pound eggplant, cut into 1-inch cubes

Salt and freshly ground black pepper

5 tablespoons extra virgin olive oil

3 yellow or red bell peppers, seeded and cut into 1-inch strips

4 small zucchini, trimmed and cut into 3/4-inch slices

2 medium yellow onions, cut into 8 wedges

4 cloves garlic, minced

5 tomatoes, peeled, seeded (page 259), and cut into 1-inch cubes

2 bay leaves

4 tablespoons chopped fresh flat-leaf parsley

1/2 teaspoon chopped fresh thyme

1 to 2 tablespoons red wine vinegar

20 fresh basil leaves, cut into thin strips

Place the eggplant in a colander and salt liberally. Leave to drain for 30 minutes. Wash the eggplant and pat dry with paper towels.

Heat 2 tablespoons of the olive oil in a large, heavy frying pan over medium heat. Add the eggplant and brown on all sides, 15 minutes. Remove with a slotted spoon and reserve. Add 1 tablespoon of the olive oil to the pan and add the bell peppers. Cook, stirring occasionally, until they begin to wilt, 5 to 7 minutes. Remove with a slotted spoon and reserve with the eggplant. Add the zucchini and cook until lightly browned, 3 to 4 minutes. Remove and reserve with the other vegetables. Add the remaining 2 tablespoons olive oil, the onions, and garlic and cook until soft, 7 to 10 minutes. Add the tomatoes, bay leaves, parsley, thyme, and pepper and simmer slowly for 20 minutes. Add the reserved vegetables to the pan and cook, stirring occasionally, for 15 minutes. Season as needed with salt, pepper, and red wine vinegar.

Place the ratatouille on a platter and garnish with the basil.

Serves 6

NOTE: Ratatouille can be served hot, warm, or at room temperature. It can be prepared 1 day in advance. Bring to room temperature or heat slightly to serve.

BRAISED ARTICHOKES STUFFED WITH SAUSAGE AND MUSHROOMS

Artichauds Barigoule

Some have big hearts, some have a distinct purple hue, some are so small they can be eaten whole, and some are so tender they can be eaten raw: artichokes are one of the most popular vegetables grown in the south of France, and a multitude of dishes have been created around them. Jean-Noel Escudier, the father of the Provençal table, described the artichoke as "a petaled cone that started as a thistle and was cultivated into a classic vegetable." This dish is a beloved classic.

6 medium artichokes, trimmed (page 259)

4 tablespoons extra virgin olive oil

1/4 cup chopped yellow onion

1/4 pound mushrooms, brushed clean and thinly sliced

1/2 pound lean pork sausage, crumbled

4 cloves garlic, minced

1/4 cup chopped fresh flat-leaf parsley

1/2 teaspoon chopped fresh thyme

10 fresh basil leaves

4 ounces country-style ham (West-phalian, Black Forest, Virginia, Smithfield, prosciutto, or Serrano), finely diced

Salt and freshly ground black pepper

3 medium yellow onions, thinly sliced

2 small carrots, peeled and thinly sliced

Bouquet garni (6 sprigs flat-leaf pars-ley, pinch of thyme, 1 bay leaf)

1 1/4 cups dry white wine, such as sauvignon blanc

Blanch the artichoke hearts in boiling salted water for 8 minutes. Drain and reserve.

To make the stuffing, heat 2 tablespoons of the olive oil in a frying pan over medium heat. Add the chopped onion, mushrooms, and sausage and sauté until the onion is soft, 10 minutes. Chop the garlic, parsley, thyme, and basil leaves together and add to the onion with the ham. Mix well. Season with salt and pepper. Stuff the centers of the artichokes and the space between the leaves with the stuffing.

In a small flameproof casserole just large enough to hold the artichokes, heat the remaining 2 tablespoons olive oil over medium heat. Add the sliced onions, carrots, salt, pepper, and bouquet garni and sauté for 2 minutes. Place the artichokes on top, stuffing side up. Sauté for 6 to 8 minutes, or until the vegetables start to brown. Turn the heat to high, add the wine, and reduce for 1 minute. Turn the heat to low, cover the pan, and cook slowly for 45 minutes, checking to make sure that the artichokes don't dry out. Uncover the artichokes, increase the heat to high, and reduce the broth until you have a syrupy sauce.

To serve, place the onions and carrots on a serving plate with the artichokes on top. Spoon the juices over the top and serve warm.

Serves 6

SALAD OF ROASTED PEPPERS, ANCHOVIES, AND BASIL LA MERENDA

Salade de Poivre, Anchois et Basilic

My only complaint at La Merenda, a little bistro tucked down an alley just steps from the Cours Selaya market in Nice, is about the little woven leather stools. They are so uncomfortable! But the food makes it all worth it. As an indication of how much I like the place, I have been known to eat here two nights in a row when I'm in Nice. It is down-home and rustic, right up my alley. The menu, written on a chalkboard, changes nightly depending upon what is available in the market. One of my favorites here is this pungent salad of roasted sweet peppers, anchovies, and basil leaves.

3 red bell peppers, roasted
  (page 259)

3 yellow bell peppers, roasted
  (page 259)

One 2-ounce can flat anchovy fillets,
  soaked in cold water 10 minutes
  and patted dry

1 clove garlic, minced

1 teaspoon red wine vinegar

5 tablespoons extra virgin olive oil

Salt and freshly ground black pepper

1/2 teaspoon chopped fresh oregano

1/3 cup pitted small black olives,
  preferably niçoise

20 to 25 fresh basil leaves

Cut the peppers into 1-inch strips. Toss with the anchovies, garlic, vinegar, olive oil, salt, and pepper. Let marinate at room temperature for 30 minutes.

Place the pepper mixture on a serving plate and sprinkle oregano over the top. Garnish with the olives and basil leaves and serve immediately.

Serves 6

WARM BEAN AND TOMATO SALAD WITH GARLIC MAYONNAISE

Haricots Verts et Tomates au Basilic, Sauce Aioli

In Provence, aïl means garlic, and oli is the local dialect for oil. Put the two together and you get aioli. Aioli is commonly eaten along the Mediterranean shore, spreading through Languedoc, where it's called aïllade and often thickened with blanched and ground walnuts. Heading farther west to Roussillon and still further along the Mediterranean to Spain, a similar sauce is called allioli. In the following recipe, the Provençal version of aioli melts over the warm beans and imparts the heady flavor of garlic. Be sure to serve plenty of bread alongside to mop up the delicious juices.

1 recipe Provençal Garlic Mayonnaise (page 256)

3 to 4 tablespoons water

1¹/₂ cups fresh shell beans (flageolets, black-eyed peas, cranberry beans, limas, cannellini, or a combination)

5 tablespoons red wine vinegar

4 tablespoons extra virgin olive oil

Salt and freshly ground black pepper

³/₄ pound green beans, ends removed

³/₄ pound yellow beans, ends removed

¹/₂ pound assorted cherry tomatoes (red, yellow, orange, pear, and grape)

20 fresh basil leaves

Whisk the aioli with the water to lighten the texture and make a barely fluid sauce.

In a saucepan, cover the shell beans with water by 2 inches. Bring to a boil and cook until tender, 20 to 30 minutes, depending upon the beans. Drain and toss with 4 tablespoons of the vinegar, the olive oil, salt, and pepper. Keep warm.

Bring a pot of salted water to a boil. Add the green and yellow beans and cook until tender but still crisp, 5 to 8 minutes. Drain. Add to the shell beans and toss together. Keep warm.

Halve the cherry tomatoes and season with salt, pepper, and the remaining 1 tablespoon vinegar. Toss together.

Place the various beans on a platter and top with the tomatoes and a spoonful of aioli. Garnish with basil and serve immediately.

Serves 6

GARDEN SALAD WITH PEARS AND ROQUEFORT CROUTONS

Salade Verte avec Poires et Croutons au Roquefort

There are many imitations of Roquefort, the French equivalent of Italian Gorgonzola. This ewe's milk cheese, with its distinctive blue veins, comes from the underground caves of Roquefort-sur-Soulzon, a small town devoted to its production. Roquefort has gained an international reputation for its pungent flavor, which is highlighted in this salad.

Vinaigrette

2 tablespoons red wine vinegar

1 shallot, minced

1 tablespoon walnut or other nut oil

4 tablespoons extra virgin olive oil

Salt and freshly ground black pepper

Croutons

3 tablespoons unsalted butter,
    at room temperature

4 ounces Roquefort cheese, at room
    temperature

2 ounces cream cheese, at room
    temperature

1 tablespoon chopped fresh flat-leaf
    parsley

2 green onions, white and green
    parts, thinly sliced

2 tablespoons finely chopped
    walnuts, toasted (page 258)

6 large slices rustic country-style
    bread, cut in half on the diagonal
    and lightly toasted

Salad

2 or 3 small heads of salad greens
    (oak leaf lettuce, frisée, mizuna,
    radicchio, arugula, and
    watercress)

Salt and freshly ground black pepper

2 pears or apples, peeled and thinly
    sliced

1/3 cup walnuts or pecans, toasted
    (page 258)

To make the vinaigrette, place the vinegar and shallot in a small bowl and let sit 10 minutes. Add the walnut and olive oils and whisk together. Season with salt and pepper and set aside.

To make the croutons, preheat the oven to 400°F. In a bowl, mash together the butter, Roquefort, cream cheese, parsley, green onions, and walnuts or place the ingredients in a food processor and pulse until the ingredients are mixed. Season with salt and pepper. Spread the mixture on the toasted bread. Place the bread on a baking sheet and toast on the top rack of the oven until golden around the edges, 30 to 45 seconds.

To make the salad, trim the heads of the salad greens. Discard any outside leaves that may be damaged. Tear the leaves into bite-size pieces, wash them, and spin dry. Season the greens with salt and pepper. In a large salad bowl, toss the greens, pears, and walnuts with the vinaigrette. Garnish the salad with the Roquefort croutons and serve immediately.

Serves 6

TOASTED GOAT CHEESE SALAD WITH SMOKED BACON

Mesclun au Fromage de Chèvre Grillée

Around Banon, in the Haute Provence, the goats graze in herb-filled pastures, giving their milk and cheese an herbaceous quality. Storing summer's sweet, creamy goat cheese in local olive oil and herbs is an ancient way of preserving it, so it can be enjoyed in the cold winter months. In this recipe, goat cheese is rolled in bread crumbs, baked, and served with smoked bacon and croutons. What a combination!

3/4 cup extra virgin olive oil

3 large sprigs of fresh thyme

2 large sprigs of fresh oregano

1 large sprig of fresh rosemary

1 large sprig of fresh savory (optional)

8 peppercorns, coarsely cracked

8 whole coriander seeds, coarsely cracked

3/4 pound fresh goat cheese, cut into 3 small round disks, 1 inch thick by 2 1/2 inches in diameter and cut in half horizontally to make 6 pieces

6 ounces thickly sliced smoked bacon, cut into 1/2-inch dice

4 thick slices rustic country-style bread, cut or torn into 1/2-inch cubes

1/2 teaspoon Dijon mustard

1 clove garlic, minced

2 tablespoons red wine vinegar

Salt and freshly ground black pepper

4 large handfuls of mesclun or mixed salad greens (red leaf, radicchio, butter, mustard green, mizuna, arugula, and oak leaf)

1 1/2 cups fine dry bread crumbs

Place the olive oil in a saucepan and heat until warm. With the back of your chef's knife, tap the sprigs of thyme, oregano, rosemary, and savory to bruise them and release their flavor. Add the herbs, peppercorns, and coriander seeds to the oil and remove from the heat. Let the oil cool. Pour two-thirds of the oil over the goat cheese rounds. Reserve the remaining oil. Let the goat cheese marinate in the refrigerator for 2 hours or up to 1 week (see Note).

Preheat the oven to 400°F. Combine the bacon and bread cubes and place on a baking sheet. Bake, tossing occasionally, until both the bread and bacon are golden, 7 to 10 minutes. Leave the oven on.

Combine the mustard, garlic, and red wine vinegar. Add the reserved olive oil and whisk together. Season with salt and pepper.

Tear the greens into bite-size pieces. Wash well and spin dry.

Season the bread crumbs with salt and pepper. Remove the goat cheese from the oil and coat with the bread crumbs. Place on a baking sheet and bake until the cheese bubbles slightly around the edges, 4 to 5 minutes.

Toss the vinaigrette with the greens. Arrange the greens on a salad plate and place the cheese in the center. Surround the cheese with croutons and bacon.

Serves 6

NOTE: This cheese is best when marinated at least 3 to 4 days before using. The oil can be reused.

AUBERGE D'AILLANE CHICKPEA SALAD WITH PROVENÇAL HERBS AND OLIVES

Salade de l'Auberge d'Aillane

We had been at the market all morning, and by the time we left Aix-en-Provence I was already starving and couldn't wait for lunch. Auberge d'Aillane is in the middle of an industrial park on the outskirts of Aix, rather tricky to find, but well worth the trip. After many wrong turns we finally arrived, about one hour after our reservation. We ran through the gardens and into the front door. The place was empty. Out from the kitchen came one of the daughters of the proprietor. I explained our predicament. With a sympathetic look, she agreed to make us lunch, but only if she could plan our menu. This was the first dish she brought, and I will never forget it.

1 cup dried chickpeas, about
   6 ounces

3 to 4 tablespoons red wine vinegar

4 cloves garlic, minced

5 tablespoons extra virgin olive oil

Salt and freshly ground black pepper

3 tablespoons mixed chopped fresh
   herbs (mint, thyme, rosemary,
   tarragon, oregano, and basil)

2 tablespoons chopped fresh
   flat-leaf parsley

$1/3$ cup pitted black olives,
   preferably niçoise (page 260)

1 small red onion, cut into
   $1/4$-inch dice

Pick over the chickpeas and discard any stones. Cover with water and soak 8 hours or overnight. Drain and place in a saucepan with enough water to cover by 2 inches. Simmer until the skins begin to crack and the beans are tender, 45 to 60 minutes. Drain and cool.

In a large bowl, whisk together 3 tablespoons of the vinegar, the garlic, and olive oil. Season with salt and pepper. Add the mixed herbs, parsley, chickpeas, olives, and onion and toss well. Season with salt, pepper, and additional vinegar, if needed.

Place on a platter to serve.

Serves 6

NOTE: This salad can be prepared 1 day in advance and stored in the refrigerator. Bring to room temperature before serving.

SHELLFISH FRITTERS WITH SPICY HOT GARLIC MAYONNAISE

Beignets de Coquillage avec Rouille

Beignets, croquettes, croquetas, bunyols, buñelos, fritto misto, *and* crokettes *are a few of the names given to the wide variety of deep-fried fritters of fish, meat, and vegetables served around the northern Mediterranean. Here I have packed these fritters with all kinds of shellfish—mussels, scallops, clams, shrimp, and oysters—and deep-fried them until golden and crispy. Dip them into the best garlic mayonnaise and you have a recipe that is absolutely addictive.*

Batter

1 cup all-purpose flour

$^1/_2$ teaspoon salt

2 eggs, separated

2 tablespoons extra virgin olive oil

$^3/_4$ cup warm beer

$^1/_4$ cup water

1 pound clams, scrubbed well

1 pound mussels, scrubbed and beards removed

$^1/_4$ pound scallops, white muscle on side removed

$^1/_4$ pound medium shrimp, peeled

12 oysters, shucked

Salt and freshly ground black pepper

1 quart corn or peanut oil for deep-frying

Lemon wedges

1 recipe Spicy Hot Garlic Mayonnaise (page 256)

Sift the flour and the salt together in a bowl and make a well in the center. In another bowl, whisk together the egg yolks, olive oil, and beer and pour into the well. Mix together just until mixed. Let rest at room temperature for 1 hour.

Bring the water to a boil in a frying pan. Add the clams and cover. Cook until the clams open, 4 to 6 minutes. Remove from the heat immediately, remove the clams from their shells, and place in a bowl. Discard the shells. Repeat with the mussels, cooking for 3 to 6 minutes. Add the shelled mussels to the clams. Reduce the heat to medium and add the scallops. Cover and cook 1 minute. Remove from the heat and cut into $^1/_4$-inch pieces. Add the scallops to the clams and mussels. Add the shrimp to the frying pan, cover, and cook 1 minute. Remove from the heat and cut in half. Add to the other shellfish. Add the raw oysters to the rest of the shellfish. Season with salt and pepper and reserve in the refrigerator.

In a deep saucepan, heat the oil to 375°F. A drop of batter should sizzle when dropped into the oil.

Beat the egg whites until stiff peaks form. Fold the whites into the batter and fold the batter into the shellfish.

Using a heaping tablespoon of batter, deep-fry a few fritters until they are golden brown, 3 to 4 minutes. Do not overcrowd the pan. Garnish with lemon wedges and serve with Spicy Hot Garlic Mayonnaise.

Makes 24 to 30 fritters to serve 8

MUSSELS IN THE STYLE OF THE CAMARGUE

Moules à la Camarguaise

The Camargue is the half-ranch, half-quagmire stretch of mysterious land that juts into the Mediterranean and divides Provence and Languedoc. It is the land of Provençal cowboys, pink flamingos, and wild horses. From this area also come the little thumbnail-size clams called tellines *that are so delicious when steamed open and doused with a parsley vinaigrette. Since* tellines *are not available in the United States I've substituted mussels, and the result is superb. Any kind of clams can also be substituted.*

3 pounds extremely fresh medium mussels, scrubbed and beards removed

Salt

1 small yellow onion, chopped

1 leek, white and 1 inch of green, chopped

3 cloves garlic, coarsely chopped

6 sprigs fresh flat-leaf parsley

Pinch of dry thyme

1 bay leaf

$1/2$ cup dry white wine, such as sauvignon blanc

2 tablespoons lemon juice

4 tablespoons extra virgin olive oil

2 cloves garlic, minced

Freshly ground black pepper

$1/3$ cup chopped fresh flat-leaf parsley

6 lemon wedges

Crusty bread

Discard any mussels that are broken or cracked. Soak in a generous quantity of salted water for 15 to 20 minutes. Place the mussels in a large pan with the onion, leek, garlic, parsley, thyme, bay leaf, and wine. Cover and steam the mussels open over high heat, shaking the pan occasionally, 3 to 6 minutes. Remove the mussels from the pan as they open and spread them, in their shells, on a baking sheet to cool. Reserve the cooking liquid and strain through several layers of cheesecloth or a coffee filter. Reduce the cooking liquid by two-thirds, 4 to 5 minutes, and reserve.

Mix together the lemon juice, olive oil, and 2 cloves garlic. Add the reduced cooking liquid and season with pepper.

Toss the mussels with the olive oil mixture and parsley and place on a platter. Garnish with lemon wedges and serve immediately with crusty bread.

Serves 6

ITALY

*P*icture the scene. A silver slice of moon lights an Italian piazza; the air is heavy with the perfume of citrus trees, wood smoke, and the serenade of distant cicadas. A warm Mediterranean breeze rustles the tablecloth at the street-side trattoria and the flowers outside the apartment upstairs. A drama is about to begin.

In the kitchens of trattorias and homes, fires are carefully built in brick ovens with brush, fruit, and nut woods; soon flat breads, pizzas, and calzone will be baked to savory perfection. Raised hearths are readied for grilling fresh fish, meat, and vegetables.

Amid carafes and tumblers of robust red wine, friends, lovers, and families are gathering for the daily ritual so important to Italian life—the sharing of good food and time at the table. In Italy, the joys of the table are unparalleled, and food holds center stage in everyday life.

The Drama Begins

The opening act is the antipasti (the singular form is antipasto), which means "before the meal." Antipasti are meant to stimulate the imagination and whet the appetite; to be savored rather than gobbled; to fan the appetite, not extinguish it. Their roots go back to the opulent feasts of the Roman Empire, when lengthy banquets of gustatory excess are rumored to have lasted for hours, sometimes days. These beginning courses were called *gustus* or *gustatio* and, much later, antipasti.

Today, antipasti can be as informal as a platter of sliced meats such as salami and mortadella, pickled peppers, olives, a morsel of cheese, and a few radishes. At home, the focus is on freshness, availability, and simplicity: you might be served a few slices of prosciutto with perfectly ripe figs or juicy melon, or some *bruschetta*. At the trattoria, the scope is much wider: deep-fried polenta sticks; white bean salads with fresh herbs and grilled fish; caponata or stewed vegetables; eggplant sandwiches; fried calamari or artichokes; rustic layered pies, or *torte*; and *crostini* topped with everything under the sun might be on the menu.

Act Two

The next act is the *primi piatti*, or first plates. This course sets the tempo and mood for the rest of the drama to follow. *Primi piatti* often consist of a starch or carbohydrate, such as polenta, risotto, and, of course, pasta. *Primi piatti* are usually served in a wide, flat bowl, and they are often called *minestra*, or the wet course, since they usually contain a sauce or some liquid. *Primi piatti* are a great favorite of the Italian table and a tough act to follow (which may explain why main courses are traditionally quite simple).

The *Bacari* of Venice

In Venice, a similar drama takes place in the *bacari*, bars where small plates known as *cicheti* are served. *Cicheti* are as old as Venice itself. The early merchants of the Rialto fish and produce markets used to start their days well before dawn, setting up their stands for trade. Naturally, they finished early and needed a little refreshment. Off to the *bacari* they went for a small glass of *ombreta*, or local wine, or prosecco, naturally sparkling wine from the Veneto, and a bite of food.

These *cicheti* might be as simple as a few stuffed olives or a bite of cheese, or as elaborate as crispy fried tuna croquettes, polenta topped with squid cooked in their own ink, trays piled with tiny sandwiches, or salt cod mashed with olive oil and garlic. Everything is consumed standing along the counter with the usual pointing and gesturing at what looks freshest and most flavorful. To understand the *bacaro*, one needs to understand Venice. This is a very social city, where the idea of hurrying doesn't exist. There is no need to make a date for the *bacari*; you run into the same people again and again. The custom that began so long ago lives on in a vital way today, and visiting the *bacari* is not only a pastime of the merchants, but also much enjoyed by almost all Venetians.

A Legacy of Invasions

The traditions of serving antipasti and *primi piatti* have their roots deep in Italy's past. Waves of invasion have stirred Italy for 3,000 years, with the Greeks, Etruscans, and Arabs leaving the most profound effects on Italy's cuisine. As a strong force in the Mediterranean before the first millennium, the Greeks maintained power over southern Italy and Sicily for several hundred years. Their legacy was tremendous: they planted wheat and olive and almond trees, they showed the southern Italians how to make wine and honey, and they introduced spit roasting.

In 500 BC, the Etruscans occupied northern Italy and introduced *pulmentum*, or polenta, which was critical to the Roman Empire's survival and later became an integral part of the Italian diet. The Arabs migrated to southern Italy from North Africa and the eastern Mediterranean in the ninth century. They brought rice, nuts, saffron and other spices, flaky pastry, couscous, and citrus. Much later, in the sixteenth century, tomatoes, coffee, peppers, and various squash and beans were introduced to Italy from the New World. These ingredients have also played a crucial role in the development of Italy's cuisine.

A Varied Geography

Italy juts out into the Mediterranean in the shape of a boot giving a swift kick toward Sicily and North Africa. Only seven hundred miles from north to south and not wider than three hundred miles at any point, Italy is nevertheless a land of varied geography, culture, people, and food. Twenty different regions can be identified, each region so different from the other that a single Italian cuisine is impossible to describe. Not only is each region unique, but even each town and village is a world unto its own. A dish with the same name might be prepared in both northern and southern Italy, but the ingredients and technique used to make it will vary dramatically. For example, in Naples, the soup *pasta e fagioli* is made with beans, pasta, garlic, celery, tomatoes, parsley, oregano, and crushed red pepper; in Bologna, it's made with beans, pasta, garlic, onions, prosciutto, and sage.

Northern Italy

The prosperous north is well irrigated and relatively lush, which allows for the grazing of cattle. The food reflects this through the use of cream, eggs, and butter. The provinces of northern Italy have made many contributions to the country's cuisine, including prosciutto or cured ham; Parmigiano-Reggiano;

pancetta, a peppered and brined bacon; balsamic vinegar from Emilia-Romagna; Gorgonzola, a very flavorful blue-veined cheese; polenta; arborio rice, a short-grained rice perfect for making risotto; basil from the hillsides of Liguria; Tuscan and Umbrian olive oil; excellent beef; truffles; wild mushrooms; pecorino or sheep's milk cheese; and tremendous quantities of fish and shellfish.

Southern Italy

Compared to the north, the rural south is sun-parched and barren. The rugged, mountainous terrain is unsuitable for farming, and poor soil conditions have left this area ravaged by economic hardship over the years. The cooking medium is olive oil. Just a hint of crushed red pepper appears in many dishes, a holdover from times when black pepper prices were so high that southern Italians grew hot red pepper to use as a substitute. Pasta is eaten all over Italy, but it reigns supreme on the southern table. Here, it is either factory-made of 100 percent semolina or freshly made with semolina, water, and/or olive oil and, for the most part, without eggs. Buffalo milk mozzarella is made here from the milk of water buffaloes grazing in the mountains above Sorrento and neighboring areas. Sweet red tomatoes are present in many dishes, and large sheets of tomato concentrate can be seen drying on many Neapolitan balconies. And in the bustling city of Naples, pizza and calzone are sold on every corner. Antipasti are not as important in the south as the north, but *primi piatti* are enjoyed here every bit as much as they are elsewhere in the country.

Sicily

Sicily is a kingdom unto its own. This broadly triangular island is the largest in the Mediterranean. It is not as barren as southern Italy, and the countryside is carefully planted in rows of abundant color producing fantastic produce, including fennel, eggplant, tomatoes, and artichokes. Citrus trees grow in profusion, and caper bushes grow wild along the shores. North Africa is just ninety miles southwest of Sicily, and its influence can be tasted in sweet-and-sour dishes, spices, raisins, pine nuts, and couscous. Anchovies and sardines are a favored accent to many dishes; again, the cooking medium is olive oil.

Sardinia

Sardinia has been repeatedly invaded and colonized over the centuries, its people driven from the coasts into the central mountains, where they have become farmers and shepherds. The last invasion of Sardinia was by the Italians just one hundred years ago. Their influence has not been felt nearly as strongly as those of the Spanish, French, and North Africans who dominated Sardinia's early history. Sardinia makes excellent pecorino. Hunting game is a sport of necessity, and blackbird and wild boar are presented in a variety of guises. Bread replaces pasta as the starch of choice.

Culinary Traditions

Italian cuisine has drawn from three distinct culinary heritages as it has developed over thousands of years. *Cucina alto-borghese*, or the cuisine of the upper classes, courts, or merchant families, with its refined principles and ingredients, was developed during the Roman Empire and prospered throughout the Middle Ages, flourishing in the Renaissance. Court cuisine contributed a refinement to today's Italian kitchen. *Cucina povera*, or the cuisine of the poor, has been cooked by the large percentage of Italy's population that lack money and other resources. *Cucina casalinga* is a term commonly used to describe the cuisine of the home. It refers to food that is informal, down-to-earth, and unadulterated, food that relies on bold flavors for its success.

These three different styles have merged somewhere in the middle to create a rich, varied, and well-respected world cuisine that relies on excellent local ingredients, peasant-style recipes, simple preparations, and assertive flavors, as seen here in these antipasto and *primi piatti* recipes.

TUSCAN THREE-ONION SOUP WITH GRILLED BREAD AND SHAVED PARMIGIANO-REGGIANO

Zuppa di Cipolle Toscane

There's so much about this soup that I love! It's a delicious mixture of sweet and sour that comes from tons of onions, balsamic vinegar, and fruity red wine. One word of caution, though: make sure the leeks are free of dirt and grit. Dirt gets lodged inside leeks as they grow, and it is virtually impossible to clean them when they are whole. The best way to deal with this problem is to chop the leeks first, place them in a bowl of cold water, and rinse them well. Drain them really well before using or, better yet, use a salad spinner to dry them.

1/4 cup extra virgin olive oil

4 ounces pancetta, cut into 1/4-inch slices

4 large yellow onions, about 2 to 3 pounds, thinly sliced

4 medium leeks, white and 3 inches of green, halved and cut into 1/4-inch slices

6 cups chicken stock (page 255)

3 to 4 tablespoons balsamic vinegar

3/4 to 1 cup fruity red wine, such as Chianti, Beaujolais, or Zinfandel

Salt and freshly ground black pepper

6 slices rustic country-style bread, toasted

2 cloves garlic, peeled

6 ounces Parmigiano-Reggiano cheese

2 tablespoons chopped fresh flat-leaf parsley

Heat the olive oil in a soup pot over medium heat. Add the pancetta and cook until some of the fat has rendered, 5 minutes. Reduce the heat to medium-low, add the onions and leeks, and continue to cook, stirring occasionally, until they have softened and are beginning to turn light golden, 30 minutes. Increase the heat to high, add the stock, and bring to a simmer. Reduce the heat to low and simmer 30 minutes.

This soup can be prepared to this point up to 1 day in advance.

Just before serving, add the vinegar, wine, salt, and pepper to taste. Rub the toasted bread with the garlic cloves. Ladle the soup into bowls and float a crouton on top of the soup. Shave or pare 4 or 5 thin slices of Parmigiano on top of each serving of soup. Garnish with the chopped parsley and serve immediately.

Serves 6

SUMMER VEGETABLE SOUP WITH PESTO

Minestrone di Riso con Pesto

Don't limit yourself to making this soup in the summertime: you can make it year-round with what-ever vegetables are available. But in the summer I like it best with a big dollop of pesto spooned on top just before serving. Pesto comes from the region of Liguria, around Genoa. Just over the French border in Provence, pistou is made with the same ingredients, excluding the pine nuts.

Soup

1¹/₄ cups dried navy beans

5¹/₄ cups water

1 small bunch of Swiss chard

¹/₂ small head of savoy cabbage

Salt and freshly ground black pepper

¹/₄ cup extra virgin olive oil plus more for garnish

3 ounces pancetta, diced

¹/₄ cup chopped fresh flat-leaf parsley

2 cloves garlic, minced

2 stalks celery, cut into ¹/₄-inch dice

1 carrot, cut into ¹/₄-inch dice

1 medium yellow onion, cut into ¹/₄-inch dice

1 medium potato, cut into ¹/₄-inch dice

¹/₂ cup green beans, trimmed and cut into ¹/₂-inch lengths

1 small zucchini, halved and cut into ¹/₄-inch slices

3 fresh or one 16-ounce can tomatoes, peeled, seeded, and chopped (page 259)

1 tablespoon tomato paste

7 cups chicken stock (page 255)

¹/₃ cup arborio rice

Pesto

5 cloves garlic, minced

2¹/₄ cups packed fresh basil leaves, washed and dried

Salt and freshly ground black pepper

1 cup grated Parmigiano-Reggiano cheese

¹/₂ cup extra virgin olive oil

5 tablespoons pine nuts, toasted (page 258)

To make the soup, soak the dried beans in cold water for 8 hours or overnight. Drain and place in a large pot with 5 cups of the water. Bring to a boil over high heat, turn the heat down to low, and simmer slowly until almost tender, 40 minutes. Turn off the heat and let the beans sit in their cooking liquid.

Cut the Swiss chard and cabbage into thin strips. Place in a saucepan with a large pinch of salt and the remaining water. Cover and simmer slowly until the leaves are wilted, 15 minutes. Drain and set aside.

Heat a stockpot over medium heat. Add the olive oil and pancetta and cook, stirring occasionally, until the pancetta renders its fat and just begins to turn golden, 10 minutes. Add the parsley and garlic and cook, stirring occasionally, for 2 minutes. Add the celery, carrot, onion, potato, green beans, and zucchini and cook for 5 minutes. Add the navy beans with their water to the stockpot. Add the Swiss chard, cabbage, tomatoes, and tomato paste. Add 6 cups of the chicken stock to cover the vegetables. Simmer slowly for 40 minutes.

Bring the remaining 1 cup stock to a simmer. Add the rice and simmer 10 minutes. Turn off the heat.

In the meantime, to make the pesto, place the garlic, basil, salt, and pepper in a blender or food processor. Process until a rough paste is formed. Add ¹/₂ cup of the Parmigiano and ¹/₄ cup of the olive oil and process until the paste is smooth. Add the pine nuts and the remaining ¹/₄ cup olive oil to make a stiff paste. Season with salt and pepper.

Ten minutes before the soup is finished, add the rice and simmer until cooked, 3 to 4 minutes. Season with salt and pepper.

Ladle the soup into bowls and spoon a large table-spoon of pesto on top. Drizzle some olive oil over the top, garnish with the remaining ¹/₂ cup Parmigiano, and serve immediately.

Serves 8

GRILLED BREAD SALAD WITH MOZZARELLA AND LEMON ANCHOVY VINAIGRETTE

Crostini di Mozzarella

Mozzarella is the second most popular cheese in Italy after Parmigiano-Reggiano. There are several types of mozzarella, but the most common variety in the United States is firm enough that if you drop it, it almost bounces. What this cheese lacks in flavor, it makes up in texture when melted. On the opposite end of the spectrum is the prized buffalo milk mozzarella, a specialty of Naples. Mozzarella di bufala has a mild distinctive flavor, is extremely expensive, and is best served fresh, perhaps with a salad of ripe tomatoes and basil. Fresh cow's milk mozzarella is somewhere in between the two; it is stringy when melted and has more flavor than the former but is less expensive than the latter. It makes a perfect addition to this recipe.

6 large slices rustic country-style bread

2 cloves garlic, peeled

3 tablespoons lemon juice

6 anchovy fillets, soaked in cold water 10 minutes, patted dry, and mashed

1 shallot, minced

5 tablespoons extra virgin olive oil

Salt and freshly ground black pepper

3/4 pound fresh cow's milk or buffalo milk mozzarella, thinly sliced

Garnishes

6 lemon wedges

Small radishes with young green tops

Grilled Japanese eggplant slices

Pitted black or green olives

Marinated artichoke hearts

Roasted red or yellow bell peppers, sliced

Cut each slice of bread on the diagonal into 2 pieces. Toast or grill the bread until golden and rub each side with the garlic cloves.

In a small bowl, whisk together the lemon juice, anchovies, shallot, and olive oil. Season with salt and pepper.

Preheat the oven to 400°F. Place the grilled bread on a baking sheet and distribute the mozzarella evenly on top. Bake on the top rack of the oven until the mozzarella begins to melt, 1 to 2 minutes.

To serve, place 2 pieces of grilled bread on each plate. Drizzle a spoonful of the lemon anchovy vinaigrette on top. Garnish with lemon wedges, radishes, eggplant, olives, artichokes, or roasted peppers. Serve the remaining vinaigrette on the side in a small bowl.

Serves 6

GRILLED BREAD WITH WILD MUSHROOMS, FONTINA, AND GORGONZOLA

Crostini con Funghi, Porcini e Formaggi

In Italy, when you talk about mushrooms you mean wild mushrooms, and in most cases you're referring to highly prized porcini mushrooms, named for their supposed resemblance to pudgy little piglets, or porci. Gathering porcini is a national autumn pastime, and during mushroom season the marketplace is not to be missed. Huge piles of creamy, golden-brown porcini fill the tables, and ladies doing their daily marketing pick and choose these beauties with a very discerning eye. Combine them with Gorgonzola for wonderful crostini.

1 tablespoon extra virgin olive oil

1 tablespoon unsalted butter

$^1/_2$ pound wild mushrooms (porcini, chanterelles, shiitake, morels), brushed clean and thinly sliced (see Note)

$^1/_2$ pound button or field mushrooms, brushed clean and thinly sliced

1 tablespoon chopped fresh thyme

1 tablespoon chopped fresh mint

1 tablespoon chopped fresh flat-leaf parsley

4 ounces fontina cheese, coarsely grated

3 ounces Gorgonzola cheese, crumbled

Salt and freshly ground black pepper

12 slices country-style bread, toasted

2 cloves garlic, peeled

Juice of $^1/_2$ lemon

Whole flat-leaf parsley leaves

Preheat the broiler. Heat the olive oil and butter in a large frying pan over medium-high heat. Add the mushrooms, thyme, mint, and parsley and cook until the liquid has evaporated and the mushrooms are dry, 7 to 10 minutes. Let cool. Add the fontina and Gorgonzola and season well with salt and pepper.

Rub each side of the toast lightly with the garlic cloves. Distribute the warm mushrooms on top of the toast. Place the mushroom toasts in a single layer on a baking sheet. Broil until the cheese melts, 30 to 60 seconds. Place on a platter and drizzle with the lemon juice.

Serve immediately, garnished with parsley leaves.

Serves 6

NOTE: If fresh wild mushrooms are unavailable, an equivalent quantity of button or field mushrooms can be substituted along with $^1/_4$ ounce dried porcini mushrooms soaked in hot water for 30 minutes. Drain the mushrooms, discarding the liquid or saving it for another use. Chop the porcinis coarsely, then add to the cooked mushrooms.

GRILLED BREAD WITH BEANS AND BITTER GREENS

Crostini con Capriata

My favorite way to serve crostini is to make an assortment and serve them together on one platter. I call it crostini misti, or mixed grilled bread. Everyone loves the surprising mixture of colors and flavors and wants to taste them all. Serve this delicious combination of beans and bitter greens with Grilled Bread with Wild Mushrooms, Fontina, and Gorgonzola (page 101), Grilled Bread with Sweet-Sour Chicken Livers (page 104), or maybe even grilled bread with sun-dried tomato purée.

3/4 cup dried white, cannelloni, or navy beans (see Note), about 5 ounces

1 bay leaf

Large pinch of dried thyme

3 tablespoons extra virgin olive oil

2 teaspoons chopped fresh sage

4 cloves garlic, minced

Salt and freshly ground black pepper

1 small bunch of Swiss chard, escarole, or beet or turnip greens

1/2 small yellow onion, minced

1/4 teaspoon crushed red pepper flakes

2 teaspoons red wine vinegar

6 to 8 large slices rustic country-style bread, toasted

2 cloves garlic, peeled

Pick over the beans and discard any stones. Cover with water and soak 8 hours or overnight. The next day, drain the beans and place them in a saucepan with the bay leaf, thyme, and enough water to cover by 2 inches. Over high heat, bring to a boil and immediately reduce the heat to low. Simmer until the skins crack and the beans are tender, 45 to 60 minutes. Drain the beans, reserving 1/2 cup of the cooking liquid.

Heat 2 tablespoons of the olive oil in a frying pan over medium heat. Add the beans, sage, half of the garlic, and the reserved cooking liquid. Cook, mashing occasionally, until the moisture evaporates and the mixture forms a paste, 5 to 10 minutes. Season with salt and pepper.

Wash the greens well and spin dry. Remove the stems and cut into 1-inch pieces. Heat the remaining 1 tablespoon olive oil in a frying pan over low heat and cook the onion until soft, 7 minutes. Add the greens and the remaining garlic and cook until wilted, stirring occasionally, 3 minutes. Season with salt, pepper, red pepper flakes, and vinegar.

Rub each side of the toast with the garlic cloves. Spread the beans on the toasted bread and top with the greens. Serve immediately.

Serves 6 to 8

NOTE: **This recipe can also be made with 2 cups canned cooked beans.**

GRILLED BREAD WITH SWEET-SOUR CHICKEN LIVERS

Crostini di Fegatini all'Agrodolce

Bruschetta, fettunta, and crostini *are three different types of grilled bread used to tame ferocious appetites. Indigenous to southern Italy,* bruschetta *celebrates the olive harvest with thick slices of rustic bread grilled over an open fire, rubbed with garlic, and brushed with green-gold olive oil and maybe a sprinkling of coarse salt.* Fettunta, *made in northern Italy, means "oiled slice" and is basically the same thing as* bruschetta. Crostini *is sliced thinner than* bruschetta *and can be topped with all kinds of flavorful combinations of ingredients: anchovies, olives, and capers; roasted eggplant with garlic and olive oil; chopped tomatoes with red wine vinegar, garlic, and herbs; and this sweet-sour chicken liver paste. This is a crostini to top all others!*

2 tablespoons extra virgin olive oil

2 ounces pancetta, finely chopped

1/4 cup minced yellow onion

1 teaspoon chopped fresh sage,
     or 1/2 teaspoon dried thyme

2 tablespoons dry Marsala or
     white wine

1 tablespoon unsalted butter

1/2 pound chicken livers, trimmed of
     veins and fat

Salt and freshly ground black pepper

1 clove garlic, minced

2 anchovy fillets, soaked in cold
     water 10 minutes, patted dry,
     and mashed

1 tablespoon chopped capers

2 to 3 teaspoons balsamic vinegar

6 large slices rustic country-style
     bread, sliced 1/4-inch thick,
     toasted

Heat 1 tablespoon of the olive oil in a frying pan over medium heat. Cook the pancetta, onion, and sage or thyme until the onion is soft, 10 minutes. Add the Marsala and simmer until the moisture evaporates. Remove from the pan, place on a work surface, and chop together until fine. Reserve.

In the same pan, heat the remaining 1 tablespoon olive oil and the butter over low heat. Place the livers in the pan side by side and cook for 2 to 3 minutes, turning them a few times. Season with salt and pepper. As soon as they are firm yet still pink on the inside, remove them from the pan and let cool. Chop the livers coarsely and combine them in a bowl with the onion mixture. Add the garlic, anchovies, capers, and vinegar to taste. Season with salt and pepper.

Cut each slice of bread on the diagonal into 2 pieces. Spread the liver paste on the warm croutons and serve immediately.

Makes 12 crostini to serve 6

GARLIC FLAT BREAD WITH SMOKED MOZZARELLA AND TOMATO VINAIGRETTE

Focaccia alla Scamorza e Pomodoro

Focaccia *derives its name from the Latin word* focus, *meaning "hearth" (originally* focaccia *were cooked directly on the hearth). As romantic as this all sounds, cooking on the hearth isn't so easy. These days focaccia is generally cooked in a wood-fired pizza oven or at home in your own oven.*

Dough

2¹/2 teaspoons active dry yeast

¹/4 cup lukewarm water (110°F)

¹/4 cup whole wheat flour

3 tablespoons extra virgin olive oil

1³/4 cups all-purpose flour

³/4 teaspoon salt

¹/4 cup water

4 cloves garlic, sliced paper-thin

Topping

4 tablespoons extra virgin olive oil

3 tablespoons balsamic vinegar

1 clove garlic, minced

Salt and freshly ground black pepper

¹/4 pound yellow cherry tomatoes, halved

¹/4 pound red cherry tomatoes, halved

7 ounces smoked mozzarella or Scamorza cheese, coarsely grated

¹/2 cup loosely packed fresh basil leaves, cut into thin strips

To make the dough, combine the yeast, lukewarm water, and whole wheat flour in a bowl. Let stand for 10 minutes, then add the olive oil, flour, salt, and water. Mix the dough thoroughly. Knead on a floured board for 10 minutes, until the dough is elastic yet still moist. Place the dough in an oiled bowl, turning it once to coat with oil. Cover the bowl with a towel and let rise in a warm place (75°F) until doubled in size, 1 to 1¹/2 hours.

Preheat the oven to 450°F and place a pizza stone on the bottom rack of the oven.

On a floured surface, divide the dough into 2 pieces and roll each piece into an 8-inch circle, ¹/2 inch thick. Transfer to a well-floured pizza peel or paddle. Sprinkle the sliced garlic on top and press into the dough. Transfer the dough from the peel onto the heated pizza stone in the oven. Bake until golden and crisp, 8 to 10 minutes. Remove from the oven and let rest on a cooling rack.

To make the topping, whisk together the oil, vinegar, and minced garlic in a bowl. Season with salt and pepper. Add the cherry tomatoes and toss together. Leave at room temperature.

The recipe can be prepared to this point up to several hours in advance.

Preheat the broiler. Place half of the cheese on top of each flat bread. Broil until the cheese is melted and the crust is golden, 1 to 2 minutes. Remove from the oven and place on a platter. Top each flat bread with half of the tomatoes, the vinaigrette, and basil. Serve immediately.

Makes two 8-inch flat breads to serve 6

BAKED CREPES WITH CREAMY WILD MUSHROOMS AND PROSCIUTTO

Crespelle Ripiene con Funghi Porcini e Prosciutto

Crespelle, Italian for "crepes," were supposedly introduced to Naples by the French courts. They're popular mainly on the Campania coast of the Mediterranean, in southern Italy, and in a few other scattered pockets throughout the country. Crespelle are easy to make as long as you have the right pan. Choose a heavy metal crepe pan and test the batter by making a crepe. The batter should be a bit thicker than heavy cream and can be adjusted with more flour or milk as necessary to get the right consistency. Once you start making the crepes, it's kind of fun. And the best part is that they can be made in advance and stored in the refrigerator for a few days.

Crepes

2 cups all-purpose flour

1/4 teaspoon salt

1 3/4 cups milk

4 eggs

4 to 5 tablespoons unsalted butter

Filling

2 cups boiling water

1/2 ounce dried wild mushrooms

6 tablespoons unsalted butter

1 medium yellow onion, minced

1/2 pound fresh button mushrooms, thinly sliced

6 ounces thinly sliced prosciutto, cut into thin strips

2 tablespoons all-purpose flour

2 cups milk

3/4 cup grated Parmigiano-Reggiano cheese

Salt and freshly ground black pepper

2 tablespoons fine dry bread crumbs

To make the crepes, put the flour and salt in a bowl and slowly add the milk, a little at a time, mixing vigorously with a fork to avoid lumps. Add 1 egg at a time, beating rapidly with a fork after each addition. Let the batter rest 30 minutes.

Oil the bottom of an 8-inch crepe pan with 1 teaspoon of the butter. Place the pan over medium heat. Stir the batter, pour 1/3 cup into the pan, and rotate the pan to completely cover the bottom. As soon as the batter has set, loosen the crepe with a spatula and flip it. When the other side is firm, remove the crepe and place it on a plate. Repeat with the rest of the batter, stirring the batter occasionally and adding butter to the pan as needed to keep the crepes from sticking. Crepes can be stacked on top of one another until ready to use.

To make the filling, pour the boiling water over the dried mushrooms and let sit 30 minutes. Drain well and reserve the water. Chop the mushrooms coarsely. Filter the mushroom water through a paper towel–lined strainer and reserve.

Heat 2 tablespoons of the butter in a frying pan over medium heat. Add the onion and cook, stirring occasionally, until soft, 7 minutes. Add the fresh mushrooms and continue to cook, stirring occasionally, until the mushroom liquid is evaporated, 10 minutes. Add the chopped soaked wild mushrooms and continue to cook 1 minute. Add the reserved mushroom water, turn the heat to high, and simmer, stirring constantly, until almost dry, 10 minutes. Reduce the heat to medium, add the prosciutto, and continue to cook 2 minutes.

Melt 3 tablespoons of the butter in a saucepan over low heat. Add the flour and stir constantly for 2 minutes. Add the milk, stirring constantly, and cook until the mixture thickens, 2 to 3 minutes. Add the mushroom mixture and mix well. Add $1/2$ cup of the Parmigiano and season with salt and pepper.

Preheat the oven to 425°F. Butter the bottom and sides of a 9 by 12-inch baking dish.

Place a crepe flat on the work surface. Spread half of it with a few tablespoons of filling. Fold in half, then quarters. Stand the triangles in a baking dish, overlapping one another with the curved side up. Repeat. Melt the remaining 1 tablespoon butter and brush on the tops of the crepes. Combine the remaining $1/4$ cup grated Parmigiano and the bread crumbs. Sprinkle over the top. Bake the crepes until golden on top, about 20 minutes. Allow the crepes to cool for 10 minutes before serving.

Makes 12 crepes to serve 6

PIZZA WITH FRESH HERB, OLIVE, AND PECORINO SALAD

Pizza con Verdure Fresche, Olive e Pecorino

This is not your typical pizza recipe: it is adapted from the restaurant Chez Panisse in Berkeley, California, where I worked for a few years. At the restaurant, we topped a hot pizza with a parsley and shaved Parmigiano salad. Here the pizza is topped with a salad of parsley, basil, chives, mint, olives, and shaved pecorino. The combination may sound odd, but once you've tried it, you will understand why it's a Chez Panisse favorite.

3 cloves garlic, minced

5 tablespoons extra virgin olive oil

1 cup loosely packed fresh basil leaves

2 cups fresh flat-leaf parsley leaves

3 tablespoons snipped fresh chives

2 tablespoons very coarsely chopped fresh mint

1/4 cup pitted and coarsely chopped cured Italian black olives (page 260)

2 tablespoons lemon juice

Salt and freshly ground black pepper

1 recipe pizza dough (page 258)

3/4 cup grated mozzarella cheese, about 3 ounces

3/4 cup grated fontina cheese, about 3 ounces

3 ounces pecorino or grana padano cheese

Combine the garlic and 2 tablespoons of the olive oil and let stand for 30 minutes.

Preheat the oven to 500°F. Place a pizza stone on the bottom rack of the oven.

Tear the basil leaves into pieces about the same size as the parsley leaves. Combine the basil, parsley, chives, mint, and olives. In a small bowl, whisk together the remaining 3 tablespoons olive oil and the lemon juice. Add one-quarter of the reserved garlic mixture and mix well. Season with salt and pepper.

On a floured surface, roll half of the dough into a 9-inch circle, 1/4 inch thick. Transfer to a well-floured pizza peel or paddle. Brush the dough to within 1/2 inch of the edge with half of the remaining garlic oil. Combine the mozzarella and fontina cheeses and spread half over the dough, leaving a 1/2-inch border around the edge. Transfer the dough from the peel directly onto the heated stone. Bake until golden and crisp, 8 to 10 minutes.

Toss the herbs and olives with the vinaigrette. Place half of the salad on top of the pizza. With a cheese shaver or vegetable peeler, shave paper-thin slices of pecorino on top of the herb salad. Serve immediately. Repeat with the remaining half of the pizza dough.

Makes two 9-inch pizzas

FLAT BREAD WITH GORGONZOLA, PINE NUTS, AND RED ONIONS

Focaccia con Gorgonzola e Pinoli

Every year I take my students with me to study in Italy and France. A few years ago I had the opportunity to take my students to visit the caves of Gorgonzola, in northern Italy, where they make the prized blue-veined cheese. Anyone who knows me knows that I happen to love Gorgonzola, so when the chance arose, we got on the bus and headed in that direction. We all looked like scientists as we put on coats, boots, and hairnets in order to step into the caves. The highlight of the tour, of course, was when they opened a big wheel of Gorgonzola and gave us each a spoonful. Honestly, I think my eyes rolled back into my head! Gorgonzola mashed with a bit of butter is a terrific filling for this focaccia.

3 tablespoons warm water (115°F)

1 teaspoon active dry yeast

1^1/$_2$ cups plus 4 tablespoons all-
    purpose flour

^{1}/$_3$ cup water

^{1}/$_2$ teaspoon salt

2 tablespoons extra virgin olive oil

3 ounces Gorgonzola cheese,
    at room temperature

2 tablespoons unsalted butter,
    at room temperature

1^1/$_2$ tablespoons pine nuts, toasted
    (page 258)

^{1}/$_4$ small red onion, thinly sliced

Combine the warm water, yeast, and 4 tablespoons of the flour in a small bowl. Let stand for 20 minutes until it gets foamy. Add the water, salt, olive oil, and the remaining 1^1/$_2$ cups flour. Mix the dough well. Knead on a floured surface until it is smooth and elastic but still moist, 10 minutes. Place the dough in an oiled bowl, turning it once to coat with oil. Cover the bowl with plastic wrap and let rise in a warm place (75°F) until doubled in volume, 1 to 1^1/$_2$ hours.

Place a pizza stone on the bottom rack of the oven. Preheat the oven to 500°F for at least 30 minutes.

Divide the dough into two pieces. On a well-floured surface, roll 1 piece of the dough into a 10 by 12-inch rectangle, ^{1}/$_8$ inch thick. Transfer to a pizza peel or paddle and arrange so that the longer side is parallel to your body and the edge of your work space. Mash the Gorgonzola, butter, and pine nuts together. Spread half the cheese on the right half of the dough, leaving a 1-inch border around the edge. Spray or brush the edges of the dough lightly with water. Fold the empty half of the dough over the Gorgonzola–butter–pine nuts mixture. Press the edges together and trim them with a sharp knife close to the edge, enclosing the cheese. Score the top of the dough in 3 or 4 places with 1-inch slits. Place half of the onion slices on top of the dough. Repeat with the other piece of dough.

Transfer the flat bread to the pizza stone and bake until lightly golden, 5 to 7 minutes. Remove from the oven and serve immediately.

Makes 2 flat breads to serve 6

PIZZA WITH SUN-DRIED TOMATO PASTE, ROASTED EGGPLANT, AND BASIL

Pizza con Estratto di Pomodoro, Melanzane Arristite e Basilico

It is believed that pizza originated in Naples during Roman times. As its popularity spread throughout Italy, each region added a bit of its own flavor to create a pizza of its own. This all-time favorite food has now been transported from Italy across mountains and oceans to be consumed in almost every country throughout the world.

5 cloves garlic, minced

4 tablespoons extra virgin olive oil

1/2 cup sun-dried tomatoes in oil, drained, coarsely chopped, oil reserved

1/2 small red onion, chopped

1/2 cup water

2 teaspoons balsamic vinegar

Salt and freshly ground black pepper

2 small Japanese eggplants, cut into 1/4-inch diagonal slices

1 recipe pizza dough (page 258)

3/4 cup grated fontina cheese, about 3 ounces

3/4 cup grated mozzarella cheese, about 3 ounces

1/3 to 1/2 cup fresh basil leaves, cut into thin strips

NOTE: The sun-dried tomato purée is a flavorful topping that can be spread on grilled or toasted bread or *crostini* and served with a mixed *crostini* platter.

Combine half of the garlic and 2 tablespoons of the olive oil and let stand for 30 minutes.

Preheat an oven to 400°F and place a pizza stone on the bottom rack of the oven.

Heat 1 tablespoon of the reserved oil from the tomatoes in a small saucepan over medium heat. Add the onion and the remaining garlic and cook until the onion is soft, 7 minutes. Add the tomatoes and the water and simmer over low heat until the tomatoes are soft, 10 minutes. Add more water if needed. Remove the onion and tomatoes from the pan and purée in a food processor or blender to obtain a smooth paste. Add 1 teaspoon of the balsamic vinegar, salt, and pepper.

Brush a baking sheet lightly with some of the remaining 3 tablespoons oil. Place the eggplant on the oiled baking sheet and brush the tops with additional oil. Bake on the top rack of the oven, turning occasionally, until very light golden, 10 to 15 minutes. Toss with 1 teaspoon minced garlic from the reserved garlic oil, the remaining 1 teaspoon balsamic vinegar, salt, and pepper.

Increase the oven temperature to 500°F. On a floured surface, roll the dough into a 9-inch circle, 1/4 inch thick. Transfer to a well-floured pizza peel or paddle. Brush the dough to within 1/2 inch of the edge with the garlic oil. Spread 4 tablespoons of the tomato paste on the oil. Reserve the extra tomato paste for another use (see Note). Combine the fontina and mozzarella cheeses and spread half on top of the tomato. Distribute half of the eggplant on the cheese. Transfer the dough from the peel directly onto the heated stone in the oven. Bake until golden and crisp, 8 to 10 minutes. Repeat with the remaining half of the pizza dough.

Remove from the oven and sprinkle the basil leaves on top.

Makes two 9-inch pizzas to serve 6 to 8

FARFALLE WITH SHELLFISH, TOMATOES, AND ARUGULA

Farfalle alle Vongole e Rughetta di Campo a l'Antica Trattoria

L'Antica Trattoria is a modest little trattoria on a small alley in Sorrento. It was highly touted to me as a place that made the best primi piatti. Naturally, I hightailed it there. When the menu was handed to me, I just couldn't decide between deep-fried seaweed with late summer vegetables; sfolino, a dried tomato–filled puff pastry turnover; or this pasta. When Paolo, the chef, emerged from the kitchen, I decided to put my decision in his hands, and I was happy I did.

3 tablespoons extra virgin olive oil

3 cloves garlic, minced

Large pinch of crushed red pepper flakes

1 pound clams, scrubbed

1 pound mussels, scrubbed and beards removed

2 pounds tomatoes, peeled, seeded, and chopped (page 259), or one 28-ounce can Italian plum tomatoes, drained and chopped

1/2 pound farfalle or bow tie pasta

2 bunches of arugula, washed and dried

Salt and freshly ground black pepper

Heat the olive oil in a large frying pan over medium-low heat. Add the garlic and red pepper flakes and cook slowly for 1 minute. Add the clams and cover. Cook, shaking the pan occasionally, until the clams open, 2 to 5 minutes, depending upon the size of the clams. Remove the clams from the pan with a slotted spoon and keep warm in a bowl. Add the mussels, cover, and cook, shaking the pan occasionally, until the mussels open, 2 to 3 minutes. Remove the mussels from the pan with a slotted spoon and add to the clams.

Using a food mill or blender, purée the tomatoes and add to the frying pan. Increase the heat to high and simmer until the liquid begins to evaporate and the sauce thickens slightly, 4 to 5 minutes. Remove from the heat.

Bring a large pot of salted water to a boil. Add the pasta and cook until al dente. Drain.

Heat the tomato sauce and add the pasta, clams, mussels, any liquid in the bottom of the bowl, and the arugula. Toss together and season with salt and pepper. Serve immediately.

Serves 6

> NOTE: **This can be prepared with all clams or all mussels.**

PASTA WITH PANCETTA, TOMATOES, AND HOT RED PEPPER

Pasta all'Amatriciana

Pasta all'Amatriciana, that is to say, pasta from Amatrice, a town in Lazio, is best when made with good-quality store-bought pasta, peppery pancetta, and lots of garlic. In Lazio, this dish is made in huge quantities on the first Sunday after August 15 to celebrate this local specialty. When a dish is this simple, it relies upon the best possible ingredients.

1/4 cup extra virgin olive oil

8 ounces thinly sliced pancetta, cut into 1/2-inch dice

3/4 teaspoon crushed red pepper flakes

4 cloves garlic, minced

1 cup dry white wine, such as Verdicchio or sauvignon blanc

1 large red onion, thinly sliced

2 1/2 pounds fresh ripe tomatoes, peeled, seeded, and chopped (page 259), or three 14-ounce cans Italian plum tomatoes, drained and chopped

4 tablespoons chopped fresh flat-leaf parsley

Salt and freshly ground black pepper

1 pound dry semolina vermicelli, spaghetti, or linguine

1/2 cup freshly grated pecorino cheese

1/2 cup freshly grated Parmigiano-Reggiano cheese

Heat the olive oil in a frying pan over medium heat and cook the pancetta, stirring occasionally, until golden but still soft, 10 minutes. Add the red pepper flakes and garlic and continue to cook, stirring, for 3 minutes. Add the wine and simmer until the wine evaporates, 5 minutes. Remove the pancetta from the pan with a slotted spoon and reserve. Add the onion to the pan and cook until soft, 5 to 7 minutes. Pass the tomatoes through a food mill or purée in a blender until smooth. Add the tomatoes and parsley to the onion. Simmer 20 minutes. Season with salt and pepper. Add the pancetta and mix well.

Note: This recipe can be prepared to this point up to 1 day in advance.

Bring a large pot of salted water to a boil. Cook the pasta until al dente. Drain and toss with the warm sauce. Place on a platter and garnish with the pecorino and Parmigiano.

Serves 6

"LITTLE EARS" WITH SICILIAN PESTO

Orecchiette con Pesto alla Siciliana

Orecchiette means "little ears," and when you see this pasta you'll understand why. This restorative dish comes from Erice, in the northwest corner of Sicily. I learned to make orecchiette when I was in the very city of Erice, and I soon realized I couldn't stop eating them.

Pasta

2 cups all-purpose flour, plus extra for rolling and tossing

1 cup semolina flour

1/2 teaspoon salt

1 1/4 cups water

Sauce

4 cups fresh basil leaves, washed and dried

3 cloves garlic, minced

1/4 cup pine nuts, toasted (page 258)

1/2 cup extra virgin olive oil

3/4 cup grated Parmigiano-Reggiano cheese

Pinch of crushed red pepper flakes

2 large tomatoes, peeled, seeded, and chopped (page 259)

Salt and freshly ground black pepper

To make the pasta, combine the all-purpose and semolina flours and the salt on a work surface. Make a well in the center. Add the water and mix together until it forms a ball. Knead 7 to 10 minutes to form a smooth and elastic dough. Wrap in plastic wrap and let rest 30 minutes.

To make the sauce, place the basil, garlic, pine nuts, and olive oil in a blender or food processor and blend at high speed until smooth, stopping and scraping down the sides as necessary. Add 1/2 cup of the Parmigiano and the red pepper flakes and pulse a few times to make a thick paste. Drain the tomatoes and fold into the pesto. Season with salt and pepper.

Cut the dough into 4 pieces and cover with plastic wrap. With both hands, roll one of the pieces into a long snake shape, 3/8 inch in diameter. With a knife, cut it into 1/4-inch pieces. Flour the work surface well. With the thumb of your right hand, press down gently in the center of each piece, rotating your thumb counterclockwise a half turn so the dough forms a round disk that is thicker on the edges and thinner in the center. The disks should be 1 inch in diameter; if they are not, let them rest 10 minutes and rotate with your thumb again to stretch them to the right size. Toss with the flour. Repeat with the remaining dough. Store on a well-floured baking sheet covered with a kitchen towel until ready to use.

Bring a large pot of boiling salted water to a boil. Add the pasta and cook until al dente, 3 to 4 minutes. Drain and toss with the pesto. Place on a platter, garnish with the remaining 1/4 cup grated Parmigiano, and serve immediately.

Serves 6 to 8

> NOTE: **If you don't want to make homemade orecchiette, substitute 1 pound of dry.**

LEMON AND HERB PANSOTI WITH WILTED GREENS

Who doesn't love ravioli? Every time I see ravioli on a menu, I order it. Pansoti are actually giant ravioli, and since they are large, they are easy to make by hand. This recipe is inspired by Peggy Smith and the late Catherine Brandel, two talented chefs I worked with for a few years when I was a cook at Chez Panisse. The trick to achieving a bright green pasta dough is to use fresh spinach that is as dry as possible.

Pasta Dough

1 bunch of spinach

2 egg yolks

1 whole egg

2¼ cups all-purpose flour

½ teaspoon salt

Filling

1 pound ricotta, drained in a cheesecloth-lined strainer for 2 hours

¼ teaspoon chopped fresh thyme

¼ teaspoon chopped fresh oregano

Pinch of chopped fresh rosemary

2 tablespoons snipped fresh chives

Grated zest of 2 lemons

1 egg, lightly beaten

½ teaspoon salt

Freshly ground black pepper

White rice or all-purpose flour for rolling the pasta

¼ cup unsalted butter

¼ cup extra virgin olive oil

2 small bunches of washed and dried greens (turnip greens, Swiss chard, mustard greens, beet greens, escarole) ribs removed and cut into 1-inch strips

Juice of ½ lemon

To make the pasta dough, remove the stems from the spinach and wash well. Dry completely in a salad spinner.

Place the egg yolks, whole egg, and spinach in a blender. Process until completely liquefied. It should measure 1 scant cup.

Combine the flour and salt on a work surface. Make a well in the center and add the spinach and egg mixture. Mix with a fork or your thumb, bringing the flour in from the sides of the well. Continue until a mass is formed. Form into a ball. Knead the dough for 3 minutes.

Cover the dough with plastic wrap and let rest for 60 minutes.

To make the filling, combine the ricotta, thyme, oregano, rosemary, chives, lemon zest, and beaten egg. Season with the salt and pepper.

Cut the dough into 4 pieces. Using a pasta machine, open the wheels to the widest opening. Roll the pasta dough through 4 or 5 times, folding in half each time. Dust with rice flour if the dough is sticky. Roll the dough until it is as wide as the machine. If you have started at the first opening, consider this #1. Now set the opening to #3. Roll the dough through #3 one time. Set the opening to #5 and roll the dough through #5 one time. Set the opening to #6 and roll the dough through #6 one time until you can just see the outline of your hand through it. Cut the dough into 6-inch squares. Spread a heaping tablespoon of filling in the center of each square. Spray the edges lightly with water. Place a square on top and seal the edges with your finger. Trim with a zigzag roller.

Heat the butter and olive oil in a large frying pan. Add the greens and toss until wilted, 5 minutes. Season with lemon juice, salt, and pepper to taste.

Bring a large pot of salted water to a boil. Cook the pansoti until al dente, 3 to 5 minutes. Place 2 on each plate and top with wilted greens and sauce.

Serves 6 to 8

POTATO GNOCCHI WITH TOMATOES AND MOZZARELLA

Gnocchi di Patate con Pomodoro e Mozzarella

Gnocchi can turn out either as light as a feather or as heavy as lead. My thanks go to Toni Romano, who taught me how to make featherlight gnocchi years ago. Toni makes some of the best gnocchi anywhere; I think the key is the way she allows the potatoes to drain and dry for 10 minutes after boiling them. She then rices the potatoes over the flour and, with the lightest touch, works the mixture together. Try them for yourself.

Gnocchi

1^1/4 pounds russet baking potatoes, peeled and quartered

Salt

4^1/2 cups all-purpose flour

1 egg, lightly beaten

Sauce

2 tablespoons extra virgin olive oil

10 medium tomatoes, peeled, seeded, and diced (page 259), or three 14-ounce cans Italian plum tomatoes, drained and chopped

^{1}/2 teaspoon dried oregano

Large pinch of crushed red pepper flakes

2 tablespoons balsamic vinegar

1 tablespoon tomato paste

^{1}/4 cup dry red wine, such as Chianti

1 teaspoon sugar

Salt and freshly ground black pepper

1 to 2 teaspoons red wine vinegar

6 ounces fresh cow's milk or buffalo milk mozzarella, diced

^{3}/4 cup grated pecorino or Parmigiano-Reggiano cheese

To make the gnocchi, place the potatoes in a saucepan and add salted water just to the level of the potatoes. Bring to a boil and cook until very soft, 25 minutes. Drain well and let sit in a colander 10 minutes.

Place the flour on a work surface. With a potato ricer or food mill, rice the warm potatoes over the entire surface of the flour. Toss together lightly with your fingers to distribute evenly.

Make a well in the center of the mixture and add the egg. Knead together to form a ball. Knead 1 minute to gather up all of the bits of flour and potato on the work surface. Let rest on the work surface with an inverted bowl over the top for 5 minutes.

Pinch off a piece of dough the size of your fist. Cover the remaining dough with the inverted bowl. Roll the piece with your hands into a long snake shape ^{1}/2 inch in diameter. Cut on a sharp diagonal into ^{1}/4-inch pieces. With the first 2 fingertips of your right hand dusted with flour and working on a floured surface, roll each piece away from you ^{1}/2 inch, using a little pressure to flatten it as you roll. Then roll the dough back toward you to form a small indentation in the center. Toss with flour. Place on a floured baking sheet. Repeat.

To make the sauce, heat the olive oil in a large frying pan over medium-high heat. Add the tomatoes, oregano, red pepper flakes, balsamic vinegar, tomato paste, red wine, sugar, salt, and pepper. Cook until the sauce thickens slightly, 3 to 4 minutes. Purée in a blender or food processor. Season with salt, pepper, and red wine vinegar. Place in a saucepan.

Bring a large pot of salted water to a boil. Cook the gnocchi until tender, 15 to 20 minutes. Heat the tomato sauce. Drain the gnocchi and toss with the tomato sauce and mozzarella. Sprinkle with the grated pecorino or Parmigiano and serve immediately.

Serves 8

PASTA PUTTANESCA WITH TUNA AND ORANGE

Pasta alla Puttanesca

Puttanesca in Italian means "in the style of a whore," and this quick and flavorful dish packs a punch with almost everything a prostitute might have on hand in the pantry. This Campanian dish is traditionally made with onions, garlic, tomatoes, anchovies, capers, and olives, although every cook has a unique version. The addition of orange zest and tuna makes this one quite different.

1/4 cup extra virgin olive oil

1 medium red onion, thinly sliced

4 cloves garlic, minced

6 tomatoes, peeled, seeded, and chopped (page 259), or 2 1/2 cups canned Italian plum tomatoes, drained and chopped

4 anchovy fillets, soaked in cold water 10 minutes, patted dry, and mashed

3 tablespoons chopped capers

2/3 cup pitted and coarsely chopped black olives (page 260)

1 tablespoon tomato paste

Pinch of grated orange rind

Juice of 1 orange

Crushed red pepper flakes

Freshly ground black pepper

One 6-ounce can tuna packed in olive oil, drained

2 tablespoons chopped fresh flat-leaf parsley

1 pound dry semolina linguine

Heat the olive oil in a frying pan over medium heat. Add the onion and cook, stirring occasionally, until soft, 7 minutes. Add the garlic and cook 1 minute. Add the tomatoes, anchovies, capers, olives, tomato paste, orange rind, orange juice, red pepper flakes, and black pepper and simmer slowly for 3 minutes. Add the tuna and parsley and simmer for 30 seconds.

Bring a large pot of salted water to a boil. Add the pasta and cook until al dente, 8 to 12 minutes. Drain and immediately toss with the sauce. Serve immediately.

Serves 6

POLENTA GRATIN WITH GORGONZOLA AND MOZZARELLA

Polenta al Forno con Gorgonzola e Mozzarella

The first time I tasted polenta, I couldn't understand what all the fuss was about. It was like the cornmeal mush I used to eat when I was a kid. The second time I tasted polenta, it was a bowl of creamy polenta with wild mushrooms, lots of sweet butter, and freshly grated Parmigiano-Reggiano cheese. It has been years since then, and the memory still lingers with me. Today, I think of polenta as miracle food; it is basically cornmeal, ground from white or yellow corn, and available at grocery stores in coarse and medium grinds. It's versatile, nutritious, comforting, and addictive, as the following recipe will demonstrate.

5 cups water

1 teaspoon salt

1 1/3 cups coarse polenta

2 tablespoons plus 1 teaspoon unsalted butter, at room temperature

Freshly ground black pepper

1/4 cup mascarpone (page 257)

4 ounces Gorgonzola cheese

4 ounces mozzarella cheese, coarsely grated

1/2 cup grated Parmigiano-Reggiano cheese

Bring the water to a boil over high heat and add the salt. Reduce the heat to medium and slowly sprinkle the polenta into the boiling water, whisking constantly. Continue to whisk the mixture until it gets too thick to use a whisk, 2 to 5 minutes. Change to a wooden spoon and continue to simmer, stirring occasionally, until the spoon can stand in the polenta, 20 to 25 minutes. Add 2 tablespoons of the butter and mix well. Season with salt and pepper.

In a bowl, mash the mascarpone, Gorgonzola, mozzarella, and half of the Parmigiano together with a fork. Season with pepper.

Preheat the oven to 425°F. Using the remaining 1 teaspoon butter, grease a 2-quart baking dish. While the polenta is still hot, spread half of it in the dish. Dab all the cheese mixture evenly on top of the polenta. Spread the remaining half of the polenta on top of the cheese. Sprinkle the top with the remaining half of the Parmigiano.

Note: This recipe can be prepared to this point up to 1 day in advance and stored in the refrigerator. Bring to room temperature before baking.

Bake on the top rack of the oven until hot and the edges are bubbling and golden, 15 to 20 minutes. Remove from the oven and serve directly from the baking dish.

Serves 6

> NOTE: This recipe can also be made in individual 4-inch round gratin dishes, decreasing the baking time to 5 to 10 minutes.

RICE "OLIVES"

Olive di Riso

A good friend of mine, Gabriele Ferron, owns one of the best riseria, Italian for "rice mill," in the Isola della Scala area of the Veneto, in northern Italy. The soil there is incredibly fertile, and the water is absolutely pure. Best of all, his pila vecia, which means "old mill," is powered by water using all pre–World War I machinery. Visiting his mill is like stepping back in time. When I am teaching in this part of Italy I always take my students to meet Gabriele, and every time I go he makes me these bite-size risotto balls that are creamy on the inside and crispy and golden on the outside. He knows they are one of my favorites! They are called rice "olives" not only because of their size, but also because they contain olive paste, a mixture of mashed olives, garlic, and olive oil. You can make it yourself in a food processor or buy it already prepared at any specialty Italian market.

2 tablespoons extra virgin olive oil

$^1/_2$ small yellow onion, minced

1 cup arborio, vialone nano, or carnaroli rice

1$^1/_4$ cups chicken stock (page 255)

1$^1/_4$ cups milk

$^2/_3$ cup olive paste

Salt and freshly ground black pepper

$^1/_2$ cup finely grated Parmigiano-Reggiano cheese

1 cup all-purpose flour

4 eggs

$^1/_2$ cup water

4 cups finely ground toasted fresh bread crumbs

Mixture of canola and olive oil for deep-frying

Heat 2 tablespoons of the olive oil over medium-low heat in a frying pan. Add the onion and sauté until soft, 7 minutes. Add the rice and continue to cook, stirring constantly, for 3 minutes.

Place the chicken stock and milk in a saucepan and heat just to a simmer. Immediately add the simmering liquid, $^1/_3$ cup of the olive paste, and salt and pepper to taste to the rice. Bring to a simmer, reduce the heat to low, cover, and cook slowly until the rice is cooked, 20 minutes. Stir in the remaining $^1/_3$ cup olive paste and the Parmigiano. Let cool completely.

Place the flour in a bowl. Whisk the eggs and water in another bowl. Place the bread crumbs in a third bowl. Season each of the three bowls with a pinch of salt. Form the rice mixture into small olive-size balls approximately 1 inch in diameter, using less than a tablespoon of the mixture for each one. Roll the rice olives in the flour, then the egg, and then the bread crumbs. Place them on a baking sheet until you are ready to cook them.

Heat 1 inch of equal amounts of canola and olive oil to 375°F in a deep heavy pan.

Fry the rice olives, a few at a time, until golden on all sides, 60 to 90 seconds. Remove and serve immediately.

Makes 50 balls to serve 12

RISOTTO WITH RED WINE

Risotto al Vino Rosso

Risotto made with red wine? Are you curious? I was, too! I tried it, and the end result was a lovely pink risotto. Traditionally made with amarone from the Veneto or Barolo from Piedmont, it is equally delicious made with more accessible, less expensive wines such as Chianti or even a fruity California Zinfandel. The addition of radicchio is optional.

3 tablespoons extra virgin olive oil

1 small yellow onion, diced

2^1/$_2$ cups chicken stock (page 255)

1^1/$_2$ cups water

2 cups red wine, such as amarone or Barolo

2 cups vialone nano or arborio rice

2 tablespoons unsalted butter

Freshly grated nutmeg

1 cup grated Parmigiano-Reggiano cheese

1 small head radicchio, halved and cut into thin strips

Salt and freshly ground black pepper

Heat the olive oil in a large heavy pot over medium heat. Add the onion and cook, stirring occasionally, until soft, 10 minutes.

In the meantime over low heat, combine the chicken stock and water in a saucepan and bring to just below a simmer on the back burner of the stove. In another saucepan, warm the wine to just below a simmer.

Add the rice to the onion and stir until it is very hot, just beginning to stick to the bottom of the pan, and completely coated with oil, 2 to 3 minutes. Add 2 ladlefuls of hot red wine and stir constantly until the wine is almost absorbed. Add a ladleful of chicken stock and stir steadily to keep the rice from sticking. Continue to add the chicken stock a little at a time, stirring until the chicken stock is gone. Then continue with the hot red wine. Continue to add the red wine until the rice is at the chalky stage, 18 to 22 minutes. Then continue to add wine and stir for an additional 2 minutes, until it is just beyond the chalky stage. (If you run out of red wine, use hot water.)

Remove the pan from the heat and add another ladleful of red wine. Add the butter, nutmeg to taste, ^{1}/$_2$ cup of the Parmigiano, the radicchio, and salt and pepper to taste. Stir quickly. Cover and let sit, off the heat, for 5 minutes.

Stir the risotto. Season to taste with salt and pepper and serve immediately with the remaining Parmigiano on the side.

Serves 8

FRITTATA WITH ROASTED SWEET PEPPERS

Fritatta di Peperoni Arrostiti

A frittata is a flat cake of eggs that's cooked slowly over low heat until it is nearly firm and set inside. At the last moment, it is placed in the oven for the final cooking. The frittata is related to the Spanish tortilla in shape and is also a cousin to the French omelette.

1 red bell pepper, roasted (page 259)

1 yellow bell pepper, roasted, (page 259)

1 green bell pepper, roasted (page 259)

2 cloves garlic, minced

3 tablespoons extra virgin olive oil

2 teaspoons balsamic vinegar

1/4 teaspoon dried oregano

Salt and freshly ground black pepper

8 eggs

3 tablespoons milk

1/2 cup grated pecorino or Parmigiano-Reggiano cheese

2 tablespoons chopped fresh flat-leaf parsley

Cut the peppers into 1/4-inch strips. Toss with the garlic, 1 tablespoon of the extra virgin olive oil, the vinegar, oregano, salt, and pepper. Let marinate 30 minutes.

In a bowl, whisk together the eggs, milk, cheese, and parsley until frothy. Add the peppers and their liquid and mix well. Season with salt and pepper.

Preheat the oven to 400°F. Heat the remaining 2 tablespoons olive oil in a 10-inch nonstick ovenproof frying pan over medium-high heat and add the eggs and peppers. Reduce the heat to medium and cook until the bottom is set and the top is still runny, 7 to 8 minutes. Occasionally lift the outer edges of the frittata so that the uncooked egg can run underneath. Place in the oven and continue to cook until the eggs are set and golden brown, 6 to 7 minutes.

Remove the frittata from the oven and loosen the bottom with a spatula. Place a serving plate over the top of the frying pan and invert the frittata onto it. Cut the frittata into wedges and serve hot or at room temperature.

Serves 6

RISOTTO CROQUETTES WITH SMOKED HAM AND MOZZARELLA

Arancini di Riso

Many years ago, when I lived in Boston, I frequented a cavernous place called Galleria Umberto in the North End, the Italian area of the city. It was here that I fell in love with arancini, a specialty of Sicily. I didn't really understand the place, though; I found it empty and cold. It wasn't until a few years ago, when I spent some time in Palermo and discovered Antica Focacceria San Francesco, that I understood Galleria Umberto. Antica Focacceria is a gymnasium of a place, completely lined with marble. The noise reverberates as people wait in line to get inside for slices of warm focaccia and these delicious arancini, the very things I used to wait in line for in Boston.

3 cups chicken stock (page 255)

1 cup water

2 tablespoons extra virgin olive oil

1 small yellow onion, minced

1 1/2 cups arborio rice

1/2 cup tomato sauce, homemade or canned

2/3 cup grated Parmigiano-Reggiano cheese

1 egg yolk, beaten

Salt and freshly ground black pepper

3 ounces smoked ham, cut into 1/8-inch dice

1/2 cup peas, blanched for 10 seconds

4 ounces smoked mozzarella or Scamorza cheese, cut into 1/4-inch dice

Corn or peanut oil for deep-frying

3 eggs, beaten

2 cups fine dry bread crumbs

Bring the chicken stock and water to a boil in a saucepan on the back burner of the stove. Reduce the heat and keep at a very slow simmer.

Heat the olive oil in a saucepan over medium heat. Add the onion and cook, stirring occasionally, until soft, 7 minutes. Add the rice and continue to stir over medium heat until the outside edge of each grain of rice is translucent and there is a tiny white dot in the center of each grain, 3 to 4 minutes. Add a ladleful of hot stock, about 1/2 cup, and stir the rice to wipe it away from the bottom and sides of the pan. When the first addition of stock has been absorbed, add another ladleful and continue to stir. Keep the grains moist at all times. Continue to add stock and stir constantly until the rice is tender. If you run out of broth, add hot water, so that the risotto is always creamy and loose.

The risotto is done when it is firm but tender, without a chalky center, 18 to 22 minutes. Continue to cook, stirring, until the stock is absorbed and the risotto is dry. Remove from the heat, add the tomato sauce and Parmigiano, and mix well. Cool completely. Add the egg yolk and mix well. Season with salt and pepper.

In a bowl, combine the ham, peas, and mozzarella. There are 2 ways to form the croquettes: 1) Pat 2 tablespoons of the rice mixture to cover the palm of one hand and place 1 tablespoon of the peas, ham, and mozzarella mixture in the center. Gently close your hand to envelop the filling. Using both hands, shape the mass into an oval about the size and shape of a large egg. Place the croquettes on a cookie sheet and continue until you have used up all the ingredients. 2) Alternatively, scoop about 2 tablespoons of the rice mixture into a small ice cream scoop. Push 2 fingers

CONTINUED

into the mixture to make a small opening and put
1 tablespoon of the filling in the hole. Close the hole
and finish shaping it by hand.

In a deep, heavy saucepan, heat 3 inches of oil to
375°F. Roll the croquettes in the beaten egg, then roll
them in the bread crumbs. Set on a cookie sheet or
waxed paper.

Deep-fry the croquettes in oil, a few at a time, until
golden brown. Remove and drain on paper towels. Serve
hot, warm, or at room temperature.

Makes 24 croquettes to serve 8

FENNEL, PROSCIUTTO, AND PARSLEY SALAD WITH SHAVED PARMIGIANO-REGGIANO

Many Italian foods rely on contrasting tastes and textures: cold versus hot, sweet versus sour, spicy versus mild, raw and crunchy versus delicate and soft. This lively salad is a perfect example, combining salty prosciutto, crunchy licorice-flavored fennel, earthy flat-leaf parsley, and tart lemon. I had been making this salad for years when I tasted a similar one in Rome at a little trattoria off Campo dei Fiori called Ditirambo. I have to admit, I ordered two!

3 bulbs fennel

2 tablespoons lemon juice

Salt and freshly ground black pepper

4 tablespoons extra virgin olive oil

3 tablespoons freshly squeezed orange juice

1 clove garlic, minced

1/2 cup fresh flat-leaf parsley leaves

1 bunch of radishes, trimmed and thinly sliced

3 ounces Parmigiano-Reggiano cheese

4 ounces prosciutto, thinly sliced

Trim the fennel and cut it in half from top to bottom. With a sharp knife, slice the fennel into paper-thin slices. Toss with 1 tablespoon of the lemon juice and a pinch of salt and reserve in the refrigerator.

In a small bowl, whisk together the olive oil, orange juice, the remaining 1 tablespoon lemon juice, and the garlic. Season with salt and pepper.

To assemble the salad, toss the fennel, parsley, radishes, salt, and three-quarters of the vinaigrette together. Place half on a serving platter. With a cheese shaver or vegetable peeler, shave half of the Parmigiano on top of the fennel. Distribute half of the prosciutto on top. Continue with the rest of the ingredients, making sure that all of the different ingredients are visible.

Serves 6 to 8

SALAD OF RADICCHIO, ARUGULA, BLOOD ORANGES, RAISINS, AND PINE NUTS

I happen to love vegetables—any type, any season—so when I saw this salad on the menu in Rome, I immediately ordered it. Sweet, sour, peppery, bitter—the combination of ingredients and flavors is so reminiscent of North Africa, one can see the significant contribution the Arabs made during their occupation of southern Italy.

1 medium head of radicchio, torn into 2-inch pieces

1 large bunch of arugula, cut into 2- to 3-inch pieces

1 large bulb fennel, sliced paper-thin

3 blood oranges (see Note)

$1/4$ cup golden or sultana raisins

1 to 2 teaspoons red wine vinegar

3 tablespoons extra virgin olive oil

Salt and freshly ground black pepper

$1/4$ cup pine nuts, toasted (page 258)

Combine the radicchio, arugula, and fennel in a bowl and place in the refrigerator. Grate $1/2$ teaspoon orange zest. Section the oranges (page 260), place the sections in a bowl, and reserve. Squeeze 4 tablespoons of orange juice from the leftover orange membrane and reserve in a bowl.

Pour boiling water over the raisins to cover and let sit 10 minutes. Drain.

Add to the orange juice the orange zest, red wine vinegar, and olive oil and whisk together. Season with salt and pepper.

Toss the salad greens and raisins with the vinaigrette. Place in a large serving bowl and garnish with the orange sections and pine nuts. Serve immediately.

Serves 6

NOTE: Blood oranges, available in the winter months, are deliciously sweet oranges with a distinctive red pulp. Any other oranges can be substituted.

WHITE BEAN SALAD WITH GREMOLATA AND GRILLED TUNA

Insalata di Cannellini con Cremolata e Tonno

Together with tomatoes and olive oil, dried beans or legumes are elements that unite the cuisines of the Mediterranean. Lentils, chickpeas, and fava beans, thousands of years old, presumably came from the Middle East. Other legumes, for example cannellini or white kidney beans, navy beans, red kidney beans, and cranberry beans, came from the New World, revealing that this Tuscan salad is a fairly new addition to the Italian repertoire of bean dishes.

2 cups (³/4 pound) dried white, navy, or cannellini beans, or two 16-ounce cans cannellini beans, drained and rinsed

2 bay leaves

Large pinch of dried thyme

6 tablespoons extra virgin olive oil

3 lemons

Salt and freshly ground black pepper

1 pound fresh tuna

3 cloves garlic, minced

¹/4 cup chopped fresh flat-leaf parsley

¹/2 small red onion, diced

1 medium bulb fennel, trimmed and cut into ¹/4-inch dice

Lemon wedges as a garnish

Pick over the beans and discard any stones. Cover with water and soak 8 hours or overnight. The next day, drain and place the beans in a saucepan with the bay leaves, thyme, and enough water to cover by 2 inches. Simmer until the skins begin to crack and the beans are tender, 45 minutes to 1 hour. Drain the beans and keep warm. In a small bowl, whisk together 4 tablespoons of the olive oil, 3 tablespoons of lemon juice, and salt and pepper to taste. Add to the warm beans and toss together.

Preheat a charcoal grill (see Note).

Peel 1 lemon with a vegetable peeler. Marinate the tuna with the lemon peel, pepper, and the remaining 2 tablespoons of olive oil for 30 minutes at room temperature.

Grate 2 teaspoons of lemon zest. Combine the lemon zest, garlic, and parsley. Place on a work surface and chop together until very fine. Combine with the beans, onion, and fennel and toss well.

Grill the tuna until it is still pink in the center, 3 to 4 minutes per side. Salt and let cool 5 minutes. Break into ¹/2- to ³/4-inch pieces. Add to the white beans. Season with salt, pepper, and additional lemon juice if needed. Serve on a platter garnished with lemon wedges.

Serves 6 to 8

> NOTE: Instead of grilling outdoors, the tuna can also be grilled in a ridged cast-iron grill pan or in a frying pan on your stovetop.

SEAFOOD SALAD WITH GARDEN HERB SAUCE

Insalata di Frutti di Mare con Salsa Verde

Every bacari, or wine bar, in Venice serves its own version of this salad, but this one happens to come from one of the oldest bacari in the city, Do Mori. Warm, cozy, and dark with copper pots hanging from the ceiling, this refuge has been catering to the workers at the Rialto market since the fifteenth century. The owner, Roberto Biscontin, can often be seen pouring terrific local wines. In between sips, you can sample this yummy salad or point to the tiny tramezzini, or triangular sandwiches, filled with everything under the Venetian sun.

$1/2$ to $3/4$ cup fish stock (page 255), bottled clam juice, or water

$3/4$ pound medium shrimp, heads removed

1 pound squid, cleaned (page 260) and cut into $1/2$-inch rings, tentacles reserved

2 pounds mussels, scrubbed and beards removed

2 pounds clams, scrubbed

Salt and freshly ground black pepper

$1/2$ cup chopped fresh flat-leaf parsley

2 tablespoons chopped fresh chives

$1/2$ teaspoon chopped fresh thyme

$1/4$ teaspoon chopped fresh oregano

$1/4$ teaspoon chopped fresh rosemary (optional)

3 tablespoons capers, chopped

2 cloves garlic, minced

2 to 4 tablespoons lemon juice

5 tablespoons extra virgin olive oil

6 slices rustic country-style bread, toasted

1 large clove garlic, peeled

Lemon wedges

Heat half of the fish stock in a frying pan over medium heat. Add the shrimp, cover, and cook until almost firm, 1 to 2 minutes. Remove from the pan with a slotted spoon and cool. Remove and discard the shells. Place the shrimp in a large bowl and reserve.

Add the squid rings and tentacles to the pan, cover, and cook until almost firm, 30 seconds. Remove with a slotted spoon and add to the shrimp. Add additional fish stock if needed.

Add the mussels to the pan, cover, and cook until the mussels open, 2 to 4 minutes. Remove the mussels from the pan with a slotted spoon as they open. Remove the mussels from the shells and discard the shells. Add the mussels to the other cooked seafood. Add the clams to the pan, cover, and cook until the clams open, 2 to 5 minutes. Remove the clams from the pan with a slotted spoon as they open. Remove the clams from the shells and discard the shells. Add the clams to the rest of the seafood.

Over high heat, reduce the cooking liquid until 2 tablespoons remain, 5 minutes. Toss the reduced cooking liquid with the seafood. Season with salt and pepper.

In a bowl, whisk together the parsley, chives, thyme, oregano, rosemary, capers, garlic, 2 tablespoons of the lemon juice, and the olive oil. Season with salt and pepper. Toss the seafood with the vinaigrette and let sit 30 minutes. Season to taste with additional salt, pepper, or lemon juice.

Rub the toasted bread lightly with the garlic. Place the seafood and vinaigrette on a platter and garnish the platter with the toasted bread and lemon wedges. Serve immediately.

Serves 6

NOTE: This salad is best when served within 1 hour. If left longer, the lemon juice will cause the herbs to turn gray.

TUSCAN BREAD SALAD WITH TOMATOES AND BASIL

Nothing is wasted in the Mediterranean, especially bread, which at certain times has been worth its weight in gold. In Italy, yesterday's stale bread is made into today's fresh and flavorful salad called panzanella. In the Middle East, a similar salad called fattoush is prepared with pita bread, cucumbers, tomatoes, green onions, and fresh herbs. In Morocco their bread salad is called shalada del khobz yabess.

$^1/_2$ pound stale, rustic country-style bread

1 cup water

6 ripe medium tomatoes, peeled, seeded (page 259), and cut into $^1/_2$-inch cubes

1 large red onion, thinly sliced

1 medium cucumber, peeled, seeded, and cut into $^1/_2$-inch dice

2 cloves garlic, minced

2 tablespoons capers

$^1/_2$ cup fresh basil leaves

3 tablespoons red wine vinegar

3 tablespoons balsamic vinegar

$^1/_2$ cup extra virgin olive oil

Salt and freshly ground black pepper

Cut the bread into 1-inch slices. Sprinkle with the water and let sit 1 minute. Carefully squeeze the bread until dry. Tear the bread into rough 1-inch pieces and let rest on paper towels for 10 minutes.

In a bowl, combine the tomatoes, onion, cucumber, garlic, and capers. Tear the basil into small pieces and add to the vegetables. Add the bread and toss carefully.

In a small bowl, combine both vinegars and the olive oil. Season with salt and pepper. Toss with the vegetables and bread and let the mixture rest in the refrigerator 1 hour. Place on a platter and serve.

Serves 6

GREECE

When twilight approaches in any bustling city in Greece, the Greek heads straight for the taverna. Armed with a million words and a thirst to boot, he perches at a waterfront table, one hand wrapped around a pearly glass of ouzo, the other picking at a plate of feta drizzled with fruity olive oil and a dash of wild oregano.

In another part of the country, maybe on the island of Zakynthos, you will find the Greek inside an old *ouzeri*, a taverna specializing in ouzo, the national drink. Shrouded in smoke, men lean on their elbows, puff on cigarettes, and engage in conversation with such seriousness that they look as though they might change the world. Little bottles of ouzo dot the table along with plates of *mezethes*, the appetizers of Greece.

Now head further north to the second largest city in Greece, Thessaloniki. The older part of town is nestled in the congested hills. Whitewashed houses look as though they must be balancing on top of one another, and tiny roads seem a nightmarish maze. Around every corner is another taverna, each boasting a wider array of *mezethes* or a fresher catch of fish. It is later in the evening, say 10 or 11 PM. Bare lightbulbs are strung together around tables perched on a precipice overlooking the city and the Mediterranean. The temperature couldn't be more perfect; it's no wonder Greeks spend most of their lives outdoors.

Drawn by the heady scent of olive oil and garlic, taverna patrons walk right into the kitchen, peek into pots of lusty stews, give the tomatoes a proverbial squeeze, or talk to the chef, who might recommend his favorite dishes. The whole family is there to help, everyone talking simultaneously about the evening's seemingly endless offerings. Choices are made, and within minutes an outside table is laden with many small plates. There are fruity white Macedonian wine and the obligatory wicker basket filled with crusty white bread. All patrons helps themselves from the communal plates of *mezethes*. It will be a long and enjoyable evening.

The Importance of *Mezethes* in Greek Social Life

These scenes thread their way throughout Greek life like tasty morsels on a skewer. The enjoyment of *mezethes*, the little snacks or tempting appetizers eaten at any time of the day, are justification for two basic constituents of

Greek social life: a good dose of wine or ouzo and congenial conversation. The Greeks like their drinks but abhor drunkenness, so they wouldn't dream of drinking *retsina* or ouzo without some sort of food. Waiters don't hover; instead, you're encouraged to linger and unwind after a long, hot day. A single plate of *mythia me risi* (mussels pilaf) or *fassolia yigantes* (giant beans with tomatoes) can be nibbled at for an hour or more.

Something to Whet the Appetite

Greek *mezethes*, which depend upon the freshest seasonal ingredients, may be hot or cold, simple or complex. They include dips, salads, farinaceous dishes, dairy and eggs, fish, game, meats, and poultry. Colorful and pungently flavorful *mezethes* are sometimes eaten as a snack or as a prelude to dinner; sometimes they are dinner itself.

Meze (the singular form of *mezethes*) means "something to whet the appetite." The word is Turkish in origin, a legacy from the Ottoman Empire that stretched into Greece, but the custom of serving *mezethes* itself dates to Greek antiquity. Plato, the Greek philosopher who lived in the fourth century BC, described a table set with many small portions of olives, fresh garbanzo beans, almonds, figs, radishes, and briny cheeses. Sounds very much like today's *mezethes* table, doesn't it? With such a lineage, it isn't hard to see why the congenial custom of serving *mezethes* has become such a fixture of daily social and culinary life in Greece.

An Ancient Land

Greece is the land of classical antiquity, mythology, romance, and fine food traditions. The oldest European cuisine, Greek food was "civilized" earlier and to a greater degree than other European cuisines. The Greeks were a bold force around the Mediterranean at the beginning of the first millennium, and they thought of cooking as an art. Their strong influence spread this philosophy to Italy, Turkey, and the Middle East.

As the Greeks weakened, however, and the Romans thrived, Greece fell to stronger powers. The Roman Empire spread through Greece and Turkey, making its Byzantine home in Constantinople (today Istanbul) in AD 330. Greek cooking was so highly respected at that point that the palaces of Constantinople employed mostly Greek cooks, setting a precedent for high gastronomic standards.

By the 1450s, the Roman Empire had declined and the Ottomans had expanded, crossing central Asia and Asia Minor to Greece. The Ottomans occupied a majority of the countries bordering the eastern Mediterranean for nearly 400 years and influenced the religious, historical, and culinary development of these countries, especially Greece. Traditional Greek recipes were given new Turkish names, for example, *dolmathes* for *thrion*, or rolled grape leaves; *keftethes* for croquettes; *borekakia* for savory pastries; and *tzatziki* for a yogurt and garlic sauce. Dishes and techniques specific to Turkey—for example, sausages called *soutzoukakia*; the art of pickling, called *toursi*; *imam bayildi*, or stuffed eggplant; and the use of yogurt, raisins, and rice for making pilaf—were transported across the Aegean to Greece. It wasn't until 1821 that the Greeks wrestled themselves free of Ottoman rule, but what remained was a Greek and Turkish cuisine that is oftentimes difficult to disentangle.

Essential Ingredients and Techniques

In the following recipes you will see that certain key ingredients are used over and over again: lemons, garlic, mint, dill, parsley, oregano, cinnamon, red wine vinegar, and, of course, the ubiquitous olive oil. Greeks have long loved the versatility, healthiness, and range of vegetables available to them, and they make a variety of vegetable dishes using eggplants, bunches of deep red beets, various shades of zucchini, silvery purple artichokes, large red and green peppers, salad greens, sweet juicy tomatoes, crisp cucumbers, fennel, and beans in all colors, shapes, and sizes.

You will also see in these recipes some ingredients and preparations unique to Greece such as *tarama* (salted and dried mullet roe), *avgolemono* sauce (an egg and lemon sauce), *skorthalia* (an emulsified garlic sauce), *rigani* (a variety of oregano stronger than the Italian version), *elitses* olives (tiny olives from Crete), kalamata olives (large almond-shaped purple-black olives from the southern Peloponnese), and phyllo (thin sheets of pastry). Rustic cheeses such as feta (a salty white sheep's milk cheese), kephalotyri (a hard yellow goat or sheep's cheese like the Italian Parmigiano-Reggiano), and kasseri (a firm golden sheep's cheese) are a few of the favored cheeses made in Greece.

From Mountaintop to Shoreline

Greece's terrain is varied—rocky hills and valleys, snowcapped mountains, a pristine cloudless sky, and a brilliant blue sea that surrounds 2,500 miles of coastline. Its perimeter is dappled with hundreds of sun-baked islands in the Aegean, Ionian, and Mediterranean seas.

Crete, the largest Greek island, floats in the Mediterranean south of Greece, and its cuisine has been influenced by Greece, Asia Minor, and Egypt. The cuisine of Rhodes is closely related to that of Turkey, its near neighbor. The Venetians once occupied several islands, including Corfu, Kephalonia, and Zakynthos off the west coast of Greece, and Venetian subtleties are evident in all of their cuisines. Balkan influences in northern Greece can be observed with the use of cabbage, hot peppers, smoked meats, and stewed dishes. Eastern Greece, bordering on Turkey, has some shades of Turkish influence with the use of sesame seeds and a love of spices.

A Greek Cuisine

Is there a true regional cuisine of Greece? The cuisines of each of its regions have very subtle differences, unlike in Italy, France, and Spain, where differences are more dramatic. In Greece, for example, a sauce such as *skordalia* is made thinner in one region, thicker in another; in some places it is thickened with potatoes, while in others it contains various nuts. But all over Greece, *skordalia* is served. A dish may vary from kitchen to kitchen, or from region to region, but sometimes these differences are barely noticeable even to the experienced cook.

An Age-Old Art

Caught between the classical past and the ever-changing present, Greece has struggled to hold onto her culinary traditions. True Greek food is rustic, and its flavors are simple and straightforward, as seen here in a variety of *mezethes*, a testament to Greece's respect for the good things in life.

YOGURT AND CUCUMBER SOUP WITH MINT AND DILL

Tzatziki is a very familiar meze served in Greece. Usually it is a thick sauce served with crusty bread or pita as a dip. Add some milk to make a soup, and you have a perfect first course for a hot and steamy day. Omit the milk, and you have a real Mediterranean standby.

3 cups whole milk yogurt

1 large cucumber, peeled, seeded, and coarsely grated

2 cloves garlic, minced

3 tablespoons extra virgin olive oil

1 tablespoon chopped fresh mint

3 tablespoons chopped fresh dill

2 cups cold milk

3 to 4 tablespoons white wine vinegar or lemon juice

Salt and freshly ground black pepper

6 paper-thin slices unpeeled cucumber

Place the yogurt in a cheesecloth-lined strainer and let drain 2 hours. Discard the liquid and place the yogurt in a bowl. Combine the drained yogurt, grated cucumber, garlic, olive oil, mint, 2 tablespoons of the dill, and the milk. Mix well. Add the vinegar or lemon juice, salt, and pepper to taste. Chill 1 hour until ice-cold.

Ladle the soup into bowls and garnish with the cucumber slices and the remaining 1 tablespoon dill.

Serves 6

LAMB BROTH WITH SUMMER VEGETABLES AND ORZO

Hortosoupa Me Manestra

There's nothing like a big bowl of soup. In Greece, soups are usually served at home rather than at the taverna. Whether it is prepared on the lighter side like this one, or filled with vegetables, meat, and grains, soup is the best comfort food.

1/4 cup extra virgin olive oil

2 medium yellow onions, diced

2 leeks, white and 2 inches of green, quartered and diced

3 stalks celery, with leaves, diced

2 carrots, peeled and diced

1/2 cup water

1/2 cup green beans, trimmed and cut into 1/2-inch dice

2 small zucchini, seeded and cut into 1/2-inch dice

1 cup peeled, seeded, and chopped tomatoes (page 259), or 3 medium tomatoes, fresh or canned

1/2 teaspoon chopped fresh oregano

Salt and freshly ground black pepper

8 cups lamb stock (page 255)

1/2 cup orzo

1/2 cup grated kefalotyri or Parmigiano-Reggiano cheese

1/4 cup chopped fresh flat-leaf parsley

Warm the olive oil in a soup pot over medium heat. Add the onions, leeks, celery, and carrots. Cook, stirring occasionally, until the onions are soft, 10 minutes. Add the water, cover, and simmer slowly for 30 minutes.

Increase the heat to high, and add the green beans, zucchini, tomatoes, oregano, salt, pepper, and lamb stock. Bring to a boil, reduce the heat to low, and simmer, covered, for 30 to 40 minutes. Add the orzo and continue to simmer 20 minutes.

Season with additional salt and pepper if desired. Serve garnished with the grated cheese and parsley.

Serves 6

COUNTRY WHITE BEAN AND VEGETABLE SOUP

Fassolatha

The pepper and olive garnish for this dish is inspired by the incomparable Mediterranean cookbook writer Paula Wolfert, but otherwise this is a classic soup made in almost every country that borders the Mediterranean. While each country adds its own nuance, the Greek cook adds a light touch of tomatoes and herbs.

1 pound dried navy beans

1 red bell pepper, roasted (page 259)

1 yellow bell pepper, roasted (page 259)

1 green bell pepper, roasted (page 259)

2 tablespoons red wine vinegar

4 tablespoons extra virgin olive oil

Salt and freshly ground black pepper

2 medium yellow onions, diced

2 cloves garlic, minced

2 medium carrots, diced

1 stalk celery, with leaves, diced

10 cups water

$^1/_4$ teaspoon dried thyme

$^1/_4$ teaspoon dried oregano

1 tablespoon tomato paste

12 kalamata olives, pitted and slivered (page 260)

Pick over the navy beans and discard any stones. Cover with water and soak 8 hours or overnight. Drain the beans and place them in a soup pot and cover with water by 2 inches. Bring to a boil, reduce the heat to low, and simmer until the skins just begin to crack, 45 to 60 minutes.

Cut the roasted peppers into $^1/_2$-inch dice. Combine the peppers, vinegar, 2 tablespoons of the olive oil, salt, and pepper and toss to mix. Let sit at room temperature 2 hours.

In a large frying pan, heat the remaining 2 tablespoons olive oil. Add the onions, garlic, carrots, and celery and cook over low heat until the onions are tender, 10 minutes. Add the water, cooked onion mixture, thyme, oregano, and tomato paste to the beans. Continue to simmer until the beans and vegetables are very tender and the liquid is reduced, 1 hour. Season with salt and pepper. Take $1^1/_2$ cups of the soup and purée in a blender or food processor until very smooth. Return to the soup pot and mix well.

Drain the peppers and mix with the olives. Ladle the soup into bowls and garnish with the pepper and olive mixture.

Serves 6

NOTE: This soup can be made up to 2 days ahead. It can also be frozen.

AVGOLEMONO SOUP WITH SPICED VEAL MEATBALLS AND RICE

Soupa Avgolemono Me Kephtehes Ke Rizi

Avgolemono, the quintessential Greek mixture of eggs (avgo) and lemon juice (lemono), *dates back to antiquity and has always been referred to as "sour sauce." They also make this sauce in Turkey, but it doesn't seem to be quite as popular there.*

1/2 pound ground veal

1 clove garlic, minced

1/3 cup grated yellow onion

1/2 teaspoon grated lemon zest

2 teaspoons minced fresh mint

1 tablespoon minced fresh flat-leaf parsley

1 egg yolk

1/2 cup dry whole wheat bread crumbs

1/4 cup milk

Salt and freshly ground black pepper

9 cups chicken stock (page 255)

1/3 cup long-grain white rice

2 eggs

Juice of 1 to 2 lemons

Chopped fresh flat-leaf parsley

Chopped fresh mint

Preheat the oven to 375°F. In a bowl, mix together the veal, garlic, onion, lemon zest, mint, parsley, and egg yolk. Add the breadcrumbs and milk and season with salt and pepper. Mix well. Form into 3/4-inch meatballs. Place on an oiled baking sheet and bake the meatballs for 10 minutes. Set aside.

Bring the stock to a boil in a soup pot. Reduce the heat to medium-low; add the rice, salt, and pepper; and simmer slowly for 10 minutes. Add the meatballs and continue to simmer until the rice is cooked, 10 minutes.

Beat the eggs and the juice of 1 lemon in a bowl until light and frothy. Add 1 small ladle of boiling broth to the egg mixture and beat vigorously. Continue to add broth a ladle at a time, beating after each addition, until you have added 5 or 6 ladlefuls. Pour this mixture back into the soup pot. Taste and add additional lemon juice, salt, and pepper if needed. Garnish with parsley and mint and serve immediately. Do not reheat this soup to the boiling point or the soup will curdle.

Serves 6

FRIED CHEESE WITH LEMON AND OLIVES

Saganaki

Fried cheese, what an idea! I tasted this dish for the first time on the island of Crete. It was my first trip to Greece, and someone told me I must try it. The name of this recipe derives from the thin, round, flat-bottomed aluminum pan that is traditionally used to cook this simple yet flavorful dish. One word of warning: eat this dish when it is hot; otherwise, it will have the texture of an old tire.

Olive oil for frying

1 1/2-pound chunk kephalotyri cheese, 1/2 inch thick (see Note)

1 cup all-purpose flour

Juice of 1 lemon

Dried oregano

Cracked black pepper

3 lemon wedges

12 kalamata olives

Heat 1/2 inch of olive oil in a small frying pan over medium-high heat. As soon as it ripples, reduce the heat to medium-low.

Cut the cheese into sticks 1/2 inch wide. Place in a bowl of water. Place the flour in a separate bowl. Remove the sticks of cheese from the water and immediately place them in the flour. Do not tap off the excess.

Fry the cheese sticks in a single layer until golden and crusty, turning them with a fork, 1 to 2 minutes per side. They should be soft all the way through but not melting.

Serve immediately on a warm platter drizzled with lemon juice. Sprinkle with oregano and cracked black pepper. Garnish with lemon wedges and olives.

Serves 6

NOTE: If kefalotyri is unavailable, Italian fontinella, Parmigiano-Reggiano, or Swiss Gruyère cheese can be substituted.

LAMB, FENNEL, AND ORANGE PIE LIKOURESSIS

Arnopitta Me Portokalia Likouressis

Maria Likouressis and her husband, Dimitri, live on the island of Zakynthos and are renowned for being two of the best cooks in all of Greece. As she prepared this lamb pie, I stood in her kitchen making a sliced lemon and olive oil salad and writing down every step of the recipe she was making. This dough needs to be made one day ahead, so plan accordingly.

Pastry

1 tablespoon active dry yeast

1 cup warm milk

3 3/4 cups bread flour

1/2 cup plus 1 tablespoon extra virgin olive oil

1/4 cup water

1 teaspoon salt

1 egg, lightly beaten

Filling

1 1/2 pounds lamb meat, cut from the leg

4 tablespoons extra virgin olive oil

8 green onions, green and white parts, thinly sliced

3 cloves garlic, minced

3 medium bulbs fennel, very thinly sliced

Salt and freshly ground black pepper

2 large bunches of greens (spinach, arugula, collard greens, Swiss chard, turnip greens, beet greens), stems removed and coarsely chopped

2 bay leaves, very finely crumbled

1 tablespoon grated orange zest

Assembly

1 tablespoon extra virgin olive oil

1/4 pound feta cheese, crumbled

2 tablespoons unsalted butter, melted

The day before you plan to serve the pie, combine the yeast and milk in a bowl and stir well to dissolve. Let sit until it bubbles, 20 minutes. Add the flour, 1/2 cup of the olive oil, the water, salt, and egg and mix until it comes together. Remove from the bowl and knead on a floured surface until smooth and elastic, 7 to 8 minutes. Alternatively, this can be made in an electric mixer using a dough hook. Oil a large bowl with the remaining 1 tablespoon olive oil. Place the dough in the bowl and turn it over to coat the top. Cover with plastic wrap and refrigerate overnight.

The next day, trim the fat from the lamb. Cut into thin strips, 1/2 inch by 1 1/2 inches. Heat 2 tablespoons of the olive oil in a large frying pan over medium-high heat. Add the lamb and cook for 2 minutes. Remove the lamb from the pan with a slotted spoon and set aside. Reduce the heat to medium-low, add the remaining 2 tablespoons olive oil to the same pan, and cook the green onions, garlic, fennel, salt, and pepper until soft, 10 minutes. Add the greens and the lamb and continue to cook until the greens wilt and the juices evaporate, 8 to 10 minutes. Mix well and season with salt, pepper, the crumbled bay leaves, and orange zest.

Preheat the oven to 375°F. To assemble the pie, brush a round 10 by 2-inch cake pan lightly with 1/2 tablespoon of the olive oil. Divide the dough into 2 pieces. On a floured surface, roll one piece of the dough into a circle 1/8 inch thick and 14 inches in diameter. Place the dough in the pan, stretching it slightly so that it comes up over the edges. Brush lightly with the remaining 1/2 tablespoon olive oil. Spread the filling evenly over the dough. Crumble the feta on top of the lamb and the greens. Roll the other piece of dough into a circle 11 inches in diameter. Place on top of the filling so that it comes up over the edges. Press the edges together and trim any excess. Roll the crust inward to form an edge.

Brush the top with the melted butter. With the point of a knife, score the top, making sure that you do not cut through the crust completely.

Bake for 15 minutes. Reduce the heat to 325°F. and continue to bake for 45 to 60 minutes. If the top gets too dark, cover with foil and continue to bake until done. Remove from the oven and let rest 20 minutes. Cut into wedges and serve hot or at room temperature.

Serves 8

SAVORY CHICKEN, LEEK, AND FETA PIE WITH MOUNTAIN HERBS

Prassopitta Me Kotopoulo Ke Feta

I stood in front of the window of the bakeshop and knew right away that I was in for a treat. I stepped inside and was immediately entranced by the sweet smells of melted butter and golden baked phyllo. Large round pans of pitta, or savory pie, each pan nearly as long as my arm, were balanced one on top of the other across the counter. With such a variety, how could I decide? There were the traditional pittas of cheese and spinach, but there were also some new variations such as stewed chicken with artichokes and one containing fennel, dill, and wilted greens. Finally, I made my selection. My slice was wrapped in wax paper imprinted with what looked like Greek hieroglyphics. Here it is.

Pastry

2¹/₂ cups all-purpose flour

1 teaspoon salt

4 tablespoons extra virgin olive oil

¹/₂ cup water

1 egg, lightly beaten

Filling

6 leeks, white and 3 inches of green, diced

¹/₄ cup extra virgin olive oil

1 bunch of green onions, green and white parts, chopped

¹/₄ cup chopped fresh flat-leaf parsley

¹/₃ cup chopped fresh dill

2 tablespoons chopped fresh mint

³/₄ pound raw boneless chicken meat, skin and fat removed, diced and patted dry with paper towels

5 ounces feta cheese, crumbled

2 tablespoons grated kefalotyri or Parmigiano-Reggiano cheese

2 egg yolks, lightly beaten

Salt and freshly ground black pepper

Assembly

1 tablespoon extra virgin olive oil

2 tablespoons all-purpose flour

1 egg yolk, lightly beaten

To make the pastry, in a bowl, combine 2¹/₄ cups of the flour and the salt. Add 3 tablespoons of the olive oil, the water, and the egg and mix well to form a ball. Flour a work surface with the remaining ¹/₄ cup flour and knead the dough for 1 minute until smooth and elastic. Alternatively, this can be done in an electric mixer using a dough hook. Oil a large bowl with the remaining 1 tablespoon olive oil. Place the dough in the bowl and turn over to coat the top. Cover with plastic wrap and let rest at room temperature for 2 hours.

Preheat the oven to 375°F. In the meantime, to make the filling, wash the diced leeks in a bowl of cold water. Drain well. Heat the olive oil in a large frying pan over low heat. Cook the leeks and green onions until soft, 20 minutes. Transfer to a bowl. Add the parsley, dill, mint, chicken, feta, kefalotyri, egg yolks, salt, and pepper and mix well.

After the dough has rested 2 hours, to assemble the pie, brush a round 10 by 2-inch cake or springform pan lightly with ¹/₂ tablespoon of the olive oil. On a floured surface, roll two-thirds of the dough into a circle ¹/₈ inch thick and 14 inches in diameter. Place the dough in the pan, stretching it slightly so it comes up over the edges. Brush lightly with the remaining ¹/₂ tablespoon olive oil. Spread the filling evenly over the dough. Roll the other piece of dough into a circle 11 inches in diameter. Place on top of the filling so that it comes up over the edges. Press the edges together and trim any excess. Roll the crust inward to form an edge. Brush the top lightly with the egg yolk. With the point of a knife, score the top, making sure that you do not cut through the crust completely.

Bake until golden brown, 40 to 50 minutes. Cool 15 minutes before serving. This can also be served at room temperature.

Serves 8

NOTE: This recipe can also be made with store-bought phyllo dough, which will result in a light and flaky finished product. You will need 12 sheets of phyllo. Place the phyllo on a work surface and cover with a slightly dampened towel. Melt 6 tablespoons butter in a saucepan. Place 1 sheet of phyllo in the cake or springform pan, letting the extra hang over the edges. Brush lightly with butter. Turn the pan one-quarter turn and place another layer of phyllo on top of the first. Brush lightly with butter. Repeat with 4 more sheets of phyllo. Spread the filling evenly over the dough. Fold the excess phyllo onto the filling. Place 1 sheet of phyllo on top of the filling, letting the extra overhang the edges. Brush lightly with butter. Turn the pan one-quarter turn and place another layer of phyllo on top of the other one. Brush lightly with butter. Repeat with 4 more sheets of phyllo. Trim the edges of the phyllo so that they hang 1 inch over the edge of the pan. Tuck between the bottom layers of phyllo and the sides of the pan. With the point of a knife, score the top, making sure that you cut through only the top few layers of phyllo. Bake according to the directions above.

BAKED OMELETTE WITH ZUCCHINI, LEEKS, FETA, AND MOUNTAIN HERBS

Sfoungato Me Kolokithia Apagio

Savory egg pies are everyday fare in the countries that border the Mediterranean to the north. In Spain they make the tortilla; in France, the omelette; and in Italy, the frittata. Greek egg pies, made with ingredients such as rice, mint, and feta, are not quite as common as the rest.

1/4 cup long-grain white rice

3/4 cup water

Salt and freshly ground black pepper

3 tablespoons extra virgin olive oil

3 leeks, white and 2 inches of green, chopped

3 unpeeled zucchini, coarsely grated

3 tablespoons chopped fresh mint

2 tablespoons chopped fresh dill

8 eggs, lightly beaten

5 ounces feta cheese, crumbled

Bring the rice, water, and a large pinch of salt to a boil over medium-high heat in a saucepan. Turn the heat down to low and simmer, covered, until the rice is cooked and the water is absorbed, 20 minutes.

Preheat the oven to 325°F. Heat 2 tablespoons of the olive oil in a large frying pan over medium-low heat and cook the leeks, covered, stirring occasionally, until soft, 10 to 15 minutes. Remove the mixture from the pan and place in a bowl. Add the remaining 1 tablespoon olive oil to the pan and, over medium heat, cook the zucchini until it softens, 5 to 7 minutes. Season with salt and pepper.

In a bowl, combine the rice, leeks, zucchini, mint, dill, eggs, feta, salt, and pepper. Mix well.

Oil a 9 by 9-inch baking dish. Pour the eggs and vegetables into the dish. Bake until golden and set, 35 to 40 minutes. Cut into squares and serve warm.

Serves 6

> NOTE: This recipe can be prepared several hours in advance and served at room temperature.

SPICY GRILLED EGGPLANT WITH OLIVE OIL AND VINEGAR

Melitzanes Tiganites

Eggplant is commonly eaten around the Mediterranean, especially in Greece. This dish is a specialty of one of my favorite ouzeris, the Greek equivalent to a tapas bar. The technique and ingredients are so typically Mediterranean that this simple dish could easily make its way onto just about any table around the sea.

9 Japanese eggplants or 2 regular eggplants

Salt and freshly ground black pepper

$1/4$ cup plus 2 tablespoons extra virgin olive oil

3 cloves garlic, minced

2 teaspoons red wine vinegar

$1/4$ teaspoon crushed red pepper flakes

2 tablespoons chopped fresh flat-leaf parsley

Heat a charcoal grill (see Note). Slice the eggplants crosswise into $1/4$-inch slices. Place in a colander and salt lightly. Let sit 30 minutes. Wash with water and pat dry. If using Japanese eggplant, omit this salting step. Place the eggplant slices on a baking sheet and brush both sides of the eggplant using $1/4$ cup of the olive oil. Sprinkle with salt and pepper.

Grill the eggplant slices over a hot fire, turning occasionally, until they are golden and tender, 10 to 12 minutes.

Combine the garlic with the remaining 2 tablespoons olive oil and the vinegar. Place the eggplant on a serving platter and brush the garlic mixture evenly over the top. Sprinkle with the red pepper flakes, salt, and parsley.

Serves 6

NOTE: Alternatively, the eggplant can be baked in the oven. Oil a sheet pan and cover with the eggplant slices in a single layer. Bake on the top rack of a 400°F oven, turning occasionally, until golden on both sides, 15 minutes.

DILLED POTATO AND LEEK CROQUETTES

Patates Krokettes

I've tasted potato croquettes in Greece, Italy, and Turkey. Each country serves its own version, essentially similar to the others but with a slight twist. These croquettes are made with leeks, dill, cheese, and a splash of vinegar.

1 1/2 pounds russet baking potatoes

3 leeks, white and 2 inches of green, coarsely chopped

Salt and freshly ground black pepper

2 egg yolks

3 green onions, white and green parts, finely chopped

1/4 cup chopped fresh dill

2/3 cup grated kefalotyri or Parmigiano-Reggiano cheese

1/2 teaspoon white wine vinegar

1 teaspoon salt

Freshly ground black pepper

Olive oil for frying

3/4 cup all-purpose flour

2 eggs, lightly beaten

2 1/2 cups fine dry bread crumbs

Dill sprigs

Boil the potatoes and leeks in a large pot of boiling salted water until the potatoes are tender, 25 to 30 minutes. Drain and let cool. Peel the potatoes. Pass the potatoes and leeks through the fine disk of a food mill or pulse a few times in a food processor until the mixture is smooth. Do not mix so long that the mixture gets gluey.

Add the egg yolks, green onions, dill, cheese, vinegar, the salt, and pepper to the potato mixture. Mix well. Cover and refrigerate 3 hours.

Heat 1/2 inch olive oil in a large frying pan to 375°F. With floured hands, shape the mixture into croquettes 1 1/2 inches long by 3/4 inch wide.

Place the flour, beaten eggs, and bread crumbs each in their own individual bowls. Season all three with salt and pepper. Dust the croquettes in the flour first, then in the egg, and then in the bread crumbs. After each croquette is breaded, place on a baking sheet. Store in the refrigerator until ready to fry.

This recipe can be prepared to this point up to 6 hours in advance.

Fry the croquettes a few at a time, turning occasionally, until golden on all sides, 3 to 4 minutes. Serve them hot on a platter, garnished with dill sprigs.

Makes 20 croquettes to serve 6 to 8

NOTE: After the croquettes have been cooked, they can be kept warm in a 400°F oven until ready to serve.

SPICY SAUSAGES WITH TOMATOES AND OLIVES

Soutzoukakia

Spicy sausages are made all over the Mediterranean. Soutzoukakia, with its hint of orange and allspice, is similar to the loukanika sausage of Greece, which itself is a variation on the Venetian luganega sausage. The cumin, coriander, allspice, and garlic in soutzoukakia are all evidence of Turkish influence. It's not surprising that all of these flavors come into play, as the Venetians and Turks vied for supremacy in western Greece for years before the Ottomans finally won.

2 leeks, white and 3 inches of green, diced

5 tablespoons extra virgin olive oil

4 green onions, finely chopped

1/2 cup fresh white bread crumbs

3/4 cup dry red wine

1 tablespoon cumin seeds

1 teaspoon coriander seeds

3 allspice berries, or 1/4 teaspoon ground allspice (optional)

1 1/4 pounds ground lamb

4 cloves garlic, minced

1 1/2 tablespoons grated orange zest

3 tablespoons chopped fresh flat-leaf parsley

1/2 teaspoon chopped fresh thyme

1 teaspoon salt

1 teaspoon freshly ground black pepper

1/4 cup all-purpose flour

One 28-ounce can chopped Italian plum tomatoes

1/2 teaspoon sugar

1/3 cup pitted and coarsely chopped kalamata olives (page 260)

Whole flat-leaf parsley leaves

NOTE: These sausages can be made 1 day in advance and reheated before serving.

Rinse the diced leeks in a bowl of cold water and drain well. Heat 2 tablespoons of the olive oil in a large frying pan over medium-low heat and cook the leeks and green onions until soft, 10 minutes.

In a bowl, soak the bread crumbs in 1/2 cup of the red wine and mix well.

Heat the cumin seeds, coriander seeds, and allspice berries in a small dry frying pan over medium heat until aromatic, 2 minutes. Pulverize to a fine powder in a spice grinder or a mortar and pestle.

Transfer the leek mixture, bread mixture, and spices to a bowl. Add the lamb, garlic, orange zest, parsley, thyme, salt, and pepper. Knead together 2 to 3 minutes. Cover and refrigerate 2 hours or overnight.

The next day, make 1 very small patty using the lamb mixture and cook in a small, lightly oiled frying pan until done. Taste it and correct with additional spices, salt, or pepper. Moisten your hands and form the sausages into flattened ovals about 2 inches long by 3/4 inch wide. Dredge the sausages lightly in flour. Heat 2 tablespoons of the olive oil in a large frying pan over medium-high heat. Cook the sausages until golden on all sides, 10 minutes. Remove the sausages and drain. Discard any fat in the pan.

Add the remaining 1 tablespoon olive oil to the pan and heat over medium heat. Add the tomatoes, the remaining 1/4 cup wine, the sugar, salt, and pepper and simmer 10 minutes. Add the sausages and simmer very slowly, covered, for 30 minutes. Taste the sauce and season with salt and pepper.

Serve warm, garnished with olives and parsley leaves.

Makes 24 sausages to serve 6 to 8

STUFFED ZUCCHINI

Stuffed vegetables are a favorite meze in Greece. This is a great make-ahead recipe. Serve it with Stuffed Tomatoes (page 155) and Avgolemono Sauce (page 157). And don't worry if they aren't served hot. In Greece, people love stuffed vegetables served at room temperature. (See photo, page 156.)

4 to 6 medium zucchini, 1^1/$_2$ inches in diameter, ends trimmed

^{1}/$_2$ medium yellow onion, coarsely grated

1 cup peeled, seeded, and chopped tomatoes (page 259), about 1 cup, fresh or canned

^{1}/$_4$ cup long-grain white rice

1^1/$_2$ tablespoons chopped fresh dill

2^1/$_2$ tablespoons chopped fresh flat-leaf parsley

^{1}/$_2$ teaspoon salt

Freshly ground black pepper

2 tablespoons extra virgin olive oil

^{1}/$_2$ cup water

Avgolemono Sauce (page 157)

Preheat the oven to 350°F. Cut the zucchini in 1^1/$_2$-inch lengths. With a melon baller, scoop out the seeds and pulp from the center, leaving the bottom of each "stump" intact. Set aside. Chop the seeds and pulp and reserve.

Combine the reserved zucchini pulp, onion, tomatoes, rice, dill, parsley, salt, and pepper to taste. Stuff the hollowed-out zucchini very loosely with filling to just below the level of the top. Do not pack the filling, as the rice will expand. Place the zucchini filling side up in a baking dish large enough to hold the squash tightly. Pour the olive oil and water into the bottom of the baking dish. Cover tightly with foil and bake until the rice is tender, 50 minutes. Remove from the oven, uncover, and place the zucchini on a serving platter. Pour the juices from the pan into a measuring cup to make the Avgolemono Sauce.

To serve, drizzle the Avgolemono Sauce over the top or pass separately.

Serves 6

> NOTE: The stuffed zucchini can be served hot or at room temperature. They can be prepared up to 1 day in advance and baked the day they will be served. The sauce, however, should always be prepared just before the dish is served.

STUFFED TOMATOES

Domates Yemistes

All around the Mediterranean, tomatoes at the peak of their season are stuffed with a variety of fillings. The best time to make stuffed tomatoes is when they are at their peak in the summer months. Choose sweet, ripe tomatoes that aren't too soft. These can be assembled up to 1 day in advance and baked just before serving. (See photo, page 156.)

6 firm medium tomatoes

5 tablespoons extra virgin olive oil

$1/2$ medium yellow onion, coarsely grated

$1/3$ pound ground veal

$1/4$ cup long-grain white rice

$1^1/2$ tablespoons chopped fresh flat-leaf parsley

$1^1/2$ tablespoons chopped fresh dill

$1/2$ teaspoon salt

Freshly ground black pepper

$1/4$ cup water

Avgolemono Sauce (page 157)

Preheat the oven to 350°F. With a small knife, cut around the top of each tomato but leave $1/2$ inch attached to form a flap. With a spoon, scrape out the pulp, chop, strain, and reserve the juices. Reserve the hollowed-out tomatoes.

Heat 2 tablespoons of the olive oil in a frying pan over medium heat. Cook the onion and veal, breaking the veal up with a wooden spoon, until the veal turns gray, 5 minutes. Add the tomato pulp to the veal and continue to cook until the juices evaporate, 2 to 3 minutes. Add the rice, parsley, dill, salt, and pepper to taste. Turn off the heat.

Stuff the hollowed-out tomatoes with the filling to just below the level of the top. Do not pack the filling, as the rice will expand. Cover with the flap. Place the stuffed tomatoes, tops facing up, in a baking dish large enough to hold the tomatoes tightly. Combine the reserved tomato juice, the remaining 3 tablespoons olive oil, and the water and pour into the bottom of the baking dish. Cover tightly with foil and bake until the rice is tender, 40 minutes. Remove from the oven, uncover, and place the tomatoes on a serving platter. Pour the juices from the pan into a measuring cup to make the Avgolemono Sauce.

To serve, drizzle the Avgolemono Sauce over the top or pass separately.

Serves 6

NOTE: The stuffed tomatoes can be served hot or at room temperature. They can be prepared up to 1 day in advance and baked the day they will be served. The sauce should never be made in advance but should be prepared just before the dish is served.

AVGOLEMONO SAUCE

What makes the stuffed vegetables of Greece unique is avgolemono sauce. This sauce is meant to accompany the Stuffed Zucchini (page 154), the Stuffed Tomatoes (page 155), or any stuffed vegetable. If you like this sauce, try the Avgolemono Soup with Spiced Veal Meatballs and Rice (page 142).

1 cup chicken stock (page 255)

Reserved juices from Stuffed Zucchini (page 154) or Stuffed Tomatoes (page 155)

2 eggs

Juice of 2 lemons

Add enough chicken stock to the reserved juices to make 1¹/₂ cups. Place in a saucepan and, over medium-high heat, reduce by one-third, 10 minutes. Keep warm.

In a bowl, whisk the eggs until light and very foamy, about 3 minutes. Beating continuously, gradually add the lemon juice a few drops at a time. Beating continuously, gradually add the hot stock to the egg–lemon juice mixture a few tablespoons at a time. When all of the stock has been added, pour the mixture into a saucepan and cook over low heat, stirring constantly, just until it thickens slightly and coats the back of a spoon, 2 to 4 minutes. Do not let the mixture boil or get too hot, or it will curdle.

Remove from the heat and keep warm in a double boiler set over warm water.

Makes 1¹/₂ cups

GRAPE LEAVES STUFFED WITH RICE, CURRANTS, AND HERBS

Dolmathes Yalantzi

Dolmathes came to Greece by way of the Ottoman Empire, which had its heyday in the sixteenth century. Originally this dish was palace food, but today dolmathes are commonplace for everyone from field workers to prosperous city dwellers in Greece, Turkey, Cyprus, and the Middle East. Dolma is a Turkish word that means "stuffed." Many different kinds of leaves can be stuffed, including lettuce, cabbage, spinach, and—my personal favorite—grape leaves.

1 jar (16 ounces) preserved grape leaves, or 7 dozen fresh young grape leaves

$1/2$ cup extra virgin olive oil

2 medium yellow onions, finely minced

$1/3$ cup pine nuts

1 cup chopped green onions, white and green parts

1 cup long-grain white rice

$1/4$ cup chopped fresh flat-leaf parsley

3 tablespoons chopped fresh mint

3 tablespoons chopped fresh dill, plus 2 dill sprigs

3 tablespoons chopped fresh fennel greens or leaves, plus 2 fennel stalks (optional)

$1/3$ cup currants

Large pinch of ground cinnamon

$1/2$ teaspoon salt

Freshly ground black pepper

2 cups water

Juice of 2 lemons

Lemon wedges

1 cup plain whole milk yogurt or Yogurt and Cucumber Salad (page 159) (optional)

NOTE: These can be made up to 1 week in advance and stored in the refrigerator. Bring to room temperature before serving.

Trim the stems from the grape leaves. Whether you are using fresh or jarred grape leaves, the procedure is the same. Bring a saucepan of salted water to a boil. Add the grape leaves and simmer for 1 minute. Cool in a bowl of cold water and then drain. Cut off the tough stems.

Heat $1/4$ cup of the olive oil in a large frying pan over medium heat and cook the onions until soft, 7 minutes. Add the pine nuts, green onions, and rice and stir until the pine nuts are toasted and the green onions are soft, 4 minutes. Stir in the parsley, mint, dill, fennel greens, currants, cinnamon, salt, pepper to taste, and 1 cup of the water. Reduce the heat to low, cover, and simmer until the rice is cooked and the water is absorbed, 15 minutes.

To shape the rolls, place a leaf, smooth side down, on a work surface and put a heaping teaspoon of the filling near the base of the leaf at the stem end. Fold the stem end and sides over the filling and roll up toward the point of the leaf, making a little bundle that resembles a small cigar. After you have used all the filling, you should have some leaves left over.

Line a heavy 4-quart saucepan with a few leaves and place the fennel stalks and dill sprigs on the bottom. Sprinkle with a pinch of salt. Pack the rolls close together, seam side down. Sprinkle each layer with the remaining $1/4$ cup olive oil and the lemon juice. Add the remaining 1 cup water and cover the tops of the rolls with leaves. Invert a small heatproof plate directly on top to help the rolls maintain their shape. Cover tightly and bring to a boil. Turn the heat down to low and simmer slowly for $1 1/2$ hours.

Remove the saucepan from the heat and allow to sit until the liquid is absorbed, 2 hours. Let cool to room temperature. Serve warm or at room temperature, garnished with lemon wedges and/or plain yogurt or Yogurt and Cucumber Salad.

Makes 5 dozen

YOGURT AND CUCUMBER SALAD

Tzatziki

Yogurt plays an important role in the eastern and southern Mediterranean and is the main component of tzatziki, the yogurt, garlic, and cucumber spread or salad that is very popular throughout Greece and the Middle East. In Greece, tzatziki is made with the highest fat content yogurt available, preferably sheep's milk yogurt. This thick, rich yogurt is hard to find in the United States, but draining yogurt for 4 hours creates an adequate alternative.

2 cups whole milk yogurt

Salt

$1/2$ medium hothouse cucumber, peeled and seeded

3 to 4 cloves garlic, minced

1 tablespoon chopped fresh mint

2 teaspoons chopped fresh dill

1 tablespoon extra virgin olive oil

1 tablespoon lemon juice

Combine the yogurt and $1/4$ teaspoon salt in a cheese-cloth-lined strainer over a bowl and let drain for 4 hours.

In the meantime, grate the cucumber with a coarse grater to make 1 cup total. Place the grated cucumber on paper towels and sprinkle lightly with salt. Let drain 30 minutes.

Combine the yogurt, cucumber, garlic, mint, dill, and olive oil. Mix well. Add the lemon juice to taste and season to taste with salt. Let sit 1 hour before using.

Makes 2$1/4$ cups

SPINACH PURÉE WITH GARLIC

On every meze table in Greece there is a mass of small bowls filled with dips, spreads, and purées of all varieties—pungent yogurt with garlic and cucumbers; smoky eggplant spread; creamy white potato, garlic, and olive oil sauce; pale rose taramasalata; and a purée of chickpeas with lemon and cumin. The presence of these dishes on the meze table is a holdover from the Turkish domination of Greece, whose influence extends even further east to Syria, Lebanon, Iraq, and Egypt. The following recipe resembles the classic skorthalia, but has the addition of spinach. It's from my friend Stavroulas, who lives in Volos, just north of Athens.

Salt and freshly ground black pepper

1 cup coarsely chopped spinach, washed and dried

1/2 cup fresh bread crumbs

1/2 cup cold water

3/4 cup plus 2 tablespoons walnuts

1/2 cup extra virgin olive oil, plus extra for drizzling

3 cloves garlic, minced

1 teaspoon lemon juice or white wine vinegar

Lemon wedges

Crusty bread

Preheat the oven to 350°F. Bring a pot of salted water to a boil. Add the spinach to the boiling water and drain immediately.

Soak the bread crumbs in the cold water and squeeze well to remove any excess moisture. Discard the water.

Place the walnuts on a baking sheet and bake 5 to 7 minutes, until they are golden and hot to the touch. Chop 2 tablespoons of the walnuts and reserve for a garnish.

Place the spinach, bread crumbs, the remaining 3/4 cup walnuts, the olive oil, garlic, and lemon juice in a blender or food processor. Blend to obtain a smooth paste. Season with salt and pepper.

Spread the purée on a plate. Sprinkle with the reserved walnuts, drizzle with olive oil, and garnish with lemon wedges. Serve with crusty bread.

Makes 1 1/2 cups

EGGPLANT SALAD

Daphne Zepos may be a Greek goddess. She got so excited about my book project that she spent several weeks in Greece translating for me. Her love of her native country is boundless, and her friendship an honor. When we got back to San Francisco she tested this amazing eggplant salad for me, and we tasted the results together. It brought me back to Greece immediately. I love the combination of flavors: the smoky eggplant, garlic, earthy cumin, and lemon juice. Her eyes sparkled, and I think for a few moments we were back in Greece together. Thanks, Daphne, for sharing your time and your love of Greece with me.

1 large eggplant, smoked (page 259)

1/2 small red bell pepper, roasted (page 259)

2 cloves garlic, minced

1/2 medium yellow onion, grated

1/4 teaspoon dried oregano

1/4 teaspoon ground cumin

2 tablespoons lemon juice

2 tablespoons extra virgin olive oil

Salt and freshly ground black pepper

Chopped fresh flat-leaf parsley

3 lemon wedges

Crusty bread

Preheat the oven to 350°F. Place the smoked eggplant on a baking sheet and bake until the pulp is soft and a skewer easily pierces the flesh, 20 minutes. Cool. Remove the skin from the eggplant and squeeze the flesh gently between paper towels to remove any excess moisture. Remove the skin, stem, and ribs from the roasted pepper and finely dice. Set aside.

In a food processor or blender, pulse the eggplant flesh a few times. Add the garlic, onion, oregano, cumin, and lemon juice. With the motor running, gradually add the olive oil. Season with salt and pepper and pulse a few more times. Place in a bowl and fold in the peppers. Let sit at room temperature for 1 hour.

To serve, mound the salad on a serving plate and garnish with the chopped parsley and lemon wedges. Serve with crusty bread.

Serves 6

LENTIL SALAD WITH RED PEPPERS, RED ONIONS, FETA, AND MINT

Fakes Salata

Lentils are very much enjoyed in Greece, the most popular dish being soupa fakes, or lentil soup, flavored with stewed tomatoes and garlic. But lentils are used in salads, too. The following recipe isn't a dish you might find in Greece, however. Granted, all of the ingredients are indigenous to Greece, but here they are assembled in a new and updated way.

1 cup dried lentils, preferably French Le Puy

3 bay leaves

4 whole cloves garlic, peeled and bruised, plus 2 cloves garlic, minced

1/4 teaspoon dried oregano

6 tablespoons extra virgin olive oil

6 tablespoons red wine vinegar

1/2 teaspoon ground cumin

Salt and freshly ground black pepper

1 small red onion, diced

1 medium red bell pepper, seeded and finely diced

3 tablespoons chopped fresh mint

6 ounces feta, crumbled

18 pitted kalamata olives (page 260)

Fresh mint sprigs

Pick over the lentils and discard any stones. Rinse the lentils and place in a large saucepan with the bay leaves, the 4 bruised garlic cloves, and oregano. Cover with water by 2 inches. Bring to a boil, reduce the heat to low, and simmer until the lentils are tender, 20 to 25 minutes. Drain and cool.

To make the vinaigrette, whisk together the olive oil, vinegar, 2 cloves minced garlic, and the cumin in a small bowl. Season with salt and pepper.

Toss the vinaigrette with the lentils, onion, red bell pepper, 1/2 teaspoon salt, and pepper. Let sit 20 minutes. Season as needed with additional salt, pepper, and vinegar.

This salad can be prepared to this point up to 6 hours in advance.

To serve, toss the lentil salad with the mint and place on a platter. Garnish with the crumbled feta, olives, and mint sprigs.

Serves 6

SALAD OF OVEN-ROASTED BEETS, RED ONIONS, AND OLIVES WITH GARLIC SAUCE

Pantzaria Skorthalia

Irene Fotiadis is a well-respected caterer who performs miracles for her clients in Thessaloniki. I was lucky enough to work with her one day as she transformed Greek classics into modern dishes. Skorthalia, which dates back to antiquity, is Greece's most popular garlic sauce; it is linked to France's aioli and rouille and to Spain's romesco and allioli by a common thread of abundant mashed garlic. Unlike the sauces of the western Mediterranean, skorthalia has a strong starchy base from the addition of either nuts and bread (as in this recipe) or mashed potatoes. Here, Irene's version of skorthalia is used as the dressing for a flavorful salad of roasted beets, red onions, and black olives.

2 bunches beets (8 to 9 beets)

$^{1}/_{2}$ cup plus 1 tablespoon extra virgin olive oil

$^{1}/_{2}$ teaspoon dried oregano

Salt and freshly ground black pepper

1 head garlic, whole, unpeeled, and cut in half crosswise, plus 3 large cloves garlic, minced

One 8-ounce loaf rustic country-style bread, crusts removed

4 cups water

$^{1}/_{2}$ cup walnuts

$^{1}/_{4}$ cup vegetable oil

3 to 4 tablespoons white wine vinegar

2 tablespoons mayonnaise (page 256)

1 small red onion, thinly sliced

24 kalamata olives

Chopped fresh flat-leaf parsley

Preheat the oven to 350°F. Wash the beets and place in a baking dish. Drizzle with 1 tablespoon of the olive oil and toss to coat. Sprinkle with the oregano, salt, and pepper. Break the garlic head into cloves and scatter over the beets. Cover with foil and bake for 1 hour, or until the beets can be easily skewered. Remove from the oven and cool the beets. Peel the beets, cut into thin slices, and drizzle with the strained oil from the baking dish.

Place the bread in a bowl and pour the water over the bread to soak. Remove the bread from the water immediately and drain for 1 hour. Squeeze the bread to remove any excess moisture. Discard the water.

Grind the walnuts in a food processor or blender. Add the bread, salt, vegetable oil, the remaining $^{1}/_{2}$ cup olive oil, 2 tablespoons of the vinegar, the mayonnaise, and garlic in a blender or food processor and purée to obtain a smooth paste. Season with salt, pepper, and additional vinegar if needed.

Place the beets, red onion, and olives on a plate. Place a spoonful of garlic sauce on the side of the plate or pass in a separate bowl. Garnish with the parsley.

Serves 6

NOTE: The beets can be cooked up to 24 hours in advance. The garlic sauce should be made the same day. Assemble just before serving.

CORFU SALAD OF ORANGE SLICES, RED ONIONS, AND KALAMATA OLIVES

Salata Kerkiras

On the island of Corfu, off the northwest coast of Greece near Albania, this salad is traditionally made with olives, sweet juicy oranges, onions, and paprika. This more modern adaptation uses mint instead of paprika, and the whole is linked together by fruity extra virgin olive oil, a splash of red wine vinegar, and a touch of garlic. The result is a masterpiece of colors and flavor.

6 seedless oranges

3 tablespoons fresh orange juice

$1/2$ teaspoon grated orange zest

1 $1/2$ teaspoons red wine vinegar

1 clove garlic, minced

$1/4$ cup extra virgin olive oil

Salt and freshly ground black pepper

$1/2$ small red onion, thinly sliced into rings

18 kalamata olives

12 fresh mint leaves

With a knife, cut off the tops and bottoms of the oranges. With one of the cut sides down, use a small knife to cut off the skin, removing all the white pith. Cut the oranges crosswise into $1/4$-inch slices.

In a small bowl, whisk together the orange juice, orange zest, red wine vinegar, garlic, and olive oil. Season with salt and pepper.

To serve, arrange the orange slices, onion, and olives on a platter. Drizzle with the vinaigrette. Pile the mint leaves on top of one another and roll up. Cut into thin ribbons. Sprinkle on the salad and serve immediately.

Serves 6

PICKLED WILD MUSHROOMS

Manitaria Toursi

Pickling is a way of preserving foods that is very common all over the Mediterranean and espe- cially in Greece, where almost every vegetable is pickled, or toursi. These vegetables "à la Grecque" are served in many kitchens around the world, but in Greece they are simply referred to as "marinated vegetables." These marinated wild mushrooms are a welcome sight on any meze table from coast to coast in Greece.

1/2 pound wild mushrooms (porcini, morels, field, or chanterelles)

1 1/2 pounds small button mushrooms

1 cup dry white wine, such as sauvignon blanc

1 cup white wine vinegar

1/2 cup extra virgin olive oil

4 cloves garlic, thinly sliced

4 bay leaves

Salt

20 whole black peppercorns, cracked with a mortar and pestle or electric spice grinder

15 coriander seeds, cracked with a mortar and pestle or electric spice grinder

6 sprigs fresh flat-leaf parsley

2 sprigs fresh oregano, or 1/4 teaspoon dried oregano

2 sprigs fresh thyme, or 1/4 teaspoon dried thyme

2 sprigs fresh fennel, or 1/4 teaspoon fennel seeds

1 tablespoon chopped fresh flat-leaf parsley

To clean the mushrooms, use a soft, slightly dampened towel or mushroom brush and brush gently. Trim any bruised spots and discard. If the wild mushrooms are large, cut to the same size as the button mushrooms.

Place the wine, vinegar, olive oil, garlic, bay leaves, 2 teaspoons salt, peppercorns, coriander seeds, parsley, and half of the oregano, thyme, and fennel in a saucepan over high heat. Bring to a boil, reduce the heat to low, cover, and simmer slowly for 45 minutes. Strain through a fine-mesh strainer, using the back of a wooden spoon to extract all the liquid from the solids. Return the liq- uid to the saucepan, discarding the solids.

To the liquid in the saucepan, add the mushrooms; the remaining oregano, thyme, and fennel; and enough water to almost cover the mushrooms. Bring to a boil, reduce the heat to low, and simmer, stirring occasionally for 3 minutes. With a slotted spoon, remove the mush- rooms and herbs and place in a bowl. Reduce the liquid until 1 cup remains, 10 minutes. Pour the hot liquid over the mushrooms and mix well. Let cool. Cover and refrigerate overnight.

Serve at room temperature, garnished with the chopped parsley.

Serves 6

SAFFRON PILAF WITH MUSSELS AND SQUID

Pilafi Me Mithia Ke Kalamaria

Saffron, the thread-like stigma of a violet-colored crocus, contributes both flavor and a distinctive yellow-orange color to various dishes. The combination of rice and saffron is certainly no stranger to Mediterranean cooking. Spanish paella, Milan's famous risotto Milanese, and this Greek specialty of saffron pilaf with mussels and squid are three familiar dishes. When you buy saffron, always buy saffron threads instead of powder. That way you know what you are getting.

3/4 cup dry white wine, such as sauvignon blanc

2 tablespoons chopped fresh flat-leaf parsley

2 bay leaves

2 pounds mussels, scrubbed and beards removed

1 pound squid or cuttlefish, cleaned (page 260)

1/4 cup extra virgin olive oil

1 medium yellow onion, minced

3 cloves garlic, minced

1 carrot, diced

8 green onions, white and green parts, thinly sliced

1 cup tomatoes, peeled, seeded, and chopped (page 259), or 3 tomatoes, fresh or canned

1 red bell pepper, roasted (page 259) and diced

1 large pinch of saffron threads, revived (page 260)

1 1/2 cups water

1 cup bottled clam juice or fish stock (page 255)

1 cup long-grain white rice

Salt and freshly ground black pepper

2 tablespoons lemon juice

1 tablespoon coarsely chopped fresh flat-leaf parsley

6 lemon wedges

Heat the white wine, parsley, and bay leaves in a frying pan. Add the mussels, cover, and cook until the mussels open. Remove the mussels as soon as they open and reserve the mussel juices. Set aside 12 mussels in their opened shells for garnish. Remove the remaining mussels from their shells, discarding the empty shells.

Slice the squid into thin rings and cut the tentacles into bite-size pieces. Wash well. Heat the mussel juices over medium-high heat and cook the squid, stirring constantly, for 30 seconds. Remove the squid and reserve. Reserve the mussel juices.

Heat the olive oil in a large frying pan over medium heat. Add the onion, garlic, carrot, and green onions and cook until the vegetables are soft, 10 minutes. Add the tomatoes, red pepper, and saffron and simmer 20 minutes. Add the water, fish stock, rice, salt, pepper, and mussel juices and cook until the rice is tender and the liquid is gone, 20 to 25 minutes.

When the rice is done, add the mussels, squid, and lemon juice and toss together. Let sit 2 minutes.

To serve, mound the rice, mussels, and squid in the center of a platter. Garnish with the reserved mussels in their shells, the parsley, and the lemon wedges.

Serves 6

PICKLED SQUID

On the tiny idyllic island of Zakynthos, ferries arrived every few hours, unloading tons of scantily clad holiday guests who had made their way to this remote island to enjoy the notorious Easter weekend. The island was ripe for what was to come—forty-eight hours of eating, drinking, celebrating, and merrymaking. Bukios, the popular outdoor taverna just off the main street, was prepared. In advance, they had put up jars and jars of their famous pickled squid. The taverna was jam-packed all weekend with island natives and knowing tourists who ate and enjoyed this pungent meze.

1¹/2 pounds medium squid, cleaned (page 260)

¹/2 cup bottled clam juice

3 tablespoons extra virgin olive oil

¹/3 cup white wine vinegar

¹/2 cup dry white wine, such as sauvignon blanc

4 cloves garlic, thinly sliced

¹/2 to ³/4 teaspoon pickling spices

¹/2 teaspoon dried oregano

Salt and freshly ground black pepper

¹/4 red bell pepper, finely diced

¹/4 green bell pepper, finely diced

1 small pickled green pepper, Greek *toursi or* peperoncini, finely diced (see Note)

2 thin slices lemon

3 lemon wedges

Whole fresh flat-leaf parsley leaves

¹/4 cup black olives (Greek elites, kalamata, or niçoise)

Slice the squid bodies into rings and leave the tentacles whole.

Over high heat, bring the clam juice to a boil in a saucepan and reduce by half, 2 minutes. Reduce the heat to low; add the olive oil, vinegar, wine, garlic, pickling spices, oregano, salt, and pepper; and simmer for 10 minutes. Add the squid and simmer, stirring occasionally, for 30 to 40 seconds. Pour the contents of the pan into a bowl. Add the red and green bell peppers, the pickled pepper, and lemon slices and mix well. Cover and refrigerate overnight.

The next day, bring the squid to room temperature. Place the squid and juices on a platter and garnish with the lemon wedges, parsley, and olives.

Serves 6 to 8

NOTE: Greek *toursi* are available in Greek and Middle Eastern grocery stores. Peperoncini, readily available in most grocery stores, can be substituted.

STEWED MUSSELS WITH FETA

Mithia Sahanaki

Feta is the most widely used cheese in Greece. Also known as farmhouse cheese, this moist, salty cheese is made with either sheep's or goat's milk. The name feta means "slice" and refers to the way the cheese is cut into blocks. This recipe calls for an unlikely combination of shellfish and feta and is absolutely delicious, although I admit that at first I never thought I would enjoy this tangy classic as much as I do. It is also great with shrimp instead of mussels.

1/4 cup extra virgin olive oil

1/2 medium yellow onion, minced

4 large tomatoes, peeled, seeded, and coarsely chopped (page 259), or 2 cups tomatoes, fresh or canned

1 cup dry white wine, such as sauvignon blanc

1/4 teaspoon dried oregano

Pinch of crushed red pepper flakes

1 teaspoon red wine vinegar

2 pounds mussels, scrubbed and beards removed

6 ounces feta cheese, crumbled

Salt and freshly ground black pepper

1 tablespoon coarsely chopped fresh flat-leaf parsley

Heat the olive oil in a large frying pan over medium heat and cook the onion, stirring occasionally, until soft, 7 minutes. Increase the heat to high. Add the tomatoes, wine, oregano, red pepper flakes, and vinegar and stir well. Bring to a boil, reduce the heat to low, and simmer until thick, 20 to 30 minutes.

Add the mussels and cover the pan. As the mussels open, remove them from the pan and keep them warm on a platter. Cook until all the mussels have opened. Remove the mussels from their shells and discard the shells.

Return the mussels to the pan. Add the feta and stir well. Simmer slowly 30 seconds. Season with salt and pepper.

Pour the mussels and sauce onto a platter and garnish with parsley. Serve immediately.

Serves 6

SALT COD ROE FRITTERS

Taramokeftethes

The lovely seaside town of Volos is renowned for its fishing fleet. Small fishing boats bob between the calm shallow inlet harboring Volos and the Aegean Sea. In Volos, I met Stavroula Spyrou, a spry little woman who specializes in cooking a bounty of seafood while talking a blue streak. Besides the fabulous walnut and garlic spread she gave me the recipe for, this simple family favorite is one she graciously shared.

1/3 cup *tarama* or salted cod roe (see Note), about 3 1/2 ounces

2 tablespoons hot water

Juice of 1/2 lemon

1 cup water

1 cup fresh bread crumbs

2 medium yellow onions, grated

5 green onions, minced

1/2 cup chopped fresh dill

1/4 cup chopped fresh flat-leaf parsley

Freshly ground black pepper

Olive or canola oil for deep-frying

3/4 cup all-purpose flour

1 teaspoon baking powder

1/4 teaspoon salt

6 lemon wedges

Fresh dill sprigs

Fresh flat-leaf parsley sprigs

Mash together the *tarama*, hot water, and lemon juice. Pour the water over the bread crumbs and immediately squeeze well to remove any excess moisture. Discard the water. In a bowl, mix the *tarama* mixture, bread crumbs, onions, green onions, dill, parsley, and pepper.

Pour the oil to the depth of 1 1/2 inches in a deep saucepan. Heat to 375°F.

Form the mixture into 1-inch balls. Combine the flour, baking powder, and salt. Dredge the balls in the flour mixture. Deep-fry a few at a time until they are golden on all sides, 3 to 4 minutes. Do not overcrowd the pan. Remove from the pan with a slotted spoon and drain on paper towels. Serve immediately, garnished with the lemon wedges and dill and parsley sprigs.

Serves 6

NOTE: **If *tarama* is unavailable, substitute domestic whitefish caviar.**

THE LEVANT

TURKEY, SYRIA, LEBANON, ISRAEL, AND EGYPT

*E*very street hawker in Istanbul has a brother or uncle ready to offer you a special price on just about anything. And as you waver between doubt and suspicion, you'll be invited to share his *meze*, or appetizer table, which is never too small or the offerings too meager to share with a new friend.

On a trip to Istanbul with friends we decided to accept one such offer, and we soon found ourselves in a heady atmosphere of mint, cumin, and coriander, seated on kilim-upholstered cushions surrounding a deep-pile Persian carpet. Almost at once, a procession of colorful small plates began to appear on a low, linen-clad table. Each dish was more amazing than the last—seasoned with pungent spices, garlic, and wild herbs; moistened with yellow-gold olive oil, sesame seed paste, and butter; or rolled in all kinds of leaves and pastry.

And just when we thought we'd eaten our last bite, another tray of small *meze* plates would emerge from the depths of the kitchen. Our host's generosity confirmed the reputation for hospitality enjoyed by people of the eastern Mediterranean, whether in Turkey, Syria, Lebanon, Israel, or Egypt. (By the way, in the end I was too full to even think about buying anything, but I did return the next day to get the basket I'd been admiring.)

Revitalizing the Spirit and Soul

Meze is true evidence of the Middle Easterner's passion for leisure and appetite for fresh, seasonal food. Although its origins can be traced to ancient Persia, where raw-tasting wines were tempered by bites of various foods, today *meze* appears in every home, café, and restaurant before the main course. *Meze* is meant to revitalize the spirit and soul and satisfy the stomach and heart. The time devoted to the enjoyment of *meze* is a time to sit back, take a deep breath, and forget one's troubles and the stresses of daily life. It's best done in a relaxed and aesthetically pleasing environment—whether a balcony in Cappadocia amidst the stark loveliness of the moonlike formations, at one of the famous fish restaurants moored to the quay under the Galata Bridge in Istanbul, or at a terrace restaurant in the herb-laden hills above Beirut where the acacia trees act as an umbrella shielding you from the penetrating sun.

The Variety of *Meze*

One of the distinguishing features of *meze* is its versatility. Give Syrian or Lebanese cooks a few impeccably fresh ingredients, and they will concoct variation upon variation of appetizing and sumptuous dishes. For example, there are more than 100 different ways to prepare eggplant.

Meze can range from very simple to refined, sophisticated, and technically complicated: from perfectly roasted and salted hazelnuts, pistachios, and chickpeas or a wedge of vine-sweetened melon with a thick slice of creamy white cheese to *börek* or savory pies made with a delicate paper-thin pastry called *yufka*.

What to Drink

The drink of choice with *meze* is a cool glass of *raki* or *arak* (*zabib* in Egypt), the Middle Eastern version of Greek ouzo or French Pernod. This anise-flavored, colorless distillation of grape mash is also known as "lion's milk" because it turns a cloudy white when water is added and, at 87 proof, it roars with strength. Islam continues to be the dominant religion in Turkey, Syria, Lebanon, and Egypt, and drinking alcohol is forbidden, although *raki* seems to escape scrutiny here.

Raki is such an integral accompaniment to first courses here that the terms "*meze* table" and "*raki* table" are interchangeable. Whatever it's called, though, the sheer volume of choices—salads, purées, stuffed vegetables and leaves, assorted olives, roasted nuts, egg pies, tiny spiced kebabs, pastries, soups, stewed legumes, deep-fried croquettes, and different vegetable dishes—is exceptional. It isn't hard to see why this appetite-whetting prelude often surpasses in quality, quantity, and flavor the main course to follow.

The Intersection of Civilizations

The countries of the eastern Mediterranean, including Turkey, Syria, Lebanon, Israel, and Egypt, have been influenced by the Middle East, Greece, the Balkans, Asia, Byzantium, and North Africa. Christians, Muslims, and Jews have intermingled here for centuries, though not always under the most congenial of circumstances.

TURKEY

Turkey, which actually straddles Asia and Europe, is the home of the Ottoman Turks, who in 1453 changed the name of the Byzantine capital from Constantinople to Istanbul and changed its religion from Christianity to Islam. Originating in Asia, the Turks swept across the Middle East, Asia Minor, and Greece and dominated these countries for nearly 400 years. The sultans' penchant for extravagance and variety was largely responsible for the level of sophistication in the Middle Eastern kitchen. At the Ottoman Turk Empire's ceremonial zenith, 1,400 cooks, mostly from other countries, were employed at Topkapi Palace in Istanbul. The Ottoman rulers were dubbed the "Frenchmen of the East" because of their dexterity in the kitchen.

Turkey is at the crossroads between Europe and Asia, where East meets West, and both have left their mark on the rich and varied cuisine of the Middle East. Istanbul is a cosmopolitan city made up of Arabs, Serbs, Jews, Venetians, Circassians, Bulgarians, Genoese, Armenians, Greeks, and Turks who continue to leave an indelible mark on the cuisine.

Tarator, a sauce of olive oil, garlic, and nuts much like the Greek *skorthalia*, is made here. Shish kebab, meat or fish skewers, and *doner* kebab, layered slices of marinated lamb roasted on a gigantic spit, are Turkish in origin. Lamb is the livestock of choice in Turkey and the rest of the countries that border the eastern Mediterranean because lambs adapt well to the barren and arid terrain. *Pilav*, in various forms, is popular, as is paprika-steeped oil used as a garnish. Some of the most delicious yogurt in the world is made in Turkey.

SYRIA AND LEBANON

The cuisines of Syria and Lebanon are closely linked. The food, the result of a melting pot of Arabic cultures, is some of the most diverse and exotic of the Mediterranean. These two countries have always been on the trade route for spices and rice between the East and the West. The food here is redolent of spices and herbs, and the aromas of mint, parsley, allspice, and cinnamon fill the air. Turkey has ruled Syria and Lebanon over the years, and thus the food continues to be influenced by Turkish dishes.

As in Turkey, briny black olives are eaten at every meal, and of course a basket of warm disk-shaped flat bread or pita bread forms the centerpiece.

Lemon and garlic are very popular ingredients. Rice, dried beans, and bulgur, an earthy cracked wheat that is hulled and parboiled, are some of the most important ingredients in the Syrian and Lebanese larder. Bulgur is the main ingredient in making *kibbeh* and *tabouleh*. Yogurt and *labneh*, a yogurt cheese, are also used often, along with tahini, or sesame seed paste, and stuffed grape and cabbage leaves. Olive oil is used in nearly every dish.

ISRAEL

Israel, the land of historical turmoil, is a Jewish state but retains an Arabic presence that is visible in its cooking. Falafel, spiced chickpea croquettes, are a favorite first course and sold on every street corner. A variety of refreshing salads are made with fruits and vegetables such as citrus and avocados. The stringent dietary restrictions of Judaism have influenced the food prepared in Israel: pork and shellfish are infrequently used, and meals that combine meat and dairy products are rare. Matzo, an unleavened cracker, makes its way into many dishes, especially during Passover.

EGYPT

When the civilization of ancient Greece was still in its infancy, Egypt was already 2,000 years old and the most sophisticated country in the West. The Nile River, the longest river in the world, has always been Egypt's defining feature, providing Egypt with transportation, irrigation for farming, an important fishing industry, and innumerable droughts and floods. It also divides Egypt from Israel. Although Egypt is part of North Africa geographically, its food is more closely related to that of the Middle East and Turkey.

Peasants constitute three-fifths of Egypt's population, and their diet consists mostly of cereal grains, legumes, seasonal vegetables, and round loaves of bread baked in beehive-shaped clay ovens. *Ful medames*, an ancient staple of both the wealthy and the poor, is made with soaked and slow-cooked brown beans that are mashed with salt and garlic and accompanied by an assortment of highly aromatic condiments, including olive oil, hard-cooked eggs, lemon wedges, and chopped parsley and onions. These ingredients transcend their humble beginnings to create a flavorful and satisfying dish.

Ta'amiya, cousin to Israeli falafel and the national dish of Egypt, is made with fava beans, garlic, onions, and red pepper; it is said to be best around the Mediterranean. One can readily find *ta'amiya* served sandwiched between bread or sold by street vendors. Cumin, coriander, mint, dill, and tahini are favored aromatics.

A Multifaceted Cuisine

Cooking techniques are simpler in Turkey, Syria, Lebanon, Israel, and Egypt than in the western Mediterranean countries of Spain, France, and Italy, but the flavor of the foods is still strong and distinctive. Over thousands of years, a multifaceted cuisine has developed and flourished. The ingredients used in these five countries are not exotic or rare, nor are the cooking techniques difficult, but the ingredients are combined in a way that produces an unusual and distinctive array of dishes, as demonstrated here in these *meze* recipes.

ONION YOGURT

Yogurt Salcasi

All over the Mediterranean, onions are a staple of the kitchen. In the Middle East, onions are eaten raw, cooked, or marinated in everything from soups, kebabs, stews, and salads and used as a garnish. The acidity of the onions in this recipe is tempered by marinating them in salt and vinegar. Later, they are combined with yogurt for a healthy sauce or condiment.

3 cups whole milk yogurt

Salt

2 medium yellow onions

1 tablespoon plus 1 to 2 teaspoons white wine vinegar

Combine the yogurt and $1/2$ teaspoon salt. Place the yogurt in a cheesecloth-lined strainer over a bowl and let it drain 4 hours.

Cut the onions in half and then across into very thin slices. Sprinkle with 1 teaspoon salt and 1 tablespoon of the vinegar. Rub the onions and salt together and let stand 30 minutes.

Place the onions in a colander and rinse with cold water. Pat dry with paper towels. Combine the yogurt and onions together and mix well. Season with salt and the remaining 1 to 2 teaspoons vinegar to taste.

Makes 2 cups

SAVORY PIE WITH CHICKEN, SULTANAS, AND SWEET SPICES

Yufkali Pilav

Rice was first introduced to Persia from Asia in the sixth century, and later its use spread to the rest of the Middle East and Greece. In the eighth century, rice was brought to Spain by the Arabs, who planted it in Andalusia, making way for the multitude of paella and rice dishes. Later, rice was transported to Italy and used there for risotto. Today rice is a staple of the Middle Eastern table for stuffings, dolmas, and pilav. In this recipe, rice is added to a phyllo pie of chicken, golden raisins, allspice, cinnamon, and cloves.

1 whole chicken, about 3 1/2 pounds

2 yellow onions, quartered

1 carrot, coarsely chopped

2 bay leaves

4 sprigs fresh flat-leaf parsley

12 black peppercorns

8 cups water

3/4 cup long-grain white rice

1 1/2 teaspoons salt

3 1/2 cups boiling water

1/2 cup pine nuts, toasted (page 258)

1/2 cup sultana or golden raisins

10 tablespoons unsalted butter, melted

1/2 pound phyllo dough

2 eggs, lightly beaten

1/2 teaspoon ground allspice

1/4 teaspoon ground cinnamon

1/4 teaspoon ground cloves

Freshly ground black pepper

Place the chicken, onions, carrot, bay leaves, parsley, peppercorns, and water in a large soup pot. Over high heat, bring to a boil. Reduce the heat to low and simmer until the meat falls off the bone, 1 hour. Turn off the heat and allow the chicken to cool in the broth. Remove the chicken from the pan. Remove the skin and bones and discard. Cut the chicken meat into bite-size pieces and place in a bowl. Moisten with 1/4 cup of the chicken broth. Reduce the remaining broth by half, 20 to 30 minutes. Strain, skim off the fat, and set aside.

Place the rice in a bowl with the salt and pour the boiling water over the rice. Let stand until the water cools to lukewarm. Drain and wash the rice under cold water. Drain.

Place 2 1/2 cups of the chicken broth, a pinch of salt, the pine nuts, and raisins in a saucepan. Bring to a boil. Add the rice, reduce the heat to low, and cook, covered, until the rice absorbs all the liquid and is cooked, 15 minutes. Remove from the heat and let stand 10 minutes.

Preheat an oven to 350°F. Brush a 9-inch spring-form pan lightly with butter. Line the pan with 1 sheet of phyllo that hangs over the outside of the pan. Brush it lightly with melted butter. Arrange 6 more sheets of phyllo on top, brushing each layer lightly with butter, and turning the pan slightly between sheets so that the overhanging phyllo is even on all sides.

In a bowl, toss the chicken, rice, eggs, allspice, cinnamon, and cloves together. Season with salt and pepper. Place the filling in the phyllo-lined pan and pat the filling down slightly. Cut 8 circles of phyllo, the same size as the circumference of the pan. Place 1 circle on top of the filling, brushing lightly with butter. Place 3 more circles on top, brushing lightly with butter between each layer. Fold the top piece of the overhanging phyllo over the phyllo circles to cover and seal the top. Brush with butter. Repeat folding all of the remaining pieces of the overhanging phyllo, brushing with butter in between each layer. Place the remaining 4 circles on top, brushing lightly with butter between each layer. Brush the top with butter. Bake for 35 to 40 minutes, until golden. Remove from the oven and let rest 10 minutes.

Cut into wedges and serve hot or warm.

Serves 6 to 8

TURKISH SPICED LAMB AND TOMATO "PIZZA"

Lahmaçun

Lahmaçun, a kind of Arabic pizza, means "dough with meat." The difference between a pizza and a lahmaçun is that when the thin-crusted lahmaçun is taken from the oven, the crust is soft and pliable. To eat this flavorful Turkish pizza, simply roll it up or fold it and eat it while still warm.

Dough

2 3/4 teaspoons active dry yeast

1 cup lukewarm water (110°F)

2 tablespoons unsalted butter, melted

2 tablespoons extra virgin olive oil

1 teaspoon salt

3 cups all-purpose flour

Filling

2 tablespoons extra virgin olive oil

1 large yellow onion, minced

1 pound ground lamb

2 large tomatoes, peeled, seeded, chopped, and drained (page 259), about 1 cup, fresh or canned

2 tablespoons tomato paste

1/3 cup chopped fresh flat-leaf parsley

1/4 cup pine nuts, toasted (page 258)

Large pinch of ground cinnamon

Large pinch of ground allspice

Large pinch of ground cloves

1/4 teaspoon crushed red pepper flakes

1/2 teaspoon salt

1/2 teaspoon freshly ground black pepper

1 tablespoon lemon juice

4 tablespoons unsalted butter, melted

To make the dough, combine the yeast and 1/4 cup of the water in a bowl and mix well. Let stand 10 minutes until the yeast is dissolved. Add the remaining 3/4 cup water, the butter, olive oil, salt, and flour. Mix well. Knead until smooth and elastic, 7 to 10 minutes. Place the dough in an oiled bowl, turning it once to coat with oil. Cover with plastic wrap and let rise in a warm place (75°F) until doubled in volume, 1 hour.

To make the filling, heat the olive oil in a large frying pan and cook the onion, stirring occasionally, until soft, 10 minutes. Add the lamb, tomatoes, tomato paste, parsley, pine nuts, cinnamon, allspice, cloves, red pepper flakes, salt, and black pepper and cook slowly, uncovered, stirring occasionally, until almost dry, 10 minutes. Add the lemon juice and mix well.

Preheat the oven to 450°F. Divide the dough into 16 egg-size pieces and place on a floured board. Working with one piece at a time, flatten the dough with your hands or roll each piece of dough into a 6-inch circle, 1/8 inch thick. Place close together on an oiled baking sheet and let rest 10 minutes.

To assemble the pizzas, spread 1 heaping tablespoon of the filling on top of each circle of dough going right up to the edges. Brush the filling lightly with melted butter. Bake the pizzas 8 to 10 minutes, until very lightly golden around the edges but still soft enough to roll or fold.

Makes 16 small pizzas to serve 6 to 8

TURKISH RAVIOLI WITH LAMB, GARLIC, MINT, AND YOGURT

Manti

When I told my friend Mieke Schweren that I had never tasted manti, *she went to work. In less than 24 hours the energetic Mieke organized eleven local women from Goreme, in central Turkey, to prepare a lavish meze table at Mieke's lovely, restored fifteenth-century restaurant, Konak Turk Evi, nestled in the hills above the small town. The sun shone through the windows and onto a table fit for a sultan, packed with village specialties—just for me. I got out my pad and pencil and immediately wrote down this fabulous recipe.*

Sauce

4 cups yogurt

1 cup chicken stock (page 255)

4 cloves garlic, minced or mashed in a mortar and pestle

3 tablespoons extra virgin olive oil

Salt and freshly ground black pepper

Dough

1 3/4 cups all-purpose flour

1/2 cup whole wheat flour

1/2 teaspoon salt

1 egg

1 egg yolk

1/2 cup water

1 cup white rice flour

Filling

1/2 pound lean ground lamb

1/2 small yellow onion, minced

3 tablespoons minced fresh flat-leaf parsley

Salt and freshly ground black pepper

12 fresh mint leaves

Place the yogurt in a cheesecloth-lined strainer and drain for 2 hours.

To make the dough, place the all-purpose flour, wheat flour, and salt in a bowl. Make a well in the center. In a bowl, mix the egg, egg yolk, and water together and pour the mixture into the well. With a fork, gradually bring the flour into the well and mix together. When it is almost combined, gather the mixture into a ball, turn it out onto a work surface, and knead to make a rough dough, 2 to 3 minutes. Place in a bowl, cover with plastic wrap, and let rest 30 minutes.

To make the sauce, place the chicken stock in a saucepan over high heat and reduce by half, 5 minutes. In a bowl, beat together half the reduced chicken stock, the drained yogurt, garlic, and olive oil until light and creamy. Season with salt and pepper. Set aside at room temperature.

To make the filling, combine the lamb, onion, parsley, salt, and pepper in a bowl. Knead together for 2 minutes and set aside.

Divide the dough into 4 pieces. Cover with an inverted bowl so they don't dry out. Lightly flour a work surface with the rice flour and, with a floured rolling pin, roll one piece of the dough until you can almost see the outline of your hand through it when you hold it up to the light. Alternatively, you can use a pasta machine, rolling the dough to the full width of the machine, about 5 inches.

Cut the dough into 2 1/2-inch squares. Place a scant 1/2 teaspoon filling in the center of each square. Lightly mist the squares with a spray bottle filled with water. Fold each square in half to form a triangle. Press together to seal the edges. Place the ravioli on a floured baking sheet in a single layer. Repeat with the remaining dough and filling.

Bring a pot of salted water to a boil. Reduce the heat to low. Drop the ravioli into the water and simmer very slowly, stirring occasionally, until the ravioli are tender and the lamb is cooked, 15 to 20 minutes. Strain and toss with the remaining reduced chicken stock.

Pile the mint leaves on top of one another. Roll up and cut into thin strips. Toss the ravioli with the yogurt sauce. Place on a platter and garnish with the mint.

Serves 8

NOTE: This dough can be made up to a week in advance and frozen. If you are not rolling the dough for 24 hours, store in the freezer and defrost when needed. If the filled ravioli are not being used for 24 hours, store the ravioli in the freezer and remove when ready to cook. Boil the ravioli while still frozen, adding 1 or 2 minutes to the cooking time.

FLAKY CHEESE-FILLED TRIANGLES WITH HERBS

Börek

Börek, boregi, briouats, briks, empanadas, pittas, and pastillas *are the various names for the small turnovers from the countries surrounding the Mediterranean. Börek is a generic term for a whole range of Turkish pastries that come in various shapes—triangles, squares, semicircles, and cigar rolls. They are made with puff pastry, leavened dough, short crust, or yufka, the Turkish version of phyllo dough, and stuffed with anything from greens and leeks to cheese and herbs. Börek are delicious on their own, but they are also an excellent accompaniment to a bowl of hot soup.*

12 ounces feta cheese

4 tablespoons grated kefalotyri or Parmigiano-Reggiano cheese

1 egg, lightly beaten

Large pinch of freshly grated nutmeg

2 tablespoons chopped fresh chives

2 tablespoons chopped fresh dill

2 tablespoons chopped fresh mint

2 tablespoons chopped fresh flat-leaf parsley

4 tablespoons pine nuts, toasted (page 258)

Salt and freshly ground black pepper

8 ounces phyllo dough

6 tablespoons unsalted butter

To make the filling, mash together the feta, kefalotyri, egg, nutmeg, chives, dill, mint, parsley, and pine nuts. Season with salt and pepper and set aside.

With scissors, cut the phyllo the long way into 3 piles of 3 by 18-inch strips. Place the strips on top of one another to form a single pile and cover with a slightly dampened towel. Melt the butter in a small saucepan.

Preheat the oven to 375°F. Take 1 strip of the phyllo and place it on the work surface. Brush it lightly with butter. Take another strip, place it on top of the first one, and brush it lightly with butter. Place a heaping teaspoon of the filling at one end about 1 inch from the edge. Fold 1 corner over the filling to meet the other side and continue to fold as you would a flag, until the whole strip is folded into a small triangular parcel. Brush the top with butter and place on a buttered baking sheet. Repeat with the rest of the phyllo.

Bake until golden brown and crisp, 15 to 20 minutes. Serve hot from the oven, warm, or at room temperature.

Makes 25 to 30 pastries to serve 6

NOTE: These can be prepared 2 weeks in advance and stored in the freezer until they are ready to use. Defrost before baking.

SPICED CHICKPEA CROQUETTES WITH TAHINI AND CUMIN SAUCE AND HERB SALAD

Falafel Or Ta'Amiya

Years ago, recipes based on beans and grains were considered peasant food. Today, such humble ingredients have crossed all socioeconomic barriers and are eaten by the rich and the poor alike. Highly seasoned with garlic, spices, and herbs, beans and grains can be taken to new heights. Falafel, the national dish of Israel, and ta'amiya, its Egyptian equivalent, are perfect examples. I have taken a classic recipe and modernized the dish with the addition of an herb salad or Onion Yogurt (page 179). Or, if you prefer, serve this falafel with the more traditional tahini sauce.

2 cups dried chickpeas, about 12 ounces (see Note)

2 tablespoons medium-fine bulgur or cracked wheat

1/4 cup boiling water

1 medium yellow onion, minced

1/3 cup chopped fresh flat-leaf parsley

1/2 bunch chopped fresh cilantro or coriander leaves

10 cloves garlic, minced

4 teaspoons ground cumin

1 tablespoon ground coriander seeds

1 teaspoon turmeric

1/4 to 1/2 teaspoon cayenne

1 teaspoon baking soda

1 1/2 teaspoons salt

1/2 teaspoon freshly ground black pepper

Vegetable oil for deep-frying

Salad

4 large sprigs fresh mint

1/2 small bunch of fresh cilantro or coriander leaves

1/2 small bunch of fresh flat-leaf parsley leaves

2 handfuls of arugula

2 tablespoons extra virgin olive oil

1 tablespoon lemon juice

Salt and freshly ground black pepper

2 cups Tahini and Cumin Sauce (page 188) or Onion Yogurt (page 179)

Pick over the chickpeas and discard any stones. Cover with cold water and soak for 8 hours or overnight. Drain.

Place the bulgur in a bowl and add the boiling water. Stir well and let stand 30 minutes.

Place the chickpeas and onion in a food processor or blender and process until they form a thick paste. Add the bulgur and its liquid, the parsley, cilantro, garlic, cumin, coriander, turmeric, cayenne, baking soda, salt, and pepper and pulse a few times to mix well. Transfer to a bowl and let rest 30 minutes.

Take walnut-size lumps of the paste and roll them into balls. Flatten slightly into patties 1 1/2 inches by 1/2 inch. Place on a baking sheet and let rest 30 minutes. The recipe can be prepared to this point up to 24 hours in advance.

Heat 1 inch of oil to 375°F. Deep-fry the falafel, a few at a time, until they are golden on both sides, 2 to 3 minutes. The falafel can be kept warm in a 350°F oven until ready to serve.

To make the optional salad, toss the mint, cilantro, parsley, and arugula in a bowl. In a small bowl, whisk together the olive oil and lemon juice. Season with salt and pepper. Toss the herbs with the vinaigrette. Place the salad on a platter and place the falafel on top. Garnish with the Tahini and Cumin Sauce or Onion Yogurt.

Makes about 25 falafel to serve 6

> NOTE: In Israel falafel are made with chickpeas, but in Egypt, where they originated, they are made with dried fava beans. Feel free to substitute fava beans for the chickpeas.

TAHINI AND CUMIN SAUCE

Salata Tahini

Tahini and cumin complement one another. This pungent sauce is versatile and an excellent accompaniment to falafel or grilled skewers of chicken, fish, pork, or beef. It's also good simply served with warm pita bread.

2 cloves garlic, minced

Juice of 1 lemon

1/3 cup tahini or sesame seed paste

4 to 5 tablespoons water

1/2 teaspoon ground cumin

2 tablespoons chopped fresh flat-
   leaf parsley

Salt

Place the garlic in a bowl and slowly whisk in half of the lemon juice. Gradually whisk in the tahini and the water. Add the cumin and parsley and mix well. Add more water if necessary. Season with salt and additional lemon juice if needed.

Makes 1 cup

WARM CHICKPEAS WITH SPINACH

Hummus Ma'Sabanegh

Although the combination of chickpeas and spinach might seem odd, it is a classic that emigrated from Persia to the Middle East and across North Africa to Spain, where it was introduced during the Moors' 700-year occupation of Spain. I happen to be very partial to this healthy Middle Eastern vegetarian meze.

1¹/₃ cups dried chickpeas, about 8 ounces

¹/₄ cup extra virgin olive oil

1 large yellow onion, minced

1 tomato, peeled, seeded, and chopped (page 259), about ¹/₂ cup, fresh or canned

3 tablespoons tomato paste

1¹/₂ pounds spinach, stems removed and chopped

2 cloves garlic, minced

1 tablespoon minced fresh mint

Salt and freshly ground black pepper

Crusty bread

Pick over the chickpeas and discard any stones. Cover with water and soak for 8 hours or overnight. Drain and place in a saucepan with enough water to cover by 2 inches. Simmer until the skins begin to crack and the beans are tender, 1 to 1¹/₄ hours. Drain.

Heat the oil in a large frying pan over medium heat. Add the onion and cook, stirring occasionally, until very soft, 15 minutes. Add the tomato and tomato paste. Cook slowly, stirring occasionally, 10 minutes. Add the spinach and chickpeas and cook until the spinach is wilted, 4 to 5 minutes. Add the garlic and mint and toss together. Season with salt and pepper.

To serve, spoon the chickpeas and spinach on a platter and serve with crusty bread.

Serves 6

NOTE: **This recipe can be prepared 1 day in advance. To serve, bring to room temperature or reheat gently.**

SLOWLY SIMMERED BROWN BEANS WITH EGYPTIAN AROMATICS

Ful Medames

In Egypt the hamman, or public baths, generate a tremendous amount of heat, and in the past they were used for cooking. After the baths were closed for the night and the fire was left to smolder, poor merchants took advantage of the leftover embers to slowly stew their beans in huge earthenware pots until dawn. In the morning, the tender, delicate beans were ready. This Egyptian peasant dish originated in the Middle Ages. Today, these beans can be simmered on the stove; it's a bit less romantic, but the beans are just as flavorful.

1¹/₂ cups small brown beans (see Note)

¹/₄ cup red or orange lentils

3 cloves garlic, minced

1 teaspoon salt

¹/₄ cup extra virgin olive oil

¹/₄ cup chopped fresh flat-leaf parsley

3 hard-cooked eggs, coarsely chopped

¹/₂ bunch of green onions, white and green parts, thinly sliced

2 tomatoes, cut into ¹/₂-inch dice

Crushed red pepper flakes

6 lemon wedges

2 tablespoons ground cumin

2 tablespoons sweet paprika

1 cup Tahini and Cumin Sauce (page 188)

Freshly ground black pepper

1 loaf rustic country-style bread

Pick over the beans and discard any stones. Cover with water and soak 8 hours or overnight. Place the drained beans and lentils in a saucepan with enough water to cover by 2 inches. Simmer the beans and lentils over low heat, covered, until the beans are very soft but not mushy, 1¹/₂ to 2 hours. As they cook, check the beans from time to time to see that they have enough water. Add boiling water if necessary.

In the meantime, mash the garlic and salt together in a mortar and pestle or with the side of a chef's knife on your work surface. Set aside.

Place the olive oil, parsley, hard-cooked eggs, green onions, tomatoes, red pepper flakes, lemon wedges, cumin, paprika, and Tahini and Cumin Sauce in individual bowls and reserve as garnishes.

When the beans are done and very little water remains, gently stir in the garlic mixture and pepper and place in a large serving bowl. Season with salt and pepper. Serve the beans with the garnishes and bread.

Serves 6

> NOTE: Egyptian brown beans, or *ful medames*, are small beans grown in Southeast Asia and Egypt. They can often be found in Greek and Middle Eastern specialty food stores. If unavailable, substitute any small beans that have a delicate flavor, for example, pinto, navy, or fava beans.

CRISPY BULGUR CROQUETTES WITH PINE NUTS AND SPICES

Kibbeh

Making kibbeh is a labor of love. If it is made the traditional way, it takes hours to pound the kibbeh mixture in a mortar and pestle to the correct texture. With the invention of the food processor, however, making kibbeh requires much less muscle power and time. The yogurt and mint sauce (or cacik) used in this recipe is made all over the eastern Mediterranean. In Greece and Turkey, it's made with cucumbers, garlic, dill, and/or mint. The Persians omit the mint and substitute dill and golden or sultana raisins. In Iraq, fresh cilantro or coriander is the herb of choice. In this Lebanese version, cucumber is omitted altogether, and a healthy dose of mint is added at the end. Anyway you make it, cacik remains a Middle Eastern favorite.

Yogurt and Mint Sauce
2 cups yogurt

Salt

3 cloves garlic, minced

2 tablespoons extra virgin olive oil

1/2 cup chopped fresh mint

Kibbeh
1 1/2 cups medium-fine bulgur or
   cracked wheat

1/2 pound lean tender lamb cubes

1 medium yellow onion, minced

Salt and freshly ground black pepper

Filling
2 tablespoons extra virgin olive oil

1 small yellow onion, minced

3 tablespoons pine nuts

1/4 teaspoon ground allspice

1/4 teaspoon ground cinnamon

Large pinch of ground cloves

Large pinch of ground ginger

Large pinch of ground nutmeg

1/4 pound lean ground lamb

Salt and freshly ground black pepper

Corn or peanut oil for deep-frying

To make the yogurt and mint sauce, combine the yogurt and 1/4 teaspoon salt. Place the yogurt in a cheesecloth-lined strainer over a bowl and drain 4 hours.

Place the drained yogurt in a bowl. Add the garlic, olive oil, and mint and mix well. Let sit 1 hour before using.

To make the *kibbeh,* soak the bulgur in cold water to cover for 20 minutes, then drain. Place the bulgur on paper towels to dry for 5 minutes.

Place the lamb, onion, salt, and pepper in a food processor and blend together 1 minute. Add the bulgur, one-third at a time, and continue to blend until the mixture forms a soft dough, 3 minutes.

To make the filling, heat the oil in a frying pan over medium heat and cook the onion, stirring occasionally, until soft, 10 minutes. Add the pine nuts, allspice, cinnamon, cloves, ginger, and nutmeg and continue to cook, uncovered, until the pine nuts are golden, 2 minutes. Add the ground lamb and cook until the lamb has lost its pink color, 4 to 5 minutes. Season with salt and pepper.

Heat 2 inches of oil in a deep saucepan to 375°F. With wet hands, take an egg-size piece of *kibbeh* and shape into a ball. With 2 fingers, make a small indentation and fill with a small knob of filling. Place a small amount of *kibbeh* on the opening to close. Shape the *kibbeh* into a small football shape.

Deep-fry a few *kibbeh* at a time until golden brown, about 2 to 3 minutes. Drain on paper towels. Place the warm *kibbeh* on a platter and serve with the sauce.

Makes 18 *kibbeh* to serve 6

BULGUR AND LAMB TARTAR ROLLED IN LETTUCE LEAVES

Cigkofte

Tasting the ultimate tartar is going to cost you a pretty penny. It isn't around the corner, but at an outstanding restaurant called Sirobom located on the Asian side of Istanbul. I remember it being kind of dark inside, our faces lit by the charcoal brazier or grill in the center of each table. We pulled up a chair and watched the chef turn kebabs over the glowing embers to golden perfection. It was mesmerizing. Fortunately, we didn't forget to order this zippy meze to enjoy while we waited for our kebabs.

1/3 cup medium-fine bulgur or cracked wheat, about 2 ounces

1 cup boiling water

1/4 pound lean lamb, cut from a rack

1 small yellow onion

1 very small tomato, peeled, seeded, and chopped (page 259)

3 cloves garlic, minced

2 tablespoons tomato paste

2 teaspoons sweet paprika

1/4 to 1/2 teaspoon cayenne

1/2 teaspoon ground cumin

Salt and freshly ground black pepper

2 green onions, white and green parts, thinly sliced

1/4 teaspoon grated lemon zest

1 tablespoon chopped fresh flat-leaf parsley

1 small head of butter, Bibb, or leaf lettuce

1/2 bunch fresh flat-leaf parsley leaves

1/2 bunch of fresh cilantro or coriander leaves

6 radishes, thinly sliced

6 lemon wedges

Place the bulgur in a bowl. Pour the boiling water over the bulgur and drain immediately. Discard the water and let the bulgur stand 10 minutes.

Finely chop the lamb with a chef's knife or with the fine blade of a meat grinder, or pulse the lamb in a food processor. Knead the lamb and bulgur together by hand for 10 minutes, or knead using an electric mixer set on slow speed for 5 to 7 minutes.

Grate the onion. Add the onion, tomato, garlic, tomato paste, paprika, cayenne, and cumin to the lamb-bulgur mixture. Season with salt and pepper. Knead again for 5 minutes (or 3 minutes with a mixer). Let rest in the refrigerator for 1 hour.

Add the green onions, lemon zest, and parsley to the lamb-bulgur mixture and mix well. Season with salt and pepper. Bring to room temperature. Take walnut-size pieces of the lamb-bulgur mixture. With your first 3 fingers and your thumb, press the mixture to make free-form shapes with finger indentations. Tear the lettuce leaves into very large pieces and place on a platter in a single layer. Top with parsley and cilantro leaves. Place one piece of the tartar on top of the herbs and lettuce. Chill for 10 minutes. To serve, garnish with the radishes and lemon wedges. Roll the tartar in herbs and lettuce leaves and drizzle with lemon juice.

Serves 6

NOTE: This recipe can be prepared up to 6 hours in advance and stored in the refrigerator until ready to serve. This dish is also excellent served with Red-Hot Smoked Tomato Relish (page 206).

CIRCASSIAN CHICKEN

Ceerkez Tavugu

Ataturk, the twentieth-century Turkish reformer and modernizer whose bronze bust and concrete statue can be seen all over Turkey, loved this chicken and walnut dish. It originated in the area of Circassia in the northern Caucasus. It's been said that the beautiful Circassian girls introduced the recipe when they were imported to Turkey as part of the sultan's harem. It not only became a favorite of the sultans and Ataturk; it is also well loved by Lebanese and Syrians.

1 whole chicken, about 3 1/2 pounds

2 yellow onions, quartered

1 carrot, coarsely chopped

2 stalks celery, coarsely chopped

2 bay leaves

4 sprigs fresh flat-leaf parsley

12 black peppercorns

6 cups water

2 tablespoons sweet paprika

1/4 teaspoon cayenne

1 tablespoon walnut oil

2 cups walnuts, toasted (page 258), plus toasted walnut halves for garnish

2 slices rustic country-style bread, crusts removed

5 cloves garlic, minced

1 teaspoon salt

Freshly ground black pepper

Place the chicken, onions, carrot, celery, bay leaves, parsley, peppercorns, and water in a large saucepan. Bring to a boil, reduce the heat, and simmer, uncovered, for 1 hour. Turn off the heat and allow the chicken to cool in the stock. Remove the chicken from the pan and reserve the stock. Remove the skin and discard. Remove the chicken meat from the bones, tear into long strips, and moisten with 1/4 cup of the chicken stock. Set aside. Place the bones in the saucepan with the stock and reduce by half, 8 to 10 minutes. Strain, skim off the fat, and reserve.

Heat 1 tablespoon of the paprika and a pinch of cayenne in a dry frying pan until aromatic, 30 seconds. Add the walnut oil and turn off the heat. Let stand 30 minutes.

Place 2 cups of the walnuts in a food processor or blender and process to obtain a rough paste. Soak the bread in 1/2 cup chicken stock and add the bread and stock to the food processor. Pulse a few times. Add the remaining 1 tablespoon paprika, the remaining cayenne, the garlic, salt, and pepper to taste. Process until smooth. Add 3/4 to 1 cup chicken stock gradually until a thick, creamy, and pourable consistency is obtained. Season with salt and pepper.

Toss the chicken pieces with half of the walnut sauce. Place on a platter and top with the remaining walnut sauce. Drizzle with the paprika–walnut oil mixture and garnish with the walnut halves. Serve at room temperature.

Serves 6

NOTE: This recipe can be made up to 1 day in advance. To serve, bring to room temperature.

PICKLED TURNIPS

I happen to love pickled vegetables. So do the Turks, Greeks, and Italians. Apicius, the first-millennium Roman cookbook writer, liked the pickled cucumbers of Cappadocia, in central Turkey, so much that he wrote about them that long ago. Other pickled vegetables include carrots, squash, peppers, eggplants, artichokes, onions, okra, cauliflower, and turnips. Flavored with garlic and pickling spices, these magenta-colored pickled turnips are striking and flavorful when served with pickled peppers.

2 pounds small white turnips, peeled and cut into quarters

2 medium beets, peeled and thinly sliced

6 cloves garlic, thinly sliced

2 tablespoons chopped celery leaves

2¼ cups water

1½ cups white wine vinegar, plus more as needed

2 tablespoons salt

1 teaspoon pickling spices

Small pinch of crushed red pepper flakes

Pack the turnips, beets, garlic, and celery leaves into sterilized jars (2 quart-size or 4 pint-size), alternating beets between the other layers at regular intervals.

Bring the water and the vinegar to a boil. Add the salt, pickling spices, and red pepper flakes and stir to dissolve the salt. Pour over the vegetables, making sure that the vegetables are completely covered with liquid. If necessary, add a little extra vinegar to cover. Seal the jars. Leave in a warm place (at least 75°F) for 7 to 10 days before eating. The pickled turnips will keep for up to 2 months. Refrigerate after opening.

Makes 2 quarts

ARTICHOKE HEARTS STEWED WITH FAVA BEANS AND LEMON

Zeytinyagli Enginar

This is a favorite dish of the Copts, a Christian religious sect from Egypt. This vegetable stew has been served for many years during Lent, when abstinence from all animal products is required. At this time of year their diet consists exclusively of wheat and vegetables, and it takes some culinary ingenuity to produce a dish as delicious as this one. If fresh fava beans are unavailable, substitute a 10-ounce package of frozen fava beans.

6 large artichoke hearts (page 259)

Juice of 3 lemons

Salt and freshly ground black pepper

3 pounds fresh fava beans, peeled

1/4 cup extra virgin olive oil

3 cloves garlic, minced

3 cups water or vegetable or chicken stock (page 255)

2 bunches peeled baby carrots or 3 carrots, cut into 1/2-inch slices

1 1/2 teaspoons chopped fresh marjoram or oregano

Cut the artichoke hearts into quarters and place them in a bowl of cold water with the juice of 1 of the lemons. Bring a pot of salted water to a boil. Add the fava beans and simmer 30 seconds. Drain. With your fingernail, puncture the skin of the fava beans. Remove the beans from the skin and discard the skins.

Place the artichoke hearts in a saucepan with the juice of 1 of the lemons, the olive oil, garlic, and water. Over high heat, bring to a boil, reduce the heat to low, and simmer very slowly for 10 minutes. Add the carrots, marjoram, salt, and pepper and continue to simmer, covered, until the artichokes are tender, 20 to 30 minutes. Add the fava beans and simmer slowly, covered, for 5 to 10 minutes. Remove the mixture from the heat, place in a bowl, and let cool. Season with salt, pepper, and lemon juice.

Place the vegetables and their sauce in a bowl and serve warm or at room temperature.

Serves 6

NOTE: This recipe can be prepared up to 1 day in advance. Bring to room temperature or gently rewarm before serving.

OKRA STEWED WITH TOMATOES, PEARL ONIONS, AND CILANTRO

Bamia Bi Banadoura

Poor okra has gotten such a bad reputation, and I must admit that its texture is a culinary challenge. In this dish, okra, a tropical plant native to Africa, is the primary ingredient. Zeytinyaglilar is the word used in the Middle East to describe a whole array of vegetable dishes that are cooked in olive oil and served at room temperature. You can use this technique for any vegetables, whatever you like, in whatever season.

3/4 pound pearl onions

6 tablespoons extra virgin olive oil

2 pounds fresh okra, stems removed

6 cloves garlic, minced

1 1/4 cups peeled, seeded, and chopped tomatoes (page 259), about 3 tomatoes, fresh or canned

Salt and freshly ground black pepper

1 cup water

1 tablespoon coriander seeds, ground in a mortar and pestle or electric spice grinder

Juice of 1 to 2 lemons

1/4 cup chopped fresh cilantro or coriander leaves

Bring a pot of water to a boil. Add the onions and simmer 1 minute. Remove the onions and peel.

Heat the olive oil in a large frying pan over medium heat. Add the onions and cook, stirring occasionally, until golden, 15 minutes. Reduce the heat to low, add the okra, and cook, stirring occasionally, for 5 minutes. Add the garlic and cook until the garlic smells aromatic, 1 minute. Add the tomatoes, salt, pepper, and water. Cover and simmer slowly for 20 minutes. Add the ground coriander seeds and the juice of 1 lemon and simmer until the liquid is reduced by half, 5 to 7 minutes. Remove from the heat and stir in the chopped cilantro. Taste and season with salt, pepper, and more lemon juice if needed. Serve warm or at room temperature.

Serves 6

NOTE: This recipe can be prepared up to 24 hours in advance. Bring to room temperature and add the fresh cilantro just before serving.

SWEET STUFFED RED ONIONS

Basal Malfouf

The beautiful Lycian Coast of Turkey has never been exploited like the Amalfi Coast of southern Italy. When I was there, we scoured this part of the Mediterranean for just about every Roman ruin there was to be found. Talking to some Turkish friends, we learned of one more ruin we didn't want to miss, although it was 2 hours away by hired boat. The weather was perfect and the water calm, so we took a ride. After viewing the spectacular ruins, we motored just a few minutes away to the exquisite island of Kekova, where we enjoyed a rustic outdoor lunch featuring these sweet stuffed onions.

6 medium red onions

Salt and freshly ground black pepper

1 teaspoon sugar

1/3 pound ground lamb

3 tablespoons pine nuts, toasted (page 258)

1/3 cup long-grain white rice, rinsed

3 tablespoons golden raisins

1/2 cup peeled, seeded, and chopped tomatoes (page 259), or 1 tomato, fresh or canned

1 tablespoon tomato paste

1/4 cup chopped fresh flat-leaf parsley

2 tablespoons chopped fresh mint

1/4 teaspoon ground allspice

1/4 teaspoon ground cinnamon

2 tablespoons extra virgin olive oil

3/4 to 1 cup chicken stock (page 255)

Juice of 1/2 lemon

Whole flat-leaf parsley leaves

Preheat the oven to 375°F. Peel the onions. Bring a pot of salted water to a boil. Add the onions and simmer 5 minutes. Remove from the water and cool. Trim 1/2 inch off the top of each onion. Trim just enough off the bottom of each onion so that it will stand upright. Using a small knife and a spoon, cut and scoop out the center of each onion, leaving a 1/2-inch-thick shell intact. Discard the centers. Season the inside with salt, pepper, and the sugar.

Combine the lamb, pine nuts, rice, raisins, tomatoes, tomato paste, parsley, mint, allspice, cinnamon, olive oil, 3/4 teaspoon salt, and pepper. Mix well. Stuff the onions three-quarters full with this mixture, distributing evenly. Place the onions close together in a baking dish. Pour the chicken stock in a saucepan and bring to a boil over high heat. Pour 3/4 cup of the stock around the onions. Squeeze the lemon juice on top. Cover with foil and bake until the onions are tender and the filling is cooked, 45 to 50 minutes. Occasionally check to see if the pan needs additional stock.

Remove the onions from the baking dish carefully and pour the juices from the baking dish over the onions. Let cool slightly. Serve warm, garnished with parsley leaves.

Serves 6

NOTE: These can be prepared 1 day in advance. To serve, rewarm gently in a 350°F oven for 20 minutes.

CUCUMBER AND FETA SALAD WITH DILL AND MINT

Salata Michoteta

An Egyptian friend of mine, Nabih, is a great cook. But, like me, he doesn't want to have to spend hours in the kitchen. When I visited him at his house in Istanbul, he made this salad for me in a matter of minutes. When it was done and I tasted it, I couldn't believe how flavorful it was. Of course I asked for the recipe. He was delighted to share it, letting me know that it was one of his family favorites. It happens to be one of my personal favorites, too, as well as a favorite of my friends and family.

8 ounces feta cheese

2 tablespoons extra virgin olive oil

1 1/2 tablespoons fresh lemon juice

Salt and freshly ground black pepper

1 large cucumber, peeled, seeded, and cut into 1/2-inch dice

1 small red onion, cut into 1/4-inch dice

1 tablespoon chopped fresh mint, plus mint sprigs for garnish

1 tablespoon chopped fresh flat-leaf parsley

1 tablespoon chopped fresh dill, plus dill sprigs for garnish

3 lemon wedges

Pita bread

Crumble the feta coarsely into a bowl and toss it together with the olive oil, lemon juice, salt, and pepper. Add the cucumber, onion, mint, parsley, and dill.

Place on a serving plate and garnish with sprigs of dill and mint and lemon wedges. Serve with warm pita bread.

Serves 6

NOTE: This recipe can be prepared up to 1 day in advance. Bring to room temperature before serving.

SYRIAN-LEBANESE BULGUR, MINT, AND PARSLEY SALAD

Tabouleh

Tabouleh, *the national dish of Syria and Lebanon, celebrates the arrival of summer. Made with bulgur, the backbone of the regional cuisine, it has an earthy, substantial quality. With the addition of parsley, lots of refreshing herbs, sweet ripe tomatoes, and crunchy cucumbers, tabouleh makes a healthy summer favorite. Scoop it up with crisp romaine leaves or triangles of pita bread instead of the usual fork.*

1 cup medium-fine bulgur or cracked wheat

2/3 cup extra virgin olive oil

4 to 5 cloves garlic, minced

3/4 to 1 cup lemon juice

1 large bunch of green onions, white and green parts, cut into 1/4-inch dice

2 large bunches of fresh flat-leaf parsley, chopped

1/4 cup chopped fresh mint

5 large tomatoes, cut into 1/4-inch dice

2 medium cucumbers, peeled, seeded, and cut into 1/4-inch dice

Salt and freshly ground black pepper

Romaine lettuce leaves or pita bread

Place the bulgur in the bottom of a large salad bowl. Mix together the olive oil, garlic, and lemon juice and drizzle over the bulgur. Layer the green onions, parsley, mint, tomatoes, and cucumbers in the bowl, in that order. Season the top layer of cucumbers well with salt and pepper and cover with plastic wrap. Refrigerate at least 24 hours and up to 48 hours.

Bring to room temperature. Season with 1 teaspoon salt. Toss together and serve with romaine lettuce leaves or warm pita bread triangles.

Serves 6 to 8

SYRIAN TOASTED BREAD AND SUMMER VEGETABLE SALAD

Fattoush

In the Mediterranean, nothing is thrown away, not even stale bread. Instead it's tossed with cucumbers, tomatoes, green onions, parsley, mint, sumac (an astringent dark magenta crushed berry), and vinaigrette to make a delicious salad the Syrians call fattoush. Its Italian cousin, panzanella, is made with tomatoes and basil, while the Greek version contains stale bread, briny kalamata olives, crushed tomatoes, and mint.

Salt and freshly ground black pepper

1 hothouse cucumber, peeled, seeded, and cut into 1/4-inch dice

Juice of 2 lemons

2 large cloves garlic, minced

1/2 cup extra virgin olive oil

3 medium tomatoes, cut into 1/2-inch dice

3 green onions, green and white parts, thinly sliced

1/3 cup chopped fresh flat-leaf parsley

1/4 cup chopped fresh mint

1 tablespoon chopped fresh cilantro or coriander leaves

2 large or 4 small loaves pita bread, toasted or stale, torn into rough 1-inch pieces

1 teaspoon sumac (optional)

Black olives (optional)

Salt the cucumber and let drain 30 minutes. Rinse under cold water and dry well.

Whisk half of the lemon juice, the garlic, and olive oil together in a small bowl. Season with 1/2 teaspoon salt and pepper. Combine the vinaigrette with the cucumber, tomatoes, green onions, parsley, mint, and cilantro. Season with salt and pepper and mix well.

Place the pita bread in a salad bowl. Sprinkle with the remaining half of the lemon juice and let sit 5 minutes. Add the vegetables and vinaigrette to the bread and mix well. Season with salt, pepper, and lemon juice. Sprinkle the sumac onto the top. Garnish with black olives and serve immediately.

Serves 6

TEL AVIVIAN CITRUS, AVOCADO, AND WATERCRESS SALAD

Salat Avocado Ve Pri Hadar

Creamy, rich avocado, peppery watercress, tart citrus, and cool mint make up this refreshing Israeli salad best served on a hot summer day.

2 large avocados

3 tablespoons lemon juice

1 tablespoon white wine vinegar

6 tablespoons extra virgin olive oil

1/4 teaspoon lemon zest

Salt and freshly ground black pepper

3 oranges

1 small grapefruit

1 small bunch of watercress or arugula, stems removed

10 large fresh mint leaves

Cut the avocados in half. With 2 hands, twist the halves of 1 avocado in opposite directions to divide into 2 pieces. Tap the pit with the sharp side of a chef's knife, remove the pit, and discard. With a large spoon, scoop the flesh from the skin. Cut the avocado into thin slices. Repeat with the remaining avocado.

To make the vinaigrette, whisk the lemon juice, vinegar, olive oil, lemon zest, salt, and pepper in a bowl. Drizzle the avocado slices with one-third of the vinaigrette.

With a knife, cut off the top and bottom of each orange and the grapefruit. Do not peel. Cut off the skin with a small knife, leaving no white pith. Cut the oranges into 1/4-inch slices. Quarter the grapefruit and then cut crosswise into 1/4-inch slices.

Place the watercress in a bowl and season lightly with salt and pepper. Toss with 1 tablespoon of the vinaigrette.

Place the avocados on a large platter. Top with the orange and grapefruit slices, alternating the colors. Drizzle the remaining vinaigrette over the top. Garnish with the watercress. Pile the mint leaves on top of one another, roll up, and cut into very thin ribbons. Sprinkle on the salad and serve.

Serves 6

HOT SPICED CHEESE PURÉE "GOREME"

Biberli Peynir Ezmesi

Cappadocia, in central Turkey, is a fairy-tale landscape formed by the wind, which has carved away at the soft rock over thousands of years to create amorphous supernatural-seeming formations. The softness of the rock has also enabled humans to carve their own cave dwellings from the stone. This is where I met Aris, who hospitably invited me inside her humble cave dwelling to show me a true Cappadocian kitchen. She showed me how she grinds wheat, stores beans and apples for the winter, and makes thick, creamy yellow yogurt. She offered me a bite of her special spicy cheese purée, and when my eyes rolled back in my head, she gave me her recipe. (See photo, page 207.)

1$^{1}/_{4}$ cups yogurt

$^{1}/_{4}$ teaspoon salt

10 ounces feta cheese

2 cloves garlic, minced

$^{1}/_{2}$ teaspoon cayenne

1 teaspoon plus a pinch of sweet paprika

1 tablespoon plus 1 teaspoon extra virgin olive oil

Freshly ground black pepper

Black olives

Pita bread, warmed

Combine the yogurt with the salt and mix well. Place the yogurt in a cheesecloth-lined strainer over a bowl and let drain 2 hours.

Place the yogurt and feta in a bowl. With a fork, mash them together to obtain a smooth paste. Add the garlic, cayenne, paprika, 1 tablespoon of the olive oil, and pepper and mix well. Alternatively, the ingredients can be puréed in a food processor or blender.

To serve, spread the purée on a serving plate. Drizzle with the remaining 1 teaspoon olive oil. Sprinkle the remaining pinch of paprika over the top and garnish with the olives. Serve with warm pita bread.

Serves 6

NOTE: This recipe can be prepared up to 24 hours in advance and refrigerated. Bring to room temperature before serving.

RED-HOT SMOKED TOMATO RELISH

Ezme Salatasi

This tomato condiment can be found on many meze tables in Turkey. The first time I tasted it, I loved its freshness and the little bit of heat that comes from the cayenne. Luckily, I began to see it again and again, and finally I managed to get the recipe. Hungarian peppers are long green sweet peppers. If unavailable, substitute any sweet green pepper or a green bell pepper. This spicy tomato relish is best eaten with warm crusty bread, pita, grilled skewers of lamb or chicken, or simply by the spoonful. (Shown with Hot Spiced Cheese Purée "Goreme," page 205.)

1 pound ripe tomatoes

1 long green sweet pepper or
   1/2 green bell pepper

1/2 cucumber, peeled and seeded

Salt and freshly ground black pepper

1/2 medium yellow onion, grated
   and drained

2 cloves garlic, minced

1 teaspoon chopped fresh mint
   (optional)

Large pinch of chopped fresh thyme
   (optional)

1/2 teaspoon sweet paprika

1/4 teaspoon cayenne

Large pinch of crushed red pepper
   flakes

1 tablespoon extra virgin olive oil

2 teaspoons red wine vinegar

Whole flat-leaf parsley leaves

Heat a cast-iron frying pan over medium heat for 5 minutes. Place the tomatoes and green pepper in the frying pan, turning occasionally, until lightly blackened and blistered, about 10 minutes. (Alternatively, the tomatoes and pepper can be cooked on a charcoal grill. Cut the tomatoes in half and, with the cut sides up, grill the tomatoes 20 minutes. Grill the pepper until black on all sides, 10 minutes.) Place the pepper in a plastic bag and steam for 10 minutes. Peel, seed, and chop the tomatoes. Place them on paper towels and let drain 15 minutes. Peel, seed, and chop the pepper.

Coarsely grate the cucumber and place in a sieve. Salt lightly and let sit 10 minutes. In a bowl, combine the tomatoes, pepper, cucumber, onion, garlic, mint, thyme, paprika, cayenne, red pepper flakes, olive oil, vinegar, salt, and pepper. Place on a work surface and chop until the mixture forms a fine paste, or pulse a few times in a food processor. Season with salt, pepper, and vinegar.

Place on a plate and garnish with parsley leaves.

Makes 1 1/2 cups to serve 6

NOTE: This recipe can be prepared up to 1 day in advance. Bring to room temperature before serving.

TURKISH SPICY HOT CHICKPEA AND GARLIC PURÉE

Hummus Bi Tahini

Toasted ground sesame seeds, also called tahini, are one of the most important ingredients in Lebanese and Syrian kitchens. Tahini is used to make the ever-popular hummus, a chickpea and garlic purée known not only in the Middle East but all over the world. In the following recipe, cayenne and paprika are added to give the dish a real kick. If you eliminate them, you will have the classic Middle Eastern hummus.

1¹/₃ cups dried chickpeas (8 ounces), or one 14-ounce can cooked chickpeas

Juice of 3 lemons

¹/₂ cup tahini or sesame seed paste

2 tablespoons water

4 tablespoons extra virgin olive oil

6 cloves garlic, minced

¹/₄ teaspoon cayenne

1¹/₂ teaspoons plus a pinch of sweet paprika

¹/₄ teaspoon cumin

Salt

1 teaspoon chopped fresh flat-leaf parsley

6 lemon wedges

5 kalamata or niçoise olives

Pita bread, warmed

Pick over the chickpeas and discard any stones. Cover with water and soak 8 hours or overnight. The next day, drain and place in a saucepan with enough water to cover by 2 inches. Simmer until the skins begin to crack and the chickpeas are very tender, 1 to 1¹/₄ hours. Drain the chickpeas, reserving the cooking liquid. Reserve a few whole chickpeas for garnish.

In a food processor or blender, purée the chickpeas, the juice of 2 of the lemons, the tahini, the water, 3 tablespoons of the olive oil, the garlic, cayenne, 1¹/₂ teaspoons of the paprika, the cumin, and ³/₄ teaspoon salt until a soft, creamy paste is obtained. Season with additional salt and lemon juice if needed.

Spread the purée on a plate and make a small well in the center. Drizzle the remaining 1 tablespoon olive oil in the well. Sprinkle with parsley and the remaining pinch of paprika. Garnish with the lemon wedges, olives, and reserved whole chickpeas. Serve with warm pita bread.

Serves 6

NOTE: This recipe can be made up to 2 days in advance. Bring to room temperature before serving.

BAKED STUFFED EGGPLANT TO MAKE A PRIEST FAINT

Imam Bayildi

The intriguing name of this dish has two possible derivations. In Turkey, there was a priest who was reputed to be both a real glutton and a true gourmet. One theory has it that the priest's cook was distraught about trying to impress his employer. With market-fresh, jet-black eggplant, he did his best. The priest loved it and ate until he "swooned away," or fainted. The second theory is that because of the priest's tight-fistedness, he was shocked at how much olive oil was used, and he fainted at the expense of the finished product.

6 Japanese eggplants, ends trimmed

4 tablespoons salt

6$^{1}/_{4}$ cups water

7 tablespoons extra virgin olive oil

3 medium yellow onions, thinly sliced

4 cloves garlic, minced

1$^{1}/_{4}$ cups peeled, seeded, and chopped tomatoes with juice (page 259), plus 2 small tomatoes, thinly sliced

5 tablespoons chopped fresh flat-leaf parsley

$^{1}/_{2}$ teaspoon dry oregano

$^{1}/_{4}$ cup currants

$^{1}/_{4}$ teaspoon ground allspice

$^{1}/_{4}$ teaspoon ground cinnamon

Freshly ground black pepper

1 teaspoon honey

2 tablespoons lemon juice

NOTE: This recipe can be prepared completely a day in advance. Store in the refrigerator and bring to room temperature or rewarm gently in a 350°F oven for 20 minutes before serving.

Cut the eggplants in half lengthwise. Make 4 evenly spaced incisions lengthwise in each eggplant half. Dissolve the salt in 6 cups of the water and soak the eggplant for 30 minutes.

Heat 2 tablespoons of the olive oil in a large frying pan and cook the onions over low heat, stirring occasionally, until very soft, 20 minutes. Add the garlic and continue to cook for 5 minutes. Add the tomatoes, 4 tablespoons of the parsley, and the oregano and simmer until almost dry, 5 to 10 minutes. Add the currants, allspice, and cinnamon. Season with salt and pepper. Set aside.

Preheat the oven to 350°F. Rinse the eggplant well. Squeeze gently and dry well with paper towels. Heat 3 tablespoons of the olive oil in a frying pan over medium-low heat and cook the eggplant on all sides until the cut side is golden brown and the eggplant is cooked through and soft, 8 to 12 minutes. With a spoon, scoop the pulp from the inside of the shell, leaving the skin and $^{1}/_{4}$ inch of the lining intact. Finely chop the pulp and add it to the tomato and onion mixture. Mix well. Season with salt and pepper.

Place the eggplant shells in a baking dish just large enough to hold them. Fill with the tomato and onion mixture. Pour the remaining $^{1}/_{4}$ cup water into the bottom of the dish. Combine the honey, lemon juice, the remaining 2 tablespoons olive oil, salt, and pepper and drizzle evenly over each eggplant. Top each stuffed eggplant with a tomato slice. Cover and bake the eggplant for 15 minutes. Uncover and bake an additional 10 minutes, adding water as necessary. Cool to room temperature. Reserve the pan juices.

To serve, place the eggplant on a platter, drizzle with the pan juices, and garnish with the remaining parsley.

Serves 6

EGGPLANT PURÉE WITH TAHINI

Baba Ghannouj

This rich, creamy purée is a combination of smoky eggplant and tahini spiked with fresh-squeezed lemon juice and plenty of crushed garlic. In Turkey, it's called mutabbul, *but throughout the world it's more commonly known by its Lebanese name,* baba ghannouj. *Though popular and available the world over, there is nothing like homemade* baba ghannouj. *If you make this recipe, you will see why.*

2 large eggplants

4 to 5 cloves garlic, minced

Salt

1/2 cup tahini or sesame seed paste

Large pinch of cumin

Juice of 2 to 3 lemons

1 tablespoon extra virgin olive oil

1 tablespoon chopped fresh flat-leaf parsley

1/4 cup kalamata or niçoise olives

Pita or crusty bread, warmed

Preheat the oven to 375°F.

Preheat an outdoor grill. When the grill is ready, place the eggplants on the grill, turning occasionally, until the skin turns black, 5 to 10 minutes. (Alternatively, this can be done using a gas stove: Place the eggplants directly on a gas burner, turning occasionally, until the skin turns black, 5 to 10 minutes.)

Place the eggplants on a baking sheet and bake until very soft, 15 to 20 minutes. (If you don't want a very smoky baba ghannouj, omit the above grilling and simply roast the eggplant in the oven until very soft, 35 to 45 minutes.) Cool the eggplant and peel the skin.

Place the pulp in a bowl and mash or pulse in a food processor to make a smooth paste. Add the garlic and salt and mix well. Add the tahini, cumin, and lemon juice to taste and mix well. Season with additional salt, lemon juice, or tahini if needed.

Spread the purée on a plate. Drizzle the olive oil on top and sprinkle with parsley. Place the olives around the sides. Serve at room temperature with warm pita or bread.

Serves 6

NOTE: **This recipe can be prepared up to 2 days in advance and stored in the refrigerator. Bring to room temperature before serving.**

SAFFRON AND RICE STUFFED SQUID

Samak Mahshi

There is a whole string of fish restaurants under the Galata Bridge in Istanbul where hawkers try to lure you in with promises of freshness and abundance. However, they mention nothing of price. Luckily I was warned by a Greek friend that the prices at some of these places can be astronomical. At one restaurant I tasted this stuffed squid dish. Not only was it very tasty, but curiously it was one of the more reasonably priced choices.

1 1/2 pounds squid, cleaned (page 260)

4 tablespoons extra virgin olive oil

1 large yellow onion, finely chopped

1/4 cup short-grain white rice

1/4 cup pine nuts, toasted (page 258)

3 tablespoons chopped fresh flat-leaf parsley

Salt and freshly ground black pepper

2 large pinches of saffron threads, soaked in 1 tablespoon warm water (page 260)

3 medium yellow onions, thinly sliced

1 cup fish stock (page 255) or bottled clam juice

2 to 3 tablespoons lemon juice

6 lemon wedges

Whole flat-leaf parsley leaves

Leave the squid bodies whole. Chop the tentacles and reserve them separately.

Heat 2 tablespoons of the olive oil in a frying pan and cook the onion until soft, 10 minutes. Add the tentacles, rice, pine nuts, parsley, salt, pepper, and a pinch of saffron. Stuff the bodies two-thirds full with the filling and close the openings by weaving a toothpick through them.

Heat the remaining 2 tablespoons olive oil in a large frying pan over medium heat. Cook the squid, stirring occasionally, for 3 to 4 minutes. Remove the squid from the pan and reserve.

Add the sliced onions to the pan and cook, stirring occasionally, until soft, 10 minutes. Reduce the heat to low and continue to cook, covered, stirring occasionally, until the onions are golden and very soft, 15 to 20 minutes.

When the onions are golden, add the remaining saffron and its liquid and a pinch of salt and pepper. Place the squid on top of the onions and add the fish stock. Bring to a boil, reduce the heat to low, cover, and simmer 20 minutes. Uncover, increase the heat to medium-high, and reduce the liquid by one-third, 2 to 3 minutes. Remove from the heat and add the lemon juice. Remove the toothpicks from the squid. Place the onions on a platter and top with the squid. Garnish with the lemon wedges and parsley.

Serves 6

NOTE: This recipe can be made up to 1 day in advance. Bring to room temperature or rewarm gently before serving.

TURKISH BATTER-FRIED MUSSELS WITH GARLIC AND PINE NUT SAUCE

Midye Tavasi

Mitko lumbered across the street with his hand outstretched, and instantly we were friends. For hours he showed me "his" city. Mitko Stoyanof is a third-generation Istanbul baker. He introduced me to many things that day, but one of my favorites was the deep-fried mussels sold on the street. When we finally made it to the front of the line, I saw a sizzling pool of golden-fried mussels. He forked over a few lira for a couple of skewers, and when I took a bite, I immediately understood the fuss.

1¹/2 cups all-purpose flour

3/4 teaspoon salt

1 egg, separated

4 tablespoons extra virgin olive oil

3/4 cup beer

1 slice rustic country-style bread, crusts removed

1/4 cup water

1/2 cup pine nuts, toasted (page 258)

2 cloves garlic, minced

2 to 4 tablespoons lemon juice

Freshly ground black pepper

40 mussels

Canola or pure olive oil for frying

Lemon wedges

Fresh flat-leaf parsley sprigs

NOTE: The sauce should be served at room temperature. It will keep in the refrigerator for up to 1 week.

Sift 1 cup of the flour and 1/2 teaspoon of the salt together. Beat the egg yolk lightly. Make a well in the center and add the egg yolk, 2 tablespoons of the olive oil, and the beer. With a whisk, mix well, but not enough to make it stringy. Let the batter rest for 1 hour at room temperature.

Soak the bread in the water for 1 minute. Squeeze dry and discard water. Place the pine nuts in a blender or food processor and pulverize until finely ground. Add bread and garlic and pulse a few times to make a paste. In a small bowl, combine remaining 2 tablespoons olive oil, 2 tablespoons lemon juice, and the remaining 1/4 teaspoon salt. With the machine running, add lemon and olive oil mixture to bread and pine nut paste in a steady stream. Season with salt, pepper, and additional lemon juice, if desired. Thin with water until thick but pourable. Let sauce sit 30 minutes before serving, thinning again with water if needed.

Scrub the mussels well. Place them in a bowl of hot water and, as the mussels just begin to open, use a knife to open them completely. Remove the mussels from their shells and discard the shells. Reserve the mussels in the refrigerator.

Heat 2 inches of oil in a deep saucepan to 375°F. With a whisk or an electric mixer, beat the egg white until stiff. Fold the egg white into the batter. Toss the mussels in the remaining 1/2 cup flour to coat and tap off any excess. Dip the mussels in the batter. Deep-fry a few at a time until golden, 1 to 2 minutes, turning them to brown evenly. Remove with a slotted spoon and drain on paper towels.

Place the mussels on a serving platter. Garnish with lemon wedges and parsley and serve immediately with the garlic and pine nut sauce.

Serves 6

NORTH AFRICA

MOROCCO, ALGERIA, AND TUNISIA

*J*ust a few miles across the Strait of Gibraltar from Spain and less than a hundred miles across the Mediterranean from Sicily lie the magical and exotic countries of the Maghreb: Morocco, Algeria, and Tunisia. Tucked into the northwestern corner of Africa, the Maghreb is virtually a world of its own. The land is bathed in sunlight from the coast to the mountains and the Sahara desert beyond. Scrub-covered red-ocher and sand-gray ridges rise out of the Mediterranean, sculpted by generations of wind erosion, goats, and lambs.

In this mystical desert oasis, respect for food and enjoyment of eating are foremost. Food is eaten with a crust of bread or with the thumb and first two fingers of the right hand, so even hand washing is a ritual: the hands are held over a bowl while warm, rose-perfumed water from a large copper kettle is poured over them. Then they are dried with a starched white linen towel.

Meals are taken communally, with plates set in the center of a round table. All people serve themselves. The meal begins with first courses of baked pastries, soups, small bites of meat on skewers, and small plates of condiments and salads, called *mukabalatt* in Arabic. *Sheladatt*, or salads, are the most common first course; rarely fewer than four and sometimes as many as twenty different salads are served, depending upon the number of guests and how the abundance of the harvest has inspired the cook.

An Exotic Feast of Color, Flavor, and Texture

The colorful small plates of North Africa are served both hot and cold. The intense flavors vary between spicy, salty, sweet, and sour. The textures vary as well, from raw and crunchy to soft and jamlike. The range of first courses is tremendous: grated carrots with orange wedges, orange flower water, and cinnamon; minced lamb with cumin, paprika, onions, and garlic; and an eggplant purée stewed in olive oil and garlic until it resembles jam. These first courses inspire the appetite and refresh the palate. Sometimes the first course plates are cleared away before the main course arrives, but at other times they are left throughout the meal.

In most cases, the focus of the table is on food rather than on alcoholic beverages, as the consumption of alcohol is forbidden in the Koran, the holy text of the Islamic religion. Although this prohibition is more closely observed in the Maghreb than in the Levant, a glass of wine or fig liqueur appears from time to time.

Moroccan Splendor and Serenity

It isn't unusual for a meal to unfold over a couple of hours. Afterward, the diners leave the table to recline, leaning on elbows and oversized embroidered pillows for support, and tell stories in a relaxed atmosphere. In the finest homes in Morocco it isn't unusual to find beautiful mosaic work on walls, floors, and ceilings and rooms filled with low, luxurious bolsters, ottomans, cushions, and hassocks of brightly woven tapestries, and the fragrance of roses and incense in the air.

The Noisy Marketplace

In contrast to such serenity, the souk, or marketplace, is the hub of life in North Africa and distinguished by an extraordinary vitality of sights, sounds, and smells. The buzz of daily activity resonates through the labyrinth of market passageways lined with shops, vendors, beggars, and donkeys. Haggling and bargaining are expected and provoked. Shop owners meticulously build pyramids of melons, pears, lemons, oranges, peaches, figs, prickly pears, onions, peppers, garlic, squash, and rosy tomatoes. Gigantic basins are piled high with all colors of olives, some preserved with lemons, others with spicy hot pepper, cumin, and garlic.

I always think of the souk as an open-air department store: the spice shop can be found next to the carpet shop, which is next door to the fishmonger, which is next to the jeweler and the fabric shop. In the main square the water seller, in his brightly woven red garb, brushes elbows with the snake charmer, the letter writer, and the newspaper reader. Makeshift restaurants serve skewers of lamb and chicken roasted on braziers or clay grills. Cauldrons of *harira*, a minestrone-like soup, simmer for hours and then are served to patrons who eat a bowl as they sit and chat with friends.

From Ancient Times

Morocco, Algeria, and Tunisia saw wave after wave of invasion for several thousand years, leaving the countries of the Maghreb with a shared culinary heritage, many similar dishes, and common ingredients.

In 800 BC, Phoenician traders en route to Spain set up trading posts on the coast of Tunisia, at the mouth of the upper basin of the Mediterranean.

One of these posts was the city of Carthage, which the Phoenicians lifted to new heights of culture, elegance, and riches. Phoenician cooking methods, recipes, and cultivation of ingredients such as the olive, grape, fig, and pomegranate go back thousands of years.

Roman Rule

The Carthaginians dominated parts of North Africa, Sicily, Spain, Sardinia, and Corsica until 200 BC, when the city fell to the Romans. In 146 BC, Rome recognized that Carthage was its potential rival in the Mediterranean and destroyed, plowed, and salted Carthage so that nothing would grow again.

The Maghreb remained under Roman rule for several hundred years, and the reverberations of this domination can be seen in the Maghrebi *diffa*, similar to the old Roman banquet, where a great succession of dishes is presented and consumed over many hours. The Roman influence can also be seen with the cultivation of the olive and the use of olive oil as a cooking medium.

After the Fall of the Roman Empire

With the collapse of the Roman Empire, the Berbers—indigenous North Africans from the mountains and deserts—became increasingly powerful in the Maghreb. Their most important culinary contribution is the soup known as *harira*. About the same time, Muslim crusaders began their movement westward out of Southwest Asia (or Arabia) and across North Africa. They conquered Tunisia in AD 670 and later conquered Algeria and Morocco. They delivered the word of Mohammed, the Islamic religion, a new Arabic language, and foods from the eastern Mediterranean: *smen*, or preserved butter; spices; dates; citrus; almonds; rice; and sugarcane. The Islamic religion and dietary restrictions spread quickly.

In AD 711, the Berbers and Muslims created a Moorish force that went across the Strait of Gibraltar to overcome Spain, and for centuries a cultural and culinary exchange existed between Morocco and Spain. Gazpacho, for example, was first introduced to Spain by the Moors as a soup of garlic, bread, water, and almonds. When the tomato and pepper were brought to Spain from the New World, they were added to the soup, and the new version was transported back to Morocco.

The Muslims remained a powerful religious and political force in the Maghreb for many centuries, with intermittent rule by the Ottoman Turks. The Maghrebi states were later declared independent states, which they remained until the beginning of the nineteenth century, when France invaded Algeria, Tunisia, and Morocco. The French brought political order, modernization, a strong Western influence, and the grapevine. In 1956 Morocco and Tunisia were finally pronounced free states, and in 1962 Algeria achieved independence from France.

Today the vast majority of North Africans are Arab-speaking and Muslim. Muslims observe fasting from sunrise to sunset during the ninth month of the Muslim calendar. This observance, called Ramadan, is a period of atonement and forgiveness. Like the Jews, Muslims abstain from eating pork.

Morocco

Compared to Algeria and Tunisia, Morocco is fairly isolated in the northwest corner of Africa, where it borders the Mediterranean Sea and the Atlantic Ocean. Sheltered from invasion by both the mountains and sea, it is the least Europeanized part of the North African Mediterranean. *Bisteeya* is the pride of the Moroccan kitchen; it is a poultry stew, usually made with pigeon, encrusted in featherlight *warka*, and dusted with cinnamon and sugar. Spices and lemons preserved in salt are indispensable in certain recipes and provide a unique floral fragrance. *Harira* is a peppery and lemony soup thickened with meat, beans, and vegetables. *Ras el hanout*, or "top of the shop," is a highly aromatic spice mixture integral to many dishes as a marinade.

Algeria

Algeria is sandwiched between Morocco and Tunisia, though its food is more similar to that of Morocco. Algeria has been strongly influenced by the French, who occupied Algeria until fairly recently, and for 130 years in total (compared to only forty years in Morocco). The French influence is seen in the Algerian production of wine and the baking of baguettes instead of the thin, round disks of rustic country-style bread common in Morocco. Stuffed vegetables, an Ottoman invention, are very much enjoyed here. Besides these differences, many of the dishes in Morocco and Algeria overlap.

Tunisia

Tunisia faces Italy and addresses the eastern basin of the Mediterranean Sea. Although its food is somewhat similar to that of Morocco and Algeria, it has some unique dishes, including *brik*, a thin deep-fried envelope of crisp pastry enclosing a raw egg; and *chakchouka*, an intensely hot deep-red soup. The fiery condiment *harissa* is also used liberally in many dishes. Women are not seen in the Tunisian kitchen as often as they are in Morocco, where the cooking, whether in a restaurant or a home, is always done by a woman.

The Cuisine of the Maghreb

Ultimately, the kitchens of the Maghreb share a great deal. One of the most popular dishes is couscous. These golden granules are made from hard durum wheat, moistened with water, rolled in finely ground flour, and formed into pellets the size of a pinhead. Couscous is the name of the granules as well as the preparation that features them. To make couscous the traditional way requires four steps: washing, steaming, allowing the couscous to rest, and then steaming the couscous again. What results is a mound of fluffy golden grains.

Other dishes common to Morocco, Algeria, and Tunisia are *tagines*, or stews; kebabs; *merguez* sausage; and *harissa*, the condiment made of red-hot peppers, garlic, and olive oil. Baked and fried pastries are made with a phyllolike dough called *warka*. Although phyllo can be substituted, the result will not be completely authentic. *Warka* dough is made by dabbing a ball of dough onto a hot metal drum, whereas Greek and Middle Eastern phyllo is a rolled pastry. Cooking implements in the Maghreb include the clay brazier, the mortar and pestle, and skewers for roasting kebabs. Spices are used liberally to enhance the brilliance of the food.

The cuisine is technically very simple, prepared without the use of stocks or rich sauces. Instead, a complexity is developed with the juxtaposition of flavors and textures. These first courses of North Africa should transport you to this enchanting land.

LAMB SOUP WITH LENTILS, HARISSA, AND CILANTRO

Shurba L'Ham Ghan'mi

In an area of the world that has gone through its share of hardship, soups have provided needed sustenance over the years. When the poor farmer had a bin of dried legumes, garden vegetables, and a lamb bone, spices were used to heighten the flavors of the finished product. This soup is heavily spiced with cumin, paprika, bay leaves, lemon peel, harissa (the spicy condiment common to Moroccan dishes), and, at the end, a generous amount of chopped cilantro, the Maghreb's favorite herb. The result is nutritious, economical, substantial, and, of course, very flavorful.

3/4 pound lamb cubes, cut into small pieces

1 tablespoon unsalted butter

1 tablespoon extra virgin olive oil

1/2 teaspoon ground cumin

1/2 teaspoon sweet paprika

2 bay leaves

One 2-inch piece of lemon peel

1/4 to 1/2 teaspoon harissa (page 223), or 1/4 teaspoon cayenne

8 cups water, or 4 cups water plus 4 cups beef stock

3/4 cup lentils (see Note)

1 medium yellow onion, diced

1 carrot, diced

Salt and freshly ground black pepper

3/4 cup chopped fresh cilantro or coriander leaves

In a soup pot, combine the lamb, butter, olive oil, cumin, paprika, bay leaves, lemon peel, harissa, and 2 cups of the water or stock. Simmer slowly, covered, until the lamb is tender, 1 1/2 to 2 hours.

Add the remaining 6 cups water or stock, the lentils, onion, and carrot. Simmer until the lentils are just tender, 20 to 30 minutes. Discard the bay leaves and lemon peel. Season with salt and pepper.

Serve immediately garnished with the cilantro.

Serves 6

NOTE: This soup can be made 1 to 2 days in advance. Any dry beans can be substituted for the lentils. If using beans, soak the beans for 4 hours or overnight before cooking.

COUSCOUS SOUP WITH CHICKEN, TOMATOES, AND MINT

Shurba Suksu

In North Africa, cooking couscous can be a very laborious process. With this soup, the couscous is simply added to simmering broth. Make sure you simmer the broth briskly and stir vigorously while adding the couscous so that the couscous doesn't lump together. Harissa, the peppery condiment paste of North Africa, can be made from scratch (page 223) or purchased in either a can or tube.

1 small (3-pound) chicken, cut into 4 pieces, skin removed

1 tablespoon extra virgin olive oil

1 tablespoon unsalted butter

1 tablespoon tomato paste

2 tomatoes, peeled, seeded, and chopped (page 259), or ³/4 cup canned Italian plum tomatoes, drained and chopped

1 yellow onion, coarsely grated

¹/2 teaspoon ground cumin

¹/2 teaspoon sweet paprika

¹/4 teaspoon turmeric

¹/4 teaspoon harissa (page 223) or cayenne

1 cinnamon stick

¹/2 teaspoon salt

¹/2 teaspoon freshly ground black pepper

8 cups water

¹/2 cup couscous

3 tablespoons chopped fresh mint

2 tablespoons chopped fresh flat-leaf parsley

2 tablespoons chopped fresh cilantro or coriander leaves

1 to 2 teaspoons lemon juice

In a soup pot, place the chicken pieces, olive oil, butter, tomato paste, tomatoes, onion, cumin, paprika, turmeric, harissa, cinnamon stick, salt, pepper, and 2 cups of the water. Over high heat, bring to a boil, reduce the heat to low, and simmer, covered, until the chicken is cooked, 45 minutes. Remove the chicken from the broth and let cool. Remove all the bones and tear the chicken into 1-inch pieces. Add the chicken back to the broth.

Add the remaining 6 cups water and, over high heat, bring the soup to a boil. Reduce the heat to low and, using a spoon, stir the broth constantly as you slowly add the couscous. Add the mint, parsley, and cilantro and simmer, stirring occasionally, for 10 minutes. Season with salt, pepper, and lemon juice and serve immediately.

Serves 6

HARISSA, A SPICY HOT CONDIMENT

Harissa

Harissa is a fiery hot condiment made from hot peppers, garlic, and olive oil. It is used in many dishes in Morocco, Algeria, and, especially, Tunisia, where they prefer their food extra-hot. You can make your own, or you can buy it either by the tube or in a small can. If I'm not making it myself, I much prefer using the harissa sold in tubes; it keeps better.

1/2 ounce dried hot red chili peppers

1 clove garlic, coarsely chopped

Large pinch of salt

3 tablespoons extra virgin olive oil

Place the peppers in a saucepan, cover with water, and bring to a boil over high heat. Reduce the heat and simmer for 2 minutes. Turn off the heat and let soak for 1 hour. Drain the peppers and cut into small pieces. Use a mortar and pestle to pound the peppers, garlic, and salt, or use a blender or food processor and process, to make a fine purée. Spoon the mixture into a jar and cover with the olive oil. Cover tightly and refrigerate.

Harissa can be kept in the refrigerator for up to a year, as long as the surface is covered with olive oil.

Makes 1/2 cup

CHICKPEA SOUP WITH SQUASH AND CILANTRO

Shurba Hammas

I have made this soup several times, and each time I make it I like it more. The final flavor is a little bit sweet, but nothing that a good handful of cilantro and a squeeze of fresh lemon juice can't balance.

1 pound chickpeas

2 tablespoons extra virgin olive oil

2 medium yellow onions, diced

2 carrots, diced

6 cloves garlic, minced

8 cups lamb stock (page 255)

1 small (1 pound) butternut squash, peeled and diced

2 large pinches of saffron threads, revived (page 260)

3/4 cup chopped fresh cilantro or coriander leaves

Salt and freshly ground black pepper

1 to 2 teaspoons lemon juice

1/4 cup fresh cilantro or coriander leaves

Pick over the chickpeas and discard any stones. Cover with water and soak 8 hours or overnight. The next day, drain and place in a saucepan with enough water to cover by 2 inches. Bring to a boil, reduce the heat, and simmer until the skins begin to crack and the beans are tender, 50 to 60 minutes.

Heat the olive oil in a soup pot over medium heat. Add the onions and carrots, reduce the heat to low, and cook, stirring occasionally, until the onions are soft, 12 minutes. Add the garlic and cook 2 minutes. Add the stock, cooked chickpeas, and butternut squash and simmer 20 minutes. Add the saffron and cilantro and simmer for 3 minutes. Season with salt, pepper, and lemon juice, as needed.

Ladle the soup into bowls, garnish with cilantro, and serve immediately.

Serves 6

MOROCCAN MINESTRONE

Harira

Ramadan is the ninth month of the Muslim year and is marked by fasting during the daylight hours. When the bells chime to announce sundown, Moroccan families gather for a substantial bowl of harira, a peppery lemon-scented soup made robust with legumes, meat, vegetables, and spices. It's thickened at the last moment with flour and a beaten egg and accompanied by wedges of lemon and fresh dates. In addition to being eaten to break fast during Ramadan, this soup can also be found simmering in big cauldrons at the market.

$^1/_2$ cup chickpeas

3 tablespoons extra virgin olive oil

$1^1/_2$ pounds beef or lamb, trimmed and cut into small cubes

2 medium yellow onions, chopped

1 stalk celery, chopped

One 28-ounce can whole tomatoes with juice

1 tablespoon tomato paste

$^1/_4$ teaspoon ground ginger

$^1/_4$ teaspoon turmeric

$^1/_4$ teaspoon ground cinnamon

$^1/_2$ teaspoon saffron threads, revived (page 260)

1 teaspoon freshly ground black pepper

9 cups water

1 cup dried lentils

1 egg, lightly beaten

$^1/_2$ cup spaghetti, broken into small pieces

Salt

3 tablespoons all-purpose flour

$^1/_4$ cup chopped fresh cilantro or coriander leaves

$^1/_4$ cup chopped fresh flat-leaf parsley

Juice of 1 lemon

1 lemon, cut into wedges

Fresh dates, pitted and halved (optional)

Pick over the chickpeas and discard any stones. Cover with water and soak 8 hours or overnight.

In a soup pot, heat the oil over medium-high heat. In batches, add the meat and cook until well browned on all sides, 7 to 10 minutes. Remove and set aside. Add the onions and celery and cook, stirring occasionally, until the onions are soft, 7 minutes.

Place the tomatoes, tomato paste, ginger, turmeric, cinnamon, saffron, and pepper in a blender or food processor and process until smooth. Add the tomato mixture and meat to the onions and celery. Add 6 cups of the water, the lentils, and chickpeas and bring to a boil. Reduce the heat to low and simmer until the meat and chickpeas are tender, 2 hours.

Thirty minutes before serving, reheat the soup, if necessary, over medium heat. Add the beaten egg and stir briskly until it forms strands. Add 2 cups of the water and the spaghetti and cook until tender, 6 to 8 minutes. Season with salt and pepper.

Bring the soup to a boil over medium-high heat. Blend the flour with the remaining 1 cup water and add to the soup pot, mixing vigorously. Simmer slowly for 5 minutes. Add the cilantro, parsley, and lemon juice and salt and pepper to taste.

Serve garnished with lemon wedges and fresh dates.

Serves 6

NOTE: This soup can be prepared up to 1 day in advance. To serve, bring it to a low boil, taste, and season with salt, pepper, and lemon juice.

MOROCCAN BAKED PHYLLO ROLLS WITH SHRIMP AND SCALLOPS

Briouats

Fried, baked, triangular, and cigarette-shaped, all kinds of stuffed pastries are made in the countries that border the eastern and southern Mediterranean. In Morocco they are called briouats; in Tunisia, briks; in Turkey, bourek and böregi; and in Greece, bourekakia. Wrapped in featherlight pastry, these first courses almost melt in your mouth. These briouats are filled with fresh scallops and shrimp, tomatoes, and Moroccan aromatics. But this is only one of many potential fillings—the possibilities are endless.

2 tablespoons extra virgin olive oil

1/4 pound fresh sea or bay scallops

1/4 pound medium shrimp, peeled

2 cloves garlic, minced

Salt and freshly ground black pepper

1/4 cup yellow onion, finely chopped

1 large tomato, peeled, seeded, and chopped (see page 259)

3 tablespoons chopped fresh flat-leaf parsley

3 tablespoons chopped fresh cilantro or coriander leaves

3/4 teaspoon ground cumin

1/2 teaspoon sweet paprika

Large pinch of cayenne

Large pinch of saffron threads, revived (page 260)

1/4 cup fresh bread crumbs

1/2 pound phyllo dough

1/2 cup unsalted butter, melted

Lemon wedges

Heat 1 tablespoon of the olive oil in a frying pan over medium heat. Add the scallops, shrimp, and half the garlic and cook, stirring occasionally, for 2 minutes. Season with salt and pepper. Remove the seafood from the pan, chop coarsely, and reserve in a bowl. In the same pan, add the remaining 1 tablespoon oil, onion, and tomato and simmer 10 minutes. Add the remaining garlic, parsley, cilantro, cumin, paprika, cayenne, saffron, salt, and pepper. Continue to simmer slowly until the moisture has evaporated, 10 minutes. Add the seafood and bread crumbs and mix well. Season with salt and pepper.

Preheat the oven to 375°F. Cut the phyllo on the short side into 4 equal strips, 4 inches wide. Cover with a slightly dampened towel until ready to use. Brush 1 strip lightly with melted butter and place another strip on top. Brush lightly with butter. Place a heaping teaspoon of filling along the short end. Fold the sides in and roll, forming a cigar shape. Brush lightly with butter. Repeat with the remaining phyllo and filling. Place on a greased baking sheet and bake until golden, 15 minutes.

Serve immediately, garnished with lemon wedges.

Makes 30 pastries to serve 6

NOTE: These pastries can also be made into triangles. Cut each sheet of phyllo into 3-inch-wide strips, brush one strip lightly with melted butter, and place another strip on top. Brush lightly with butter. Place a heaping teaspoon of filling at one end and fold one corner over the filling to meet the other side and continue to fold as you would a flag, until the whole strip is folded into a small triangular parcel. Brush lightly with butter and proceed as above to bake.

TUNISIAN SWEET AND HOT PEPPER TOMATO RELISH

This sweet and hot pepper and tomato relish is similar to Red-Hot Smoked Tomato Relish (page 206). In fact, it is probably a derivative of that condiment, since so many foods of North Africa have been influenced by the eastern Mediterranean. I like to keep a bowl of this in my refrigerator and use it as a condiment with grilled fish, chicken, lamb, and beef.

3 ripe tomatoes, peeled, seeded, and chopped (page 259)

3 large red peppers, roasted (page 259)

2 cloves garlic, minced

1 teaspoon ground cumin

1/4 teaspoon harissa (page 223) or cayenne

1 tablespoon extra virgin olive oil

2 tablespoons lemon juice

1/4 cup chopped fresh flat-leaf parsley

Salt and freshly ground black pepper

1/2 baguette, cut into 1/2-inch slices on the diagonal

Place the tomatoes in a frying pan over high heat and cook until thickened, 6 to 8 minutes. Remove from the pan and place in a bowl.

Mince the roasted peppers and add to the tomatoes. Add the garlic, cumin, harissa, olive oil, lemon juice, and parsley. Mix well. Season with salt and pepper and place in a serving dish. Serve with baguette slices.

Serves 6

NOTE: This can be made 1 day before serving. If you make it in advance, however, do not add the garlic until you are ready to serve it.

BAKED PHYLLO TRIANGLES WITH LAMB AND MOROCCAN SPICES

Briouats

My favorite Moroccan kitchen has to be the one at the palatial Mamounia Hotel in Marrakesh, where I learned to make warka, the pastry used to make briouats and bisteeya. All the chefs there made certain that I didn't leave the kitchen until I learned to make warka perfectly. We rolled this mixture of lamb, onions, and a pinch of just about every spice in the pantry into the warka to make these fantastic briouats, but I suggest that the reader who hasn't been tutored in making warka substitute store-bought phyllo dough.

3/4 pound lean ground lamb

1/4 cup minced yellow onion

2 cloves garlic, minced

4 teaspoons ground cumin

1 teaspoon ground ginger

1 teaspoon sweet paprika

3/4 teaspoon ground cinnamon

Large pinch of cayenne

Large pinch of saffron threads, revived (page 260)

2 tablespoons chopped fresh flat-leaf parsley

2 tablespoons chopped fresh cilantro or coriander leaves

Salt and freshly ground black pepper

1 egg, lightly beaten

1/2 pound phyllo dough

1/2 cup unsalted butter, melted

Combine the lamb, onion, garlic, cumin, ginger, paprika, cinnamon, cayenne, saffron, parsley, cilantro, salt, and pepper in a frying pan and, over medium heat, cook, stirring occasionally, until the lamb is cooked and the moisture has completely evaporated, 6 minutes. Drain off the fat and discard. Add the egg and stir until it is cooked, 1 minute.

Preheat the oven to 375°F. With scissors or a knife, cut the phyllo the long way into 3 piles of 3 by 18-inch strips. Place the strips on top of one another to form a single pile and cover with a slightly dampened towel. Take 1 strip of the phyllo and place it on the work surface. Brush it lightly with butter. Take another strip, place it on top of the first one, and brush it lightly with butter. Place a heaping teaspoon of filling at one end. Fold 1 corner over the filling to meet the other side and continue to fold as you would a flag, until the whole strip is folded into a small triangular parcel. Repeat with the rest of the phyllo and filling. Place on a greased baking sheet and bake until golden, 15 minutes.

Serve immediately, warm or at room temperature.

Makes 30 pastries to serve 6

NOTE: These pastries can also be made into rolls. Cut 3-inch-wide strips of phyllo. Brush 1 strip lightly with butter and place another strip on top. Brush lightly with additional butter. Place a heaping teaspoon of filling along the short end. Fold 1/2 inch of the long sides in and roll, forming a cigar shape. Brush lightly with butter and bake as directed above.

TUNISIAN POTATO, SCALLION, AND FRIED EGG TURNOVERS

Briks

The first time my Tunisian friend, Abou, made briks for me I didn't understand the concept. No one told me that they are, indeed, properly cooked when the egg yolk is still runny and drips down your chin. Once this was established, I decided I loved these turnovers. Try them yourself. Briks are simple to prepare and can be made with all kinds of fillings.

3/4 pound red potatoes, peeled and covered with cold water

Salt and freshly ground black pepper

6 green onions, white and green parts, finely chopped

2 tablespoons chopped fresh flat-leaf parsley

1/2 preserved lemon, finely diced, optional (page 234) (See Note)

7 tablespoons unsalted butter

6 sheets phyllo dough

6 small eggs

1 egg white, lightly beaten

Olive oil

Lemon wedges

Bring a saucepan of water to a boil over medium-high heat. Add the potatoes and salt and simmer until soft, 20 minutes. Drain the potatoes and mash. Add the green onions, parsley, preserved lemon, and 1 tablespoon of the butter. Season with salt and pepper. Mix well.

Melt the remaining 6 tablespoons butter. Place the phyllo on a work surface and cover with a slightly damp towel. Working with 1 sheet of phyllo at a time, place 1 sheet on the work surface and brush the sheet lightly with butter. Fold the sheet in quarters to make a 6 by 8-inch rectangle. Brush lightly with butter and fold the short side in 2 inches to make a perfect square. Brush the folded 2-inch part lightly with butter. Divide the potato mixture into 6 equal parts and place one part on half of the square. Make a small indentation in the center of the potato and break the egg into it. Brush the edges of the pastry with egg white. Fold the square in half, making a triangle. Seal the edges by pressing firmly. Repeat with the remaining phyllo and filling.

Heat 1/4 inch of olive oil in a large frying pan over medium-high heat. Immediately fry the turnovers until golden, 2 to 3 minutes per side. Remove with a slotted spoon and drain on paper towels. Serve immediately, garnished with lemon wedges.

Makes 6 turnovers to serve 6

NOTE: If preserved lemons are unavailable, substitute 1 teaspoon lemon juice and 1/2 teaspoon grated lemon zest.

FLAKY MOROCCAN CHICKEN PIE

Bisteeya

The crowning jewel of the Moroccan table is the bisteeya, *a glorious pie made with pigeon, lemon-flavored eggs, chopped almonds, and sugar. A very substantial first course, bisteeya is one of the most sophisticated and elaborate Moroccan dishes. This recipe is a little bit lengthy and uses lots of butter, but it's worth the effort.*

14 tablespoons unsalted butter

One 3- to 3¹/₂-pound chicken, cut into 4 pieces, skin removed

1 large yellow onion, minced

1 teaspoon salt

1 teaspoon freshly ground black pepper

3³/₄ teaspoons ground cinnamon

1¹/₂ teaspoons ground ginger

1¹/₄ teaspoons ground cumin

¹/₄ teaspoon cayenne

¹/₂ teaspoon saffron threads, revived (page 260)

¹/₂ teaspoon turmeric

¹/₄ cup chicken stock (page 255)

4 eggs, lightly beaten

¹/₄ cup chopped fresh cilantro or coriander leaves

¹/₄ cup chopped fresh flat-leaf parsley

1 cup whole almonds, blanched

4 tablespoons powdered sugar

³/₄ pound phyllo dough

In a large frying pan over medium-high heat, add 2 tablespoons of the butter, the chicken pieces, onion, salt, pepper, 2 teaspoons of the cinnamon, the ginger, cumin, cayenne, saffron, turmeric, and chicken stock. Bring to a boil, reduce the heat to low, and simmer, covered, until the chicken is tender and cooked through, 45 minutes. Remove the chicken from the pan and let cool. Remove all the bones and tear the chicken into 1-inch pieces. Discard the bones. Bring the liquid in the pan to a simmer over medium heat, add the eggs, and stir gently until the eggs are cooked and most of the liquid has evaporated, 4 to 5 minutes. Add the chicken, cilantro, parsley, salt, and pepper and mix well.

Preheat an oven to 375°F. Place the almonds on a baking sheet and toast until light golden and hot to the touch, 5 to 7 minutes. Coarsely chop them by hand or in a blender or food processor. Mix the almonds with 3 tablespoons of the sugar and ³/₄ teaspoon of the cinnamon. Set aside. Reserve the remaining 1 tablespoon sugar and 1 teaspoon cinnamon for a garnish.

Melt the remaining 12 tablespoons butter. Brush a 12-inch pizza pan or pie plate lightly with butter. Place 1 sheet of phyllo on the bottom of the pie plate so that it completely covers the bottom of the plate and extends over one side by several inches. Brush the whole sheet lightly with butter. Continue with 7 more sheets, rotating the pan slightly between each sheet and brushing butter on each sheet. Spread the chicken and egg mixture on the phyllo. Sprinkle with the almond mixture.

Fold the overhanging phyllo up over the chicken and almonds and brush with butter. Place 1 sheet of phyllo on the top of the pie plate so that it completely covers the top of the pie and extends over one side by several inches. Brush the whole sheet lightly with butter. Continue with 7 more sheets, rotating the pan slightly between each sheet and brushing butter on each sheet. Tuck the overhanging edges under the pie.

The pie can be prepared to this point up to several hours in advance.

Preheat the oven to 350°F. Bake the pie until golden brown, 18 to 20 minutes. Remove from the oven. Pour off any excess butter. Place a large plate on top of the pie and flip it over. Slide it back into the pie plate and continue to bake until golden brown, 18 to 20 minutes. Remove from the oven and turn over onto a serving plate. Let cool 15 minutes before serving.

To serve, combine the remaining 1 tablespoon sugar and 1 teaspoon cinnamon and dust the top of the pie. Cut into wedges and serve.

Serves 8

PRESERVED LEMONS

Hamed M'Raked

Mounds of preserved or confit lemons are sold in the markets of Morocco. These lemons are indispensable in Moroccan kitchens and offer a unique floral fragrance and taste. The lemons are pickled in salt and lemon juice, transforming the peel into an edible ingredient that is essential in many dishes. Preserved lemons are used in tagines, or stews, with olives as a condiment, and in vegetable salads. The pulp, used much less frequently than the peel, adds an unusual flavor to vinaigrettes. (See photo, page 241.)

8 lemons (see Note)

1/2 cup kosher salt

2 cinnamon sticks

4 bay leaves

Freshly squeezed lemon juice,
     as needed

Wash the lemons and cut each into quarters from the top to within 1/2 inch of the bottom, taking care to leave the four quarters joined at the stem end. Sprinkle the insides of the lemons liberally with salt.

Place 1 tablespoon salt on the bottom of a canning jar and pack in the lemons, pushing them down and adding more salt as you go. Add the cinnamon sticks and bay leaves between the lemons. If there isn't enough juice from the lemons, add extra freshly squeezed juice to bring the level up to the top of the jar, leaving approximately 1/2 inch of airspace. Close the jar.

Let the lemons sit in a warm place for 3 weeks, turning the jar upside down occasionally to distribute the salt and juices.

To use the lemons, remove from the brine and discard the pulp. Wash the peels before using them. Some white crystals will form on the top of the lemons in the jar; this is normal. The lemons do not need to be refrigerated and will keep for 1 year.

Makes 1 quart

> NOTE: Meyer lemons are used in Morocco, but I have successfully substituted the commonly available Eureka and Lisbon lemons.

MOROCCAN PIZZA BREAD WITH HERB SALAD

Ghobz Maghribi Wa'Shelada

Salads are a way of life in the Maghreb because vegetables and fruits are so luscious and inexpensive. But don't go to Morocco thinking that you will find this pizza on a menu. This is a true Joanne Weir recipe. I have taken a traditional Moroccan combination of herbs called bekkoula, made a salad, and paired it with Moroccan bread called khobz.

Bread

1¹/₂ teaspoons active dry yeast

¹/₂ teaspoon sugar

1 cup warm water (115°F)

2 cups all-purpose flour

¹/₂ cup whole wheat flour

¹/₄ cup cornmeal

1 teaspoon salt

1 teaspoon sesame seeds

³/₄ teaspoon aniseed, ground in a mortar and pestle or spice grinder

Salad

1¹/₄ cups arugula, stems removed

³/₄ cup fresh flat-leaf parsley leaves

³/₄ cup fresh cilantro or coriander leaves

4 tablespoons extra virgin olive oil

2 to 3 tablespoons lemon juice

¹/₂ preserved lemon, finely diced (page 234) (optional)

2 cloves garlic, minced

2 teaspoons sweet paprika

Large pinch of cayenne

Salt and freshly ground black pepper

To make the bread, stir together the yeast, sugar, water, and 1 cup of the all-purpose flour in a large bowl. Let proof for 1 hour, until it becomes quite frothy and has developed a very yeasty aroma.

Add the remaining 1 cup all-purpose flour, the whole wheat flour, cornmeal, salt, sesame seeds, and ground aniseed and mix well with a wooden spoon. Turn out onto the work surface and knead until smooth and elastic, 7 to 10 minutes. (Alternatively, the dough can be made in an electric mixer: In the mixer bowl, combine the yeast, sugar, water, and 1 cup of the all-purpose flour. Let proof 1 hour. Add the remaining 1 cup all-purpose flour, the whole wheat flour, cornmeal, salt, sesame seeds, and ground aniseed and mix on low speed using a dough hook until smooth and elastic, 5 to 7 minutes.)

Place the dough in an oiled bowl, turning once to coat with oil. Cover with plastic wrap and let rise in a warm place (75°F) until doubled in volume, 1 to 1¹/₂ hours.

Preheat the oven to 375°F. To make the salad, place the arugula, parsley, and cilantro on your work surface in one pile and chop together very coarsely. In a small bowl, whisk together the olive oil, lemon juice, preserved lemon, garlic, paprika, cayenne, salt, and pepper.

Punch the dough down and form into a smooth ball. Place on an oiled sheet pan and flatten slightly. Let rest 10 minutes. Pat the dough into a 9- to 10-inch circle. Prick the loaf in 4 places with the tines of a fork. Bake until golden, 20 to 25 minutes. Remove from the oven and place on a serving plate.

Toss the greens with the vinaigrette and place on top of the bread. Serve immediately, cut into wedges.

Makes one 9- or 10-inch round bread to serve 6

TUNISIAN OMELETTE WITH HOT SAUSAGE, PEPPERS, AND EGGPLANT

Ajja

The French left their mark in Tunisia with the introduction of the omelette and a ratatouille-like stew. When you put the two together, the combination is spicy and delicious. Imagine eggs with garlic; tomato; harissa, the killer hot red pepper condiment; and hot sausage. I love to serve this omelette before a meal like you would a Spanish tortilla or an Italian frittata. It's also great for breakfast, for lunch with a salad, or even for dinner.

1 small eggplant, about 8 ounces

Salt and freshly ground black pepper

4 tablespoons extra virgin olive oil

1/2 small yellow onion, diced

1 green bell pepper, cored and diced

1/2 pound spicy sausage (Magreb Lamb Sausage—recipe follows—chorizo, or hot Italian sausage), removed from its casing and crumbled

2 cloves garlic, minced

1/4 teaspoon harissa (page 223) or cayenne

2 tomatoes, peeled, seeded, and chopped (page 259), or 1 cup canned Italian plum tomatoes, drained and chopped

8 eggs

1 tablespoon water

Preheat the oven to 375°F. Peel the eggplant and cut into 1/2-inch cubes. Salt liberally, place in a colander, and let drain 30 minutes. Wash well and pat dry with paper towels. Toss with 2 tablespoons of the olive oil and place on an oiled baking sheet. Bake, turning occasionally, until golden, 15 to 20 minutes.

Heat 1 tablespoon of the olive oil in a frying pan over medium heat. Add the onion, pepper, and sausage and cook, stirring occasionally, until the vegetables are almost soft, 10 minutes. Add the garlic and continue to cook 1 minute. Add the eggplant, harissa, and tomatoes and simmer on high heat until most of the liquid in the pan has evaporated, 3 to 5 minutes. Season with salt and pepper.

Whisk the eggs with salt, pepper, and the water until foamy. Heat the remaining 1 tablespoon olive oil in a 10-inch omelette pan until the pan is very hot and the oil is rippling, 1 minute. Add the egg mixture and let cook 5 seconds. As the eggs begin to set, lift up the outer edges of the omelette with a fork and let the liquid run underneath. Continue until it is almost set but still slightly soft inside, a total of 30 to 45 seconds. Quickly spread the eggs with the sausage and vegetable stew.

To serve, fold the omelette onto a serving plate to form a slight roll. Serve immediately.

Makes 1 large omelette to serve 6

MAGHREB LAMB SAUSAGE

Merguez

Merguez sausage originated in Tunisia, but today it is made in Algeria and Morocco as well. In Tunisia, where they like very spicy food, the merguez is murderous. It's tasty on its own, grilled on a charcoal fire, or stewed with sweet peppers and fresh summer tomatoes. In addition to the Tunisian Omelette with Hot Sausage, Peppers, and Eggplant, these sausages are perfect part-nered with Tunisian Sweet and Hot Pepper Tomato Relish (page 228).

1 pound lamb, cubed (see Note)

1/4 pound lamb or pork fat (available at a butcher shop)

4 cloves garlic, minced

1 tablespoon sweet paprika

1 teaspoon ground cumin

1/2 teaspoon harissa (page 223) or cayenne (or to taste)

1/2 teaspoon ground cloves

1/2 teaspoon ground cinnamon

1/4 teaspoon ground nutmeg

1 1/2 teaspoons salt

1 teaspoon freshly ground black pepper

3 tablespoons chopped fresh cilantro or coriander leaves

1 tablespoon chopped fresh flat-leaf parsley

1 teaspoon chopped fresh thyme

1/2 cup water

Sausage casings (optional, see Note)

1 tablespoon extra virgin olive oil

Place the lamb, lamb fat, and garlic in a food processor and process until chopped and well mixed. Add the paprika, cumin, harissa, cloves, cinnamon, nutmeg, salt, and pepper. Process together until well mixed. Add the cilantro, parsley, thyme, and 1/4 cup of the water and pulse several times.

Heat a small frying pan over medium heat. Make a small, thin patty of the lamb mixture and cook until it's cooked through, 1 to 2 minutes. Let cool and taste. Season the lamb mixture with salt, pepper, and additional spices, if needed.

If you have a sausage attachment on your electric mixer, use it to stuff the sausage casings with the lamb mixture, twisting and tying at 3-inch intervals. (See Note for preparing sausages without casings.) Place the sausages on a sheet pan in the refrigerator for 24 hours.

To cook the sausages in the casings, heat the remaining 1/4 cup water and the olive oil in a frying pan over medium-high heat. Prick the sausages and cook, turning occasionally, until the water evaporates, the sausages render some fat, and they are cooked through, 10 minutes.

The sausages can be served hot or at room temperature. Slice on the diagonal and serve.

Serves 6

NOTE: Beef and beef fat can be substituted.

If you choose not to use sausage casings, the sausage mixture can also be formed into long sausage-like shapes and threaded onto bamboo skewers. These can be brushed with oil and grilled on a charcoal grill or cooked under a hot broiler, turning occasionally.

WARM SPICED LENTILS

La Adiss Har

In Morocco I met dozens of Mohammeds, including my guide, my butcher, my spice dealer, and my driver. My driver Mohammed was very quiet at the beginning, but after a week he finally began to open up, and a week after that he invited me to his home for a traditional lunch of couscous his wife had prepared. In the Moroccan home, there are a great many customs, and I wanted to do everything right. When we walked into the dining room, Mohammed removed his shoes, so I removed mine. When he ate these warm lentils with the first three fingers of his right hand, so did I. "Delicious!" I said. Mohammed smiled in his usual shy way and handed me a piece of paper. His wife had already written out the recipe for me.

1¹/₂ cups lentils, preferably French Le Puy

4 whole cloves

1 medium yellow onion, peeled

2 bay leaves

One 2-inch piece of lemon peel

¹/₄ cup extra virgin olive oil

1 large red onion, minced

3 cloves garlic, minced

2 tomatoes, peeled, seeded, and chopped (page 259)

1 teaspoon ground cumin

1 teaspoon ground ginger

¹/₂ teaspoon turmeric

¹/₂ teaspoon sweet paprika

¹/₄ teaspoon cayenne

¹/₄ cup chopped fresh flat-leaf parsley

¹/₄ cup chopped fresh cilantro or coriander leaves

1 to 2 tablespoons lemon juice

Salt and freshly ground black pepper

6 lemon wedges

Pick over the lentils and discard any stones. Place the lentils in a large saucepan and cover with water by 2 inches. Stick the cloves in the onion. Add the onion, bay leaves, and lemon peel to the lentils. Bring to a boil over high heat. Reduce the heat to low and simmer until the lentils are just tender, 20 to 30 minutes. Remove and discard the onion, bay leaves, and lemon peel. Drain and discard the water.

Heat the olive oil in a large frying pan over medium heat. Add the red onion and cook, stirring occasionally, until almost soft, 5 minutes. Add the garlic, tomatoes, cumin, ginger, turmeric, paprika, and cayenne and cook for 3 minutes. Add the parsley, cilantro, and the lentils; stir together and heat for 2 minutes. Season with the lemon juice, salt, and pepper. Garnish with the lemon wedges and serve immediately.

Serves 8

FAVA BEAN PURÉE

Bessara is inspired by the Middle East, where they make hummus, a purée of chickpeas, tahini, garlic, and lemon juice. This version is unique because spices are sprinkled on the bread, which is then dipped into the purée. Take it from me: once you begin eating bessara, it is difficult to stop.

1¹/3 cups dried fava (see Note) or kidney beans, about 8 ounces

3 cloves garlic, minced

1/4 cup extra virgin olive oil

1 1/2 teaspoons ground cumin

1 teaspoon sweet paprika

1/4 teaspoon cayenne

1 tablespoon chopped fresh flat-leaf parsley

2 tablespoons chopped fresh cilantro or coriander leaves

3 to 4 tablespoons lemon juice

1 green onion, white and green parts, minced

Salt and freshly ground black pepper

Garnishes

1 tablespoon extra virgin olive oil

3 lemon wedges

2 tablespoons chopped green onions

1 tablespoon ground cumin

1 tablespoon sweet paprika

1 small loaf rustic country-style bread

Pick over the fava beans and discard any stones. Cover with water and soak 8 hours or overnight. The next day, if you are using fava beans, remove the skins. Place the beans in a saucepan with enough water to cover by 2 inches. Simmer until the fava beans are tender, 1 to 1¹/2 hours. If you are using kidney beans, simmer 45 to 60 minutes. Add additional water if necessary. Drain.

Place the beans, garlic, and olive oil in a food processor or blender and process until smooth. Transfer to a bowl and add the cumin, paprika, cayenne, parsley, cilantro, lemon juice, and green onion. Mix well and season with salt and pepper.

Place the purée on a serving platter and garnish with olive oil, lemon wedges, and green onions. Serve the cumin and paprika in small bowls or on a separate plate.

To serve, sprinkle the bread liberally with cumin and paprika and then dip the bread into the bean purée or spread with a knife.

Serves 6

NOTE: Fava beans can be purchased in groceries that specialize in Italian ingredients.

ALGERIAN EGGPLANT JAM

Betanjal M'Charmel

Eggplant jam is made all over the Maghreb; this almost-caramelized version comes from Algeria. In this recipe, the eggplant slices are brushed with olive oil and baked in the oven, but very often in North Africa the eggplant slices are fried in olive oil. I have changed the method of cooking the eggplant to reduce the amount of olive oil. This dish is definitely one of my favorites. (Shown with Preserved Lemons, page 234.)

3 medium eggplants, about 3 pounds

Salt and freshly ground black pepper

5 tablespoons extra virgin olive oil

3 cloves garlic, minced

2 teaspoons sweet paprika

1$^{1}/_{4}$ teaspoons ground cumin

$^{1}/_{8}$ teaspoon harissa (page 223), or $^{1}/_{4}$ teaspoon cayenne (optional)

1$^{1}/_{2}$ cups water

3 to 4 tablespoons lemon juice

1 tablespoon chopped fresh flat-leaf parsley

3 lemon slices or tomato wedges

Rustic country-style bread, warmed

Preheat the oven to 375°F. Cut the stems off the eggplants. With a vegetable peeler or sharp knife, peel the skin in $^{1}/_{2}$-inch-wide strips vertically so that you have striped eggplants. Discard the peels. Slice the eggplants horizontally into $^{1}/_{2}$-inch slices. Place in a colander and salt each slice. Let stand 30 minutes. Rinse well and pat dry with paper towels.

Brush a baking sheet liberally with 1 tablespoon of the olive oil. Brush the eggplant slices lightly with 2 tablespoons of the olive oil. Place the eggplant slices in a single layer on the baking sheet. Bake, turning occasionally, until they are a light golden brown on both sides, 20 to 30 minutes.

Place the eggplant slices in a bowl and, with a fork or potato masher, mash the eggplant with the garlic, paprika, cumin, harissa, water, salt, and pepper. Heat the remaining 2 tablespoons olive oil in a large frying pan over medium-low heat. Cook the mashed eggplant slowly, stirring occasionally, until the moisture has evaporated, 20 minutes. Stir the lemon juice into the eggplant and cook 1 minute longer. Season with salt and pepper.

Place the warm or room-temperature eggplant on a platter and garnish with the parsley and lemon slices or tomato wedges. Serve with warm bread.

Serves 6

NOTE: This recipe can be prepared 1 day in advance. Store in the refrigerator until ready to use and bring to room temperature before serving.

WARM OLIVES WITH PRESERVED LEMONS

Zartoun Bel' Hamed M'Rakhed

Dar Marjana is a very special restaurant tucked into the labyrinth of Marrakesh. Chouki, the hospitable proprietor, greeted us at the door. We were seated in the courtyard, which was crowded with palm and olive trees. We were serenaded by music as Chouki brought a glass of light green fig liqueur, a potent aperitif, and a small plate of these sumptuous olives. I looked up to a clear blue-black sky and a full moon.

3/4 cup cracked green olives

3/4 cup cured black olives

1/4 cup extra virgin olive oil

2 cloves garlic, minced

1/2 teaspoon ground cumin

1/4 teaspoon sweet paprika

1/8 teaspoon harissa (page 223)
   or cayenne

1 whole preserved lemon (page 234),
   diced

1 to 2 tablespoons lemon juice

1 tablespoon chopped fresh cilantro
   or coriander leaves

1 tablespoon chopped fresh flat-leaf
   parsley

Place the olives in a saucepan and cover with water. Bring to a boil and immediately drain. Repeat the process 1 more time.

Heat the olive oil in a small saucepan over medium heat. Add the garlic, cumin, paprika, harissa, preserved lemon, and olives. Cook over medium heat for 1 minute. Remove from the heat and transfer to a bowl. Add the lemon juice, cilantro, and parsley and toss together.

Makes 1 1/2 cups to serve 6

NOTE: These olives can be prepared 3 to 4 days in advance and stored in the refrigerator. Bring to room temperature or rewarm when ready to serve.

BEET, ORANGE, AND WALNUT SALAD

Shelada Baiba Alchin Wa'l Gharghaa

Salads in Morocco, Algeria, and Tunisia might consist of anything, including fried lamb's brains; grilled liver, potatoes, green onions, and lemon; or leftover lamb meatballs stewed with hot tomatoes. This excellent salad is a colorful combination of beets, oranges, toasted walnuts, and romaine lettuce.

1 pound beets

3 tablespoons extra virgin olive oil

3 oranges

$^1/_2$ cup walnut halves

2 tablespoons walnut oil (see Note)

Pinch of sugar

Salt and freshly ground black pepper

1 head of romaine lettuce

$1^1/_2$ tablespoons red wine vinegar

Preheat the oven to 375°F. Wash the beets and place in a baking dish. Drizzle with 1 tablespoon of the olive oil. Cover the dish with foil and bake until a skewer can be inserted easily into the beets, 45 to 60 minutes. Remove from the oven and cool. Slip off the skins and discard. Cut the beets into wedges.

With a knife, cut off the top and bottom of 2 oranges. Do not peel. Cut off the skin with a knife, leaving no white pith remaining. Section the oranges (page 260). Squeeze the remaining membrane to extract the juice and reserve the juice separately.

Toss the walnuts in 1 tablespoon of the walnut oil, sugar, salt, and pepper. Place on a baking sheet and toast until they are very hot to the touch and smell nutty, 5 to 7 minutes. Chop very coarsely.

Wash the lettuce, discard the outer leaves, and cut in half crosswise.

Whisk together the orange juice, the remaining 2 tablespoons olive oil, the remaining 1 tablespoon walnut oil, and the red wine vinegar. Season with salt and pepper.

Toss the lettuce with three-quarters of the vinaigrette and place on a platter. Toss the beets with the remaining vinaigrette. Arrange the beets, orange sections, and walnuts on top of the lettuce. Serve immediately.

Serves 6

NOTE: You can substitute other nut oils, such as hazelnut or almond oil, for the walnut oil. Nut oils, available at specialty food stores, should be stored in the refrigerator.

COUSCOUS SALAD WITH TOMATOES AND HOT GREEN PEPPERS

Shelada Suksu be' Metasha W'lfalfla Khadra

Couscous is the pillar of North African cookery. It is a staple in the same way that rice or bulgur is in the Middle East; pasta, polenta, or rice is in Italy; and rice is in Greece and Spain. Couscous is a fine pellet made from semolina flour, each golden grain a bit larger than the head of a pin. Some chefs call it "Moroccan pasta" because it is made with the same durum wheat used to make pasta. Here, cooked couscous is combined with roasted green peppers, tomatoes, and cucumbers. The resulting salad is similar to Middle Eastern tabouleh and perfect for a summer picnic.

1 1/2 cups couscous

1/2 cup water

1/2 teaspoon salt

2 green bell peppers, roasted (page 259) and diced

2 cups coarsely chopped cherry tomatoes or 2 large tomatoes, peeled, seeded, and diced (page 259)

1 small cucumber, peeled, seeded, and diced

1 hot green or red chili pepper (jalapeño or serrano), minced

1/4 cup chopped fresh flat-leaf parsley

1/4 cup chopped fresh cilantro or coriander leaves

5 tablespoons extra virgin olive oil

2 to 4 tablespoons lemon juice

1 teaspoon ground cumin

1/4 teaspoon sweet paprika

3 cloves garlic, minced

Freshly ground black pepper

Wash the couscous in cold water and drain immediately. Lift and rake the grains with your fingertips to separate them. Let rest 10 minutes.

Heat water in the bottom of a soup pot fitted with a steamer. The steamer should fit snugly into the pot, and the bottom of the steamer should not touch the water. Line the steamer with 3 layers of cheesecloth that cover both the bottom and the sides of the steamer and go up over the top. Add the couscous to the steamer and steam for 20 minutes, fluffing the grains halfway through the cooking.

Remove the couscous from the steamer and put it into a baking pan. Combine the water and salt. Sprinkle the couscous with the salt water. Lift and rake the grains with your fingertips to separate them. Let rest 10 minutes.

Place the steamer back in the soup pot and return the couscous to the cheesecloth-lined steamer. Steam slowly for 15 minutes. Remove the steamer and the couscous. Let the couscous cool completely.

The couscous can be prepared to this point up to 2 days in advance.

Place the couscous in a bowl and add the peppers, tomatoes, cucumber, chili pepper, parsley, and cilantro.

In a small bowl, whisk together the olive oil, lemon juice, cumin, paprika, and garlic. Season with salt and pepper. Toss with the couscous and vegetables. Season with salt and pepper.

Serves 6

TOMATO, ONION, AND PRESERVED LEMON SALAD

Shelada Bel Matesha, Basllaw' L'Hamed M'Rakhed

The first time I tasted this dish, I couldn't get enough. When the main course, mechoui, arrived and the salad was left on the table, I was delighted. Mechoui is a whole roasted lamb served golden brown and crisp on the outside and tender and moist inside, sprinkled with cumin and coarse salt. To go back and forth from the cool, refreshing tomato salad to the lamb was a delicious revelation to me. It was at that moment that I realized I was witness to the simplicity and harmony of Moroccan cooking.

10 ripe tomatoes, peeled, seeded (page 259), and cut into $1/2$-inch dice

1 small red onion, cut into $1/2$-inch dice

$1^1/2$ preserved lemons (page 234)

4 tablespoons extra virgin olive oil

3 tablespoons lemon juice

2 large cloves garlic, minced

$1/4$ cup chopped fresh flat-leaf parsley

$1/4$ cup chopped fresh cilantro or coriander leaves

$3/4$ teaspoon ground cumin

$1/4$ teaspoon sweet paprika

$3/4$ teaspoon salt

Freshly ground black pepper

Combine the tomatoes, onion, and preserved lemons in a bowl.

Whisk together the olive oil, 2 tablespoons of the lemon juice, garlic, parsley, cilantro, cumin, and paprika. Season with the salt, pepper to taste, and additional lemon juice if needed. Toss the vinaigrette with the vegetables and marinate 30 minutes.

Serve at room temperature.

Serves 6

FENNEL SALAD WITH PRESERVED LEMONS AND GARLIC

Shelada al Basbaas

We had been driving for hours when we came to the beautiful white hilltop town of Moulay Idriss, which lies in the countryside between Fez and Rabat. We were famished. It was a beautiful day, sunny and very warm, so we decided to eat our lunch outside at one of the cafés in the town square. My first bite of this cool and refreshing salad revealed assertive flavors combined with such simplicity, the hallmark qualities of the Moroccan table.

2 to 3 large bulbs fennel, trimmed

1/4 preserved lemon (page 234), diced

2 cloves garlic, minced

2 to 3 tablespoons lemon juice

3 tablespoons extra virgin olive oil

Salt and freshly ground black pepper

1/4 cup fresh cilantro or coriander leaves

Cut the fennel into paper-thin slices and toss with the preserved lemon.

In a small bowl, whisk together the garlic, lemon juice, olive oil, salt, and pepper. Add the vinaigrette to the fennel and toss well. Garnish with cilantro or coriander leaves.

Serves 6

> NOTE: The fennel may be sliced up to 1 hour in advance. Toss it with lemon juice to prevent discoloration.

MOROCCAN CARROT, RADISH, AND ORANGE SALAD

When I was young, I used to steal the orange flower water from the kitchen cabinet and dab it behind my ears, making believe it was perfume. Orange flower water comes from the blossoms of the bergamot orange tree. In Morocco, it is often mixed with warm water and splashed on the hands to perfume them after a meal. Orange flower water is also used in many North African recipes such as this one, where it provides a lovely and unusual floral aroma and taste.

2 oranges

2 carrots, peeled and cut into paper-thin slices

12 red radishes, trimmed and cut into paper-thin slices

Juice of $1/2$ orange

Juice of $1/2$ lemon

2 tablespoons extra virgin olive oil

1 teaspoon orange flower water

$1/4$ teaspoon ground cinnamon

Small pinch of cayenne

1 tablespoon powdered sugar

Salt and freshly ground black pepper

2 tablespoons coarsely chopped fresh flat-leaf parsley

With a knife, cut the top and bottom off the oranges. Do not peel. Cut off the skin with a knife, leaving no white pith remaining. Cut the oranges crosswise into $1/4$-inch slices. Place in a bowl with the carrots and radishes.

In a small bowl, whisk together the orange juice, lemon juice, olive oil, orange flower water, cinnamon, cayenne, sugar, salt, and pepper.

Add the vinaigrette to the oranges, carrots, and radishes and toss together. Place on a platter, garnish with parsley, and serve.

Serves 6

ORANGE, BLACK OLIVE, AND CILANTRO SALAD

Shelada Alchin, Zaitun Wa' L'Khazbout

Orange and olive groves compete for space all along the Mediterranean coast. This symbiotic relationship produces wonderful first course salads such as Corfu Salad of Orange Slices, Red Onions, and Kalamata Olives (page 165) and this salad of oranges, black olives, preserved lemons, and cilantro, so distinctly North African.

6 oranges

1/4 cup extra virgin olive oil

1 small clove garlic, minced

Pinch of cayenne

Salt and freshly ground black pepper

1/2 cup cured black olives

1/2 small red onion, thinly sliced

1/2 preserved lemon (page 234), diced (optional)

6 tablespoons fresh cilantro or coriander leaves

With a knife, cut off the tops and bottoms of 5 oranges. Do not peel. Cut off the skin with a knife, leaving no white pith remaining. Cut the oranges crosswise into 1/4-inch slices.

Juice the remaining orange and add the juice to the olive oil. Whisk together with the garlic, cayenne, salt, and pepper.

Place the orange slices on a platter. Garnish with the olives, onion, and preserved lemon. Drizzle with the vinaigrette and garnish with the cilantro. Serve immediately.

Serves 6

MUSSELS STEAMED WITH CUMIN AND TOMATOES

Sometimes the best dishes are the simplest ones. To accomplish this feat is not as easy as it seems: you need to choose the freshest, most flavorful ingredients. I love these mussels just like this, or served with warm pita bread and a salad.

2 pounds mussels, scrubbed and beards removed

3 tablespoons extra virgin olive oil

1/2 cup water or bottled clam juice

1 small yellow onion, minced

2 cloves garlic, minced

2 tomatoes, peeled, seeded, and chopped (page 259), or 1 cup canned Italian plum tomatoes, drained and chopped

1 tablespoon tomato paste

2 tablespoons chopped fresh flat-leaf parsley

1 teaspoon ground cumin

1 teaspoon sweet paprika

1/4 teaspoon crushed red pepper flakes

Salt and freshly ground black pepper

1/4 teaspoon grated lemon zest

2 to 3 teaspoons lemon juice

6 lemon wedges

Heat a large frying pan over high heat. Add the mussels, olive oil, water or clam juice, the onion, garlic, tomatoes, tomato paste, parsley, cumin, paprika, and red pepper flakes. Cover and simmer until the mussels open, 3 to 4 minutes. As the mussels open, remove them from the pan with tongs and place in a bowl. When all of the mussels have opened, uncover the pan, increase the heat to high, and reduce the tomato sauce by one-quarter, 3 to 5 minutes.

Add the salt, pepper, lemon zest, and lemon juice to taste. Add the mussels and toss well.

Serve immediately, warm, or at room temperature, garnished with the lemon wedges.

Serves 6

BRAISED CLAMS WITH PRESERVED LEMONS AND CILANTRO

Mahara Bel' Lhamed Wa' Khazbour

Preserved lemons are a flavor enhancer that provide a bit of sweet, acid, and salt to an otherwise simply flavored dish. Here, preserved lemons pair well with clams, cilantro, parsley, and garlic in this quick and easy dish.

3 tablespoons extra virgin olive oil

³/4 cup water

³/4 cup bottled clam juice

1 small red onion, minced

2 cloves garlic, minced

¹/4 cup chopped fresh flat-leaf parsley

¹/2 preserved lemon (page 234), diced

3 pounds clams, scrubbed well

Salt and freshly ground black pepper

¹/4 cup chopped fresh cilantro or coriander leaves

1 teaspoon lemon juice

6 lemon wedges

Heat a large frying pan over high heat. Add the olive oil, water, clam juice, onion, garlic, and parsley. As soon as it comes to a boil, reduce the heat to low and simmer slowly for 5 minutes. Add the preserved lemon and clams and simmer, covered, until the clams open, 3 to 5 minutes. As the clams open, remove them from the pan and place in a bowl. When all of the clams have opened, add the salt, pepper, cilantro, and lemon juice to taste. Add the clams and juice on the bottom of the bowl and toss well.

Serve immediately, warm, or at room temperature, garnished with lemon wedges.

Serves 6

GRILLED TUNA SKEWERS WITH MOROCCAN SPICES

K'Ban Thon Be' Chermoula

Chermoula is a Moroccan marinade used to enhance the flavors of the food. The recipe for cher-moula varies from cook to cook, but it is usually made of parsley, cilantro, garlic, onions, saffron, sweet and hot pepper, cinnamon, and cumin. Chermoula is a natural with grilled tuna, but it also goes well with swordfish, cod, shellfish, and all kinds of poultry. It is best to marinate the fish or poultry for at least 2 hours and remember to soak the skewers before you place them on the hot grill. This recipe is simple and just wonderful.

1 1/2 pounds fresh tuna

1 teaspoon ground cumin

1 teaspoon ground sweet paprika

1/2 teaspoon turmeric

1/4 teaspoon cayenne

2 cloves garlic, sliced

1/4 cup chopped onion

Salt and freshly ground black pepper

1/3 cup chopped fresh cilantro or coriander leaves, plus sprigs for garnish

1/3 cup chopped fresh flat-leaf parsley

1/4 cup lemon juice

3 tablespoons extra virgin olive oil

Lemon wedges

Soak twelve 4- or 5-inch skewers in water for 30 minutes. Cut the tuna into 1-inch cubes and set aside.

In a blender or food processor, purée the cumin, paprika, turmeric, cayenne, garlic, onion, salt, pepper, cilantro, parsley, lemon juice, and olive oil. Pour over the tuna and mix well. Let marinate 2 hours in the refrigerator.

Start a charcoal grill (see Note). Divide the tuna into 12 portions and thread the tuna onto the skewers. Set the brochettes on a platter until ready to grill. Reserve the marinade.

This recipe can be prepared to this point up to 6 hours in advance.

Grill the tuna brochettes over a medium-hot fire for 5 to 7 minutes, turning every few minutes and brushing occasionally with the marinade. Remove from the fire and place on a platter. Garnish with the lemon wedges and cilantro sprigs and serve immediately.

Serves 6

NOTE: These brochettes can also be cooked under the broiler for 5 to 8 minutes. Turn every few minutes and brush occasionally with the marinade.

MEDITERRANEAN BASICS

CHICKEN STOCK

5 pounds chicken parts (backs, necks, wings), excess fat removed

1 large yellow onion, peeled and coarsely chopped

1 carrot, peeled and coarsely chopped

12 sprigs fresh flat-leaf parsley

Pinch of dried thyme

1 bay leaf

Place all of the ingredients in a stockpot. Add enough water to cover the chicken and vegetables by 2 inches.

Bring to a boil. Skim foam from the top and discard. Reduce the heat and simmer very slowly, uncovered, for 4 to 5 hours. As the liquid evaporates, replenish to the original level. Strain the stock and discard the solids. Place the stock in the refrigerator. The following day, skim the fat from the top and discard it.

The stock can be frozen for 1 to 2 months.

Makes 10 to 12 cups

LAMB OR BEEF STOCK

3 pounds lamb or beef bones

8 cups water

2 bay leaves

1 yellow onion, coarsely chopped

1 carrot, coarsely chopped

Place the lamb bones, water, bay leaves, onion, and carrot in a soup pot. Over high heat, bring to a boil. Reduce the heat and simmer slowly for 2 to 3 hours. Replenish the water to the original level as needed. Strain and discard the bones and vegetables.

The stock can be frozen for 1 to 2 months.

Makes 8 cups

FISH STOCK

2 to 2 1/2 pounds fish bones, such as snapper, grouper, cod, perch, sole, trout, pike, or salmon

1 cup dry white wine, such as sauvignon blanc

1 small yellow onion, peeled and coarsely chopped

1 small carrot, peeled and coarsely chopped

12 sprigs fresh flat-leaf parsley

Pinch of fresh or dried thyme

1 bay leaf

Remove the liver, gills, fat, skin, tail, and any traces of blood from the fish bones. Wash the bones and place in a stockpot with the remaining ingredients. Fill the pot with water to the level of the bones. Bring to a boil. Skim the foam from the top and discard. Reduce the heat and simmer, uncovered for 40 minutes. During cooking, crush the bones with a wooden spoon occasionally.

Strain immediately through a fine-mesh strainer. Remove the fat from the surface by running a spoon over the surface, or place a paper towel over the top and lift to remove the fat.

The stock can be frozen for 1 to 2 months.

Makes 5 cups

MAYONNAISE

1/2 cup extra virgin or pure olive oil

1/2 cup mildly flavored oil, such as sunflower, safflower, corn, vegetable, or canola oil

1 egg yolk

2 teaspoons Dijon mustard

Salt and freshly ground black pepper

Juice of 1/2 lemon

Place the olive oil and mildly flavored oil in a liquid measuring cup together. In a bowl, whisk the egg yolk, mustard, and 1 tablespoon of the combined oils together until an emulsion is formed. Drop by drop, add the oil to the emulsion, whisking constantly. Continue to add the oil in a slow, steady stream, whisking until all of the oil has been added. Season with salt, pepper, and lemon juice.

Makes 1 1/4 cups

PROVENÇAL GARLIC MAYONNAISE   Aioli

3 to 4 cloves garlic, minced or mashed with a mortar and pestle

1 recipe Mayonnaise

Add the garlic to the mayonnaise and whisk together well.

Makes 1 1/4 cups

SPICY HOT GARLIC MAYONNAISE   Rouille

1 red bell pepper, roasted (page 259)

1 slice rustic country-style bread, crusts removed

2 tablespoons bottled clam juice

Large pinch of saffron threads, revived (page 260)

Large pinch of cayenne, or to taste

3 cloves garlic, minced or mashed in a mortar and pestle

3/4 cup extra virgin or pure olive oil

3/4 cup mildly flavored oil, such as corn, safflower, sunflower, vegetable, or canola oil

1 tablespoon Dijon mustard

2 egg yolks

1/4 cup chopped fresh flat-leaf parsley

1 tablespoon tomato paste

3 to 4 tablespoons lemon juice

Salt and freshly ground black pepper

Purée the pepper in a blender or food processor until it forms a fine paste. Drizzle the slice of bread with the clam juice. Sprinkle with the saffron and cayenne. Add the mashed garlic and bread to the pepper and pulse a couple of times to make a rough paste.

In a liquid measuring cup, combine the olive oil and the mildly flavored oil. Combine the mustard, egg yolks, and 1 tablespoon of the oil in a bowl. Whisk until an emulsion is formed. Drop by drop, add the remaining oil to the emulsion, whisking constantly. Do not add the oil too quickly; wait until the emulsion is homogeneous before adding more oil. Add the parsley, tomato paste, and the red pepper, bread, and garlic paste. Season with lemon juice, salt, pepper, and additional cayenne if desired.

Makes 2 cups

SPANISH GARLIC MAYONNAISE
Allioli Negat

1 egg yolk, at room temperature

1 cup extra virgin olive oil

5 cloves garlic, minced or mashed in a mortar and pestle

Salt and freshly ground black pepper

2 to 3 tablespoons white wine vinegar

Place the egg yolk in a bowl and whisk in 1 tablespoon of the oil. Drop by drop, add the remaining oil to the egg yolk, whisking constantly until all of the oil has been emulsified before adding more. Add the garlic, and season with salt, pepper, and vinegar to taste.

Makes 1¼ cups

NOTE: **This recipe can be made up to 6 hours in advance.**

CRÈME FRAÎCHE

1 cup heavy cream

2 tablespoons buttermilk

Warm the cream in a saucepan to 95°F. Stir in the buttermilk. Pour into a glass jar and cover loosely. Let sit in a warm place (75°F) until the cream has thickened slightly, 12 to 14 hours. Cover and store in the refrigerator. It will keep for 10 days in the refrigerator.

If you've got some crème fraîche and you want to make more, follow the above directions but substitute 2 tablespoons of the crème fraîche for the buttermilk.

Makes 1 cup

MASCARPONE

2 cups heavy cream

⅛ teaspoon tartaric acid (see Note)

NOTE: **Tartaric acid is available at pharmacies.**

Place the cream in the top of a double boiler and heat to 180°F. Remove the double boiler from the heat. Stir in the tartaric acid and stir continuously for 30 seconds. Remove the top of the double boiler and continue to stir for 3 minutes.

Place a kitchen towel–lined strainer over a deep bowl. Slowly pour the cream mixture into the strainer. It should not seep through the cloth but instead stay in the strainer. Place the bowl and strainer in the refrigerator and let cool undisturbed for 12 hours. Cover with plastic wrap and let the mascarpone sit in the refrigerator for 1 to 2 days before using.

Makes 2 cups

PIZZA DOUGH

1 1/2 teaspoons active dry yeast
Pinch of sugar
1/4 cup lukewarm water (110°F)
2 cups all-purpose flour
1/2 teaspoon salt
1 tablespoon olive oil
1/2 cup water

In a bowl, whisk together the yeast, sugar, lukewarm water, and 1/4 cup of the flour. Let proof for 10 minutes.

Add the remaining 1 3/4 cups flour, salt, olive oil, and water and mix well with a wooden spoon. Turn out onto a work surface and knead until smooth and elastic, 7 to 10 minutes. The dough should feel moist to the touch.

Alternatively, this dough can be made in an electric mixer or food processor. If you're using a mixer, knead the dough with a dough hook for 5 to 7 minutes. In the food processor, process the dough for 1 minute.

Place the dough in an oiled bowl, turning once to coat with oil. Cover with plastic wrap and let rise in a warm place (75°F) until doubled in volume, 2 to 2 1/2 hours.

**Makes two 9- to 10-inch pizzas or
1 large rectangular pizza**

TOASTING NUTS

1 cup pecans, walnuts, or almonds

Preheat the oven to 375°F. Place the nuts on a baking sheet and bake until light golden, 5 to 7 minutes.

Makes 1 cup

TOASTING PINE NUTS

Always toast pine nuts in a frying pan on top of the stove. They will brown too quickly if toasted in the oven.

1 cup pine nuts

Place the pine nuts in a dry frying pan over medium heat. Stir constantly until golden, 2 to 3 minutes.

Makes 1 cup

SMOKING EGGPLANT

Pierce the eggplant several times with a fork. If you have a gas stove, you can rest the eggplant directly over the gas jets or skewer the eggplant with a large fork and turn it over the gas flame. Alternatively, you can place the eggplant on a charcoal-fired grill, turning occasionally, until the skin is completely black and blistered all over.

Using either one of these methods, it will take 20 to 25 minutes to achieve a very smoky flavor, 15 minutes for a medium smoky flavor, and 5 minutes for a lightly smoky flavor. If neither a gas stove nor a charcoal-fired grill is available, the eggplant can be broiled, turning periodically, until the skin is black and blistered, 10 to 15 minutes. However, the result will not taste as smoky.

PEELING AND SEEDING TOMATOES

Bring a large pot of water to a boil. Score the bottom of each tomato, cutting an X through the skin with a sharp knife. Place the tomatoes in boiling water for 30 seconds, then remove with a slotted spoon. Place in a bowl of ice water (this step is optional). With a knife, remove the core from the stem end of each tomato, then peel off the skin. With the stem end facing up, cut the tomatoes in half horizontally. Cupping each half in the palm of your hand, squeeze out the seeds. Discard the seeds, skin, and core.

TRIMMING ARTICHOKES

With a serrated knife, cut through the leaves of the artichoke crosswise (perpendicular to the stem), removing about half of the artichoke just above the choke. Discard the top half. Tear off and discard the dark green outer leaves around the base of the artichoke until you get to the light green leaves. With a paring knife, trim the torn edges of the base of the artichoke. Scoop and scrape out the hairy choke. Discard the parings and the hairy choke. Set the artichoke hearts in a bowl of water with the juice of 1 lemon added to prevent discoloration.

ROASTING PEPPERS

Preheat the broiler.

Cut the peppers in half and place them, cut side down, on a baking sheet. Broil the peppers until they are completely black, 6 to 10 minutes.

Alternatively, the peppers can be pierced with a large fork and held directly over the flame of a gas stove, turning occasionally, until the skin on all sides is completely black, 5 to 6 minutes. Place the charred peppers in a plastic or paper bag, close the bag, and steam them for 10 minutes. When the peppers are soft, remove them from the plastic bag and, with a knife, scrape off and discard the black skin. (I prefer not to wash them under running water, as this removes some of the flavor.) Cut the peppers in half and remove and discard the membrane and seeds.

Finally, the peppers can also be roasted on an outdoor charcoal grill. Follow the steps above.

PITTING OLIVES

Place the olive on a work surface and, with your thumb, press the olive until you feel the pit. This loosens the pit and makes it much easier to locate. Remove it with your fingers and discard. Alternatively, larger olives such as Greek kalamata olives can be pitted with a cherry pitter.

SECTIONING ORANGES

With a knife, cut the top and bottom off the orange. Place one of the cut sides down on a work surface. Starting at the top and following the contour of the orange down, cut off the skin, leaving no white pith remaining. Cut the peeled orange into sections between the remaining membranes.

REVIVING SAFFRON

I recommend buying saffron threads instead of saffron powder. The best method for bringing out the flavor of saffron is to crush the threads with a mortar and pestle and then soak them in a small amount of warm water. Use both the water and the ground saffron threads. Or you can warm a small, dry frying pan over medium-high heat. Add the saffron threads and shake the pan until the saffron is just aromatic, 30 to 60 seconds.

CLEANING SQUID

Wash the squid. Separate the body from the head by tugging gently. (If the ink is needed for the recipe, reserve the black ink sacs intact and place in a cheesecloth-lined strainer. With the back of a spoon, press to extract the ink into a bowl.) With your fingers, pull any remaining insides and the transparent quill bone from the body and discard. Remove the tentacles by cutting just below the eyes of the head. Remove the small, round beak by turning the head inside out and pressing the center. Discard. Remove the skin from the body by scraping with a knife.

INDEX